Marketing and Psychology

This lively and engaging book helps marketers create more effective strategies and campaigns. It explores why customers behave the way they do, drawing on hundreds of psychological theories and showing how these can be applied to marketing practice.

The book presents a broad framework, grouping psychology theories together into a simple to follow 'ABC' approach: Understanding your audience, communicating brand perception, and helping customers to make the right choice – while posing key questions to consider. Understanding the basics of psychology gives invaluable insight into customer behaviour, whether in B2C, B2B, or nonprofit contexts. Written by authors with expertise in both marketing psychology and marketing practice, the book presents the latest research in a way that is accessible to all, guiding readers through the psychology underpinning marketing, to understand human behaviour and explain what we know about how customers think.

Offering effective strategies to develop successful marketing plans, *Marketing and Psychology* is essential reading for marketing practitioners, from early career to seasoned professionals. It will also be relevant reading for students of marketing, consumer psychology, and advertising.

Tom Bowden-Green spent 11 years in PR agency roles before moving to academia in 2013. He completed a PhD at the University of Bath and is now a Senior Lecturer teaching marketing and psychology at Bristol Business School, UWE Bristol, UK.

Luan Wise is a seasoned industry practitioner with 25 years of agency, client side, and consultancy experience. She is a chartered marketer, fellow of the Chartered Institute of Marketing (FCIM), and is currently pursuing a PhD by Portfolio at the University of Lancashire, UK.

"It's my bible for understanding the hundreds of behavioural biases. The ultimate reference guide to decode human decision-making."

Phill Agnew, *host of the No.1 marketing podcast 'Nudge'*

"This book is essential reading for marketers intent on advancing their strategic capabilities. The ABC approach presents a robust, practical framework grounded in psychological theory, making it highly relevant to today's marketing landscape. Whether you are at the outset of your marketing career or bring years of experience, the insights offered are both accessible and readily applicable, making this book an invaluable addition to your professional toolkit."

Chris Daly, *CEO Chartered Institute of Marketing*

"You'll refer to this book time and again. It's the equivalent of having two experts on staff who research, distil, and prompt you to use countless psychological principles to sharpen your marketing strategy. Fantastic!"

Nancy Harhut, *Chief Creative Officer, HBT Marketing;*
Author of 'Using Behavioral Science in Marketing'

"A really neat idea. I like the simplicity of the ABC approach."

Alan Tapp, *Professor of Marketing*

"If you're serious about marketing, this book is non-negotiable. It gives you the psychology you need to stop guessing and start creating work that actually connects."

Katy Howell, *CEO of Immediate Future*

"This is exceptional. Rarely does a book come along that covers this subject in a way that is both comprehensive and very readable. I have been waiting for a book like this and would recommend it therefore to both practicing marketers, academic colleagues from across the business spectrum, and engaged students."

Jonathan Deacon, *Professor of Marketing*

"This book is packed with brilliant brain hacks that will make your comms and marketing unforgettable. You learn how to tell better stories, be bolder with humour, and be inspired by behavioural science insights that work in real life. It's smart, useful, and I'll be stealing ideas from it for years to come."

Hel Reynolds, *Chief Unboring Officer, Comms Creatives*

Marketing and Psychology

Understanding Customer Behaviour with the ABC Approach

Tom Bowden-Green and Luan Wise

Routledge
Taylor & Francis Group

LONDON AND NEW YORK

Designed cover image: Getty © OksanaTelesheva

First published 2026
by Routledge
4 Park Square, Milton Park, Abingdon, Oxon OX14 4RN

and by Routledge
605 Third Avenue, New York, NY 10158

Routledge is an imprint of the Taylor & Francis Group, an informa business

© 2026 Tom Bowden-Green and Luan Wise

The right of Tom Bowden-Green and Luan Wise to be identified as authors of this work has been asserted in accordance with sections 77 and 78 of the Copyright, Designs and Patents Act 1988.

For Product Safety Concerns and Information please contact our EU representative GPSR@taylorandfrancis.com. Taylor & Francis Verlag GmbH, Kaufingerstraße 24, 80331 München, Germany.

Trademark notice: Product or corporate names may be trademarks or registered trademarks, and are used only for identification and explanation without intent to infringe.

British Library Cataloguing-in-Publication Data
A catalogue record for this book is available from the British Library

ISBN: 978-1-032-89116-3 (hbk)
ISBN: 978-1-032-89114-9 (pbk)
ISBN: 978-1-003-54122-6 (ebk)

DOI: 10.4324/9781003541226

Typeset in ITC New Baskerville Std
by KnowledgeWorks Global Ltd.

Contents

Figures

About the authors

Dr Tom Bowden-Green

After starting his career in college marketing with Sony Music, Tom spent 11 years in PR agency roles before moving into academia in 2013. In his most senior role, he was an Associate Director at Grayling for several years. He completed a PhD at the University of Bath, examining the behaviour of customers in online environments, and he is now a Senior Lecturer teaching marketing and psychology at Bristol Business School (UWE Bristol).

Tom's teaching experience includes undergraduate and postgraduate university students, doctoral supervision, and leading delivery on a wide range of executive education and CPD courses. He also established and led the MSc in Digital Marketing at Bristol Business School for many years. Tom has published several research papers in leading psychology and marketing journals, and his current research is focused on applying psychology in a wide range of marketing contexts.

Luan Wise

Luan is a seasoned industry practitioner with 25 years of agency, client-side, and consultancy experience. She is a chartered marketer, fellow of the Chartered Institute of Marketing (FCIM) and is currently pursuing a PhD by Portfolio at the University of Lancashire, focusing on B2B marketing and technology adoption. Luan is a LinkedIn Learning Course Instructor, Meta Lead Trainer, and delivers training for professional bodies and organisations across the world. Her 2024 TEDx talk focused on the role of social media as a force for good.

Marketing and Psychology: Understanding Customer Behaviour with the ABC Approach is Luan's sixth book – she has previously published *Relax! It's Only Social Media, Planning for Success: A Practical Guide to Setting and Achieving your Social Media Marketing Goals, Using Social Media for Work: How to Maintain Professional Etiquette Online, Smart Social Media: How to Grow your Business with Social Media Marketing,* and she also contributed a chapter to *The Future of Charity Marketing.*

Acknowledgements

We would like to extend our thanks to everyone who contributed their experiences, and case studies to this book. Your contributions have greatly enriched our work, and we deeply appreciate your time and effort in reviewing our manuscript and sharing your feedback.

We are especially grateful to:

Alison, Daryl, Ross, Helen, Jonathon, Steve, Elizabeth, Ian, Andrew, Phil, Helena, and Ruth – thank you for your generous insights that helped bring this book to life.

A special thank you to our early reviewers: Phill, Nancy, Alan, Katy, Jonathan, Hel, and Chris. Your thoughtful feedback has been invaluable in shaping the final version of this book.

We also want to express our gratitude to Emilie and the team at Routledge for their guidance and support throughout the publication process.

From Tom: I would like to say a special thank you to my wife and children, and to apologise for the hours spent sat outside the campervan with a laptop, at various locations around Europe and the UK. Hopefully, the end result is worth it.

From Luan: Thank you to Tom for inviting me to collaborate on this project – it's been a joy to work on with you. And, as always, thank you to my husband, Steven, for your encouragement and the behind-the-scenes support that helps make everything possible.

Introduction

This is a book for marketers who want to create more effective strategies and campaigns. Whether you are at the start of your career or an experienced professional, the concepts we've included are designed to support your thinking and strengthen your approach.

We believe that understanding the basics of psychology will give you invaluable insight into the mind of your customers, including consumers and businesses. Since customers are at the heart of everything marketers do, we're confident that applying this learning will help you to develop successful marketing plans.

This book focuses solely on how to incorporate psychological knowledge, rather than how to write a strategy. However, we present a broad framework, grouping psychology theories together so that you can incorporate valuable insights into your strategy and planning. We call this framework, simply, the ABC approach.

This is a topic we're really passionate about. We both enjoy digesting the very latest research, engaging with academic discussion, and spotting real-life examples of theory in practice. If this book whets your appetite to learn more about marketing and psychology, please visit our website and sign up for our regular updates where we distil everything we continue to learn into bite-size chunks.

www.marketingandpsychology.com

DOI: 10.4324/9781003541226-1

THE ABC APPROACH TO MARKETING AND PSYCHOLOGY

Before we begin chapter 1, we want to introduce you to our ABC approach to incorporating psychology when preparing your marketing plan. To write this book, we scoured academic papers and collected many, many psychology books over several years. We then had the challenge of putting all this academic theory into some kind of structure. We couldn't include every single journal article, but we wanted to consider what goes through customers minds at each stage of the buying process by drawing on the myriad of studies and theories that seek to explain human behaviour. We also wanted to present those theories in an accessible way for marketers to apply to a marketing plan. The result was a simple and memorable acronym for remembering the key considerations: (A) Audience, (B) Brand perception, and (C) Choice. This is the general structure to the book.

As a marketer, you'll know that consideration of the audience (or the 'target market') is usually the first step in marketing planning. There is also plenty of academic literature about differences between people according to aspects such as personality and mindset. Plus, people react to their social surroundings. Understanding the audience (A) is therefore our starting point.

Traditional 'funnel' approaches to marketing then tend to represent the first stage of customer interaction as 'attention' or 'awareness'. In other words, a brand needs to show a customer that it exists. What impression do customers have when they first hear about your organisation, product, or service? We call this brand perception (B). Typically, this might involve some form of marketing communications activity, such as advertising. Again, there are lots of academic theories that explain how people react to a range of content styles and formats, as well as different communicators; we try to cover as many as we can.

Finally, when customers reach the point at which they are ready to purchase (the 'conversion' stage of a marketing funnel), they need to make a decision – often evaluating a range of options. Decision-making is another big area of psychology, which we draw on for this last section of the book, focusing on choice (C).

So, the acronym ABC is a simple way of summarising some core areas of psychology that marketers should consider, and in an order that will help you to incorporate theory as you write your strategy and plan your next successful campaign.

STRUCTURING YOUR THINKING

Before you execute tactics, you need to plan. Planning is where strategy takes shape; it's the bridge between setting objectives and delivering tactical activity. A good plan connects the why with the how, aligning goals with meaningful actions.

This is neither a book about tactics, nor a detailed book on marketing planning. There are plenty of great books that cover various aspects of strategic planning such as market segmentation, persona development, or customer-journey mapping. This book is just about how to incorporate psychological insights. However, we do suggest some questions to consider when incorporating psychological insights, grouped within the ABC approach. We then use these to structure the proceeding chapters:

- **Audience**
  - o Can you segment your audience according to their psychological traits?
  - o How does your audience feel?
  - o Are other people likely to influence the way your audience thinks?
- **Brand perception**
  - o How will you attract an audience's attention and guide their first impressions?
  - o Who will communicate on behalf of your brand?
- **Choice**
  - o Will people remember your brand when they consider a purchase?
  - o How do people evaluate available options before purchasing?

Psychology has a role to play across every stage of your marketing strategy, from identifying audience insights to understanding what drives purchase decisions. Psychology theory helps marketers move beyond guesswork. It provides evidence-based insights to help understand why people behave the way they do – what drives attention, how people form attitudes, and what influences decision-making. When you understand these underlying mechanisms, you'll be better equipped to design messages, experiences, and campaigns that truly connect.

A marketer's own worldviews may be inherently biased and, as authors of this book, we also recognise that our worldviews have guided us too. However, we know (and hope) this won't be the only resource you refer to. As new psychology research is published daily, we actively encourage you to explore a diverse range of perspectives, experiences, and research (our website www.marketingandpsychology.com is a good starting point). Applying psychology is not a one-off task. It's an ongoing process – one that requires curiosity, critical thinking, and a willingness to challenge assumptions.

THE STARTING POINT: AUDIENCE

As you will see in chapter 2, our starting point is to consider the audience – the 'A' of our ABC approach. Marketers are taught early on that understanding audiences is fundamental to effective marketing. But while the concept sounds straightforward, the reality is far more complex.

In their series of white papers, Ian Murray and Andrew Tenzer remind readers just how easily marketers can misjudge the people they're trying to reach. In the Aspiration Window (2020), Murray and Tenzer suggest, *"Advertising and marketing people see and interpret the world differently and, despite the abundance of market research, behavioural data and 'insight' at our disposal, we are persistently bad at estimating the basic values and drivers of mainstream behaviour"*.

This disconnect is a powerful reminder that audience understanding isn't just about collecting data – it's about recognising that your perspective as a marketer might be skewed. That's why audience insight forms the first section of this book.

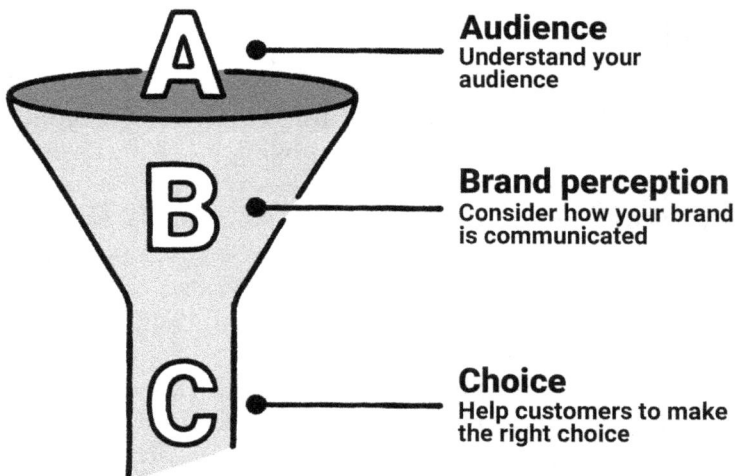

Audience
Understand your audience

Brand perception
Consider how your brand is communicated

Choice
Help customers to make the right choice

Figure 0.1 The ABC Approach to Marketing and Psychology

COMMUNICATING WITH POTENTIAL CUSTOMERS: BRAND PERCEPTION

Customers cannot buy your product or service if they don't know about your brand. To quote one of the leading academics in this area, a brand is "a name that influences buyers" (Kapferer, 2008). This influence then affects subsequent information such about the product or service. Most marketing funnels suggest that the marketing process truly begins when a brand generates 'awareness' or gains 'attention'; so, after identifying an audience, you need to engage them somehow. Bear in mind that whatever you do will affect how your brand is perceived – from the tone of voice you use to the platforms you choose, every decision shapes the impressions people form about your organisation.

There are many psychological theories that will ensure your communication is effective. We explore these from chapter 5 onwards. In practical terms, you will need to consider the tactics you can employ to convey this brand, utilizing psychological theory. Typically, these tactics would fall within what most marketers call 'marketing communications', such as advertising, public relations, and events, both offline and online. If you are familiar with the 4P's of marketing popularised by Philip Kotler (1994), most of the activity to shape brand perception would be classed as 'promotion'.

MAKING A DECISION: CHOICE

The final stage of most marketing funnel models is to generate a sale, or some other form of 'conversion', such as registering for an event or signing up for a free-product trial. We describe this as resulting from a customer's evaluation of options, i.e., making a choice. Some marketing funnels include repeated conversions (known as 'retention' or 'loyalty'), but this still broadly involves a decision following an assessment of the options available. Again, if you want to think practically about the 4P's of marketing, making a choice incorporates factors such as the product itself, the influence of the place, and, very importantly, the price (especially in comparison to other options).

By following the ABC approach, as you plan your marketing activity (before you begin designing specific tactics or create your messaging), you will pinpoint the audience you are trying to engage and how they think. Then you will consider relevant psychological theories to engage and convince your customers at each stage of their journey, from brand perception to their final evaluation of the options and decision.

Lastly, we hope you enjoy reading the book and learning how to apply the theories we introduce you to. If you have questions, please don't hesitate to reach out to us. You can connect with either of us on LinkedIn or email us both at info@marketingandpsychology.com.

INTRODUCTION REFERENCES

Kapferer, J.N. (2008). *The new strategic brand management: Creating and sustaining brand equity long term.* Kogan Page Publishers.

Kotler, P. (1994), *Marketing Management, Analysis, Planning, Implementation, and Control.* Prentice-Hall.

Murray, I. and Tenzer, A. (2025). *The Aspiration Window.* Reach Solutions. https://www.everydaypeopleresearch.com/thought-leadership

1 Marketing and Psychology in Practice

In this first chapter we introduce you to psychology, explaining how the field has grown and why it is important for marketing. We also discuss technological changes that have affected customer behaviour and how these changes affect marketers that apply psychology to their work.

Imagine your customer having a quick coffee break, with all sorts of thoughts passing through their mind. Their best friend's car is so much nicer; if only they could watch a movie at home rather than go out to dinner tonight; hopefully nobody has noticed that they need a haircut; what food do they have in the fridge? As they sit and scroll on their smartphone, an advert appears. The light from the screen passes through the cornea of their eye, refracting through the lens until it reaches the retina sending a signal to the optic nerve in the brain. The synapses pass electrochemical signals to each other through the lateral geniculate nucleus to the primary visual cortex, triggering the frontal lobe to recognise the image. Dopamine flows through the brain and the motor cortex directs the forefinger to tap on the advert. They remember the brand on the screen from a previous email they saw last month. Perhaps they should click to find out more, especially given that the product is half price for the next 24 hours!

This scenario is psychology in action.

Psychology affects who humans are, what they pay attention to, and why they decide to buy.

Psychology is the study of mind and behaviour. When marketers want to understand how customers think, psychological research offers a glimpse into a customer's mind to understand why and what they purchase. In this book, we're going to introduce many theories to help

DOI: 10.4324/9781003541226-2

you understand your customers; theories that are underpinned by academic research, supported with real-life examples.

You may not realise it, but you encounter marketing psychology every day – whether it's the way a café prices its coffee, a countdown timer urging you to "buy now before the offer ends", or an ad for a new online tool that will support you in being more productive at work.

You might have read or listened to people like Rory Sutherland, Katy Milkman, Phill Agnew, or Richard Shotton, whose work helps an understanding of how psychology (sometimes referred to as behavioural science) really drives decisions.

There are examples of marketers using psychology everywhere – helping brands connect, persuade, and stay memorable.

1.1 WHERE DID PSYCHOLOGY COME FROM?

Many current psychological theories were first published in the twentieth century. Before this, there was little scientific clarity about the drivers of behaviour. What controlled a person's behaviour? Their heart? Their soul? Perspectives on this differed. As understanding of the brain evolved, the case of Phineas Gage is a well-cited landmark. Whilst building an American railway in the nineteenth century, an explosion sent a metal pole through Phineas' skull – and, of course, injured his brain. Miraculously, he survived for some time afterwards, but the change in his personality helped lead to the realisation that the brain determines who people are.

Towards the end of the 1900s, physiologist and philosopher Wilhelm Wundt began experiments to assess influences on the 'psyche', now known as 'psychology'. Physician William James then published the first textbook on the topic, titled 'The Principles of Psychology' (1890).

The twentieth century saw many studies undertaken as researchers sought to understand how and when the brain affects behaviour. The writings of Sigmund Freud played a big role in appreciating the influence of the brain beyond conscious thought, but many of the theories accepted today were developed far later. The field of psychology has moved through various paradigms. A prominent area of research was around learning, with famous 'behaviourist' studies including Pavlov's dog and the 'Skinner box' demonstrating that brains can be 'conditioned' to acknowledge and respond to new stimuli. Gordon Allport and his peers also sought to identify consistent personality traits to explain differences and similarities in behaviour.

Social psychology emerged as researchers examined interactions between people, whilst cognitive psychologists focused on how decisions are made. Now, psychologists of different disciplines sit side by side, focusing on distinct contexts of thought and behaviour. For more on the roots of psychology, we recommend reading *The Story of Psychology* by Morton Hunt (1994).

Today, psychologists understand that observable behaviour results from processes in the brain. Very often people talk of 'left', 'right', or 'lizard' brains to describe different aspects of human thought and behaviour. While these might illustrate a specific point, none alone accurately describes a brain.

A person's brain is really a collection of around 128 billion brain cells (called neurons) connected through synapses in a way that is unique to each person. Each neuron releases chemicals to send instant signals across the brain. Individually, neurons don't have specific responsibilities. Neuroscientists identify areas of the brain where neurons group together to serve specific functions, such as the primary somatosensory cortex, which processes tactile information to create a sense of touch and the prefrontal cortex, which is involved in decision-making and social behaviour.

Where patterns of brain activity occur, they lead to observable patterns of behaviour or thought, i.e., patterns visible to researchers studying psychology.

1.2 EFFECTIVE MARKETING UTILISES PSYCHOLOGY

Without an understanding of psychology, marketing risks missing the mark – failing to connect with the very people it's designed to reach. Marketing is not just about campaigns or content; it shapes how people perceive brands, form opinions, and make decisions. When marketers overlook the principles of human behaviour – how people think, feel, and act – their activity becomes less effective, less relevant, and easier to ignore. Psychology provides the foundation for marketing that resonates and endures. It helps marketers understand audience motivations, overcome barriers to action, and create meaningful connections across every touchpoint – from first impressions to long-term loyalty.

In a world where attention is limited and choice is abundant, applying psychological insight is not a nice to have – it's fundamental to marketing that works.

Many people in marketing utilise psychology insights without knowingly following a theory; marketing is about understanding people, drawing on experience, and sometimes following a gut instinct. As Jonathon Ford, VP Digital at global sports and culture agency IMG, suggests; *"You're a bit like a chef; you've got all of these different ingredients you*

could choose from, so often the way you make the decision is based on your
expertise and an inherent instinct for what will work."

It's reassuring though that there is a world of psychological research
to support many of these instincts.

As you read this book, you may therefore recognise many of the
theories as we explain them. Recognising that there is theory to
underpin your marketing activity ensures you're making decisions based
on insights rather than gut feeling. In turn, as you read and learn more,
your intuition will become more expansive and better qualified. The
knowledge you gain will be applied over many years and many
campaigns.

While writing this book, we talked to marketers working in a wide
range of industries and discovered a real passion for understanding and
applying psychology through marketing campaigns. You'll see a case
study at the beginning of each chapter, plus many other examples
throughout.

Daryl Fielding has led global brand strategies and marketing
campaign for brands including Ford, Dove, Milka, Cadbury, and
Vodafone. During our conversation (for the case study in chapter 5)
she highlighted the challenge of relying on customers for insights;
"Customers often won't be able to tell you if you ask them directly." Instead,
she recommends:

> *"finding other ways of really understanding your customer such as observa-*
> *tional insights, or from reading well-designed research studies in academia*
> *that can provide an absolute wealth of information on a topic that is broad*
> *and relevant to whatever product or service you are marketing; this is also*
> *a particularly good source of information if you haven't got a big budget for*
> *research."*

We also spoke to Steve Manser, Head of Marketing at giftware brand
DCUK. Steve loves working for a smaller brand because it gives him the
freedom to experiment – testing out marketing-psychology theories and
ideas from case studies he's picked up from podcasts and books. His
expertise is so renowned that colleagues even suspect his clothing is
some form of psychological persuasion, for example using T-shirt
colours to influence product design decisions (he confirmed that this
was not his intention!).

Use of psychology in marketing is not just about driving sales.
Understanding how the mind works can also influence behaviour
changes that improve people's daily lives. For example, initiatives like
the Couch to 5K app encourage people to adopt healthier lifestyles by

making fitness more accessible, while public safety campaigns, such as urging people to stay home during severe weather events, help protect communities. These efforts tap into people's motivations and emotions, guiding them to make better decisions for our well-being and safety.

As Ruth Dale, a behavioural change expert and founder of Hidden Voices Heard says:

> *"Psychology shows us that people don't always do what they intend, even when they want to. This gap – the intention gap – is where marketing can step in. It is our role is to bridge this gap, using insight and empathy to connect, influence, and inspire action. In health behaviour change this is where the real magic happens."*

Similarly, Ross Middleham, Creative Lead at the Met Office, highlights the importance of understanding emotions to communicate factual information:

> *"Weather is a constant conversation because it's always changing. To stay relevant, we need to tap into what people care about – their emotions, their daily lives, and what's happening in the world around them – especially at the moment they care most."*

1.3 MARKETING IN A DIGITAL WORLD

Before the rise of digital technology, marketing was largely confined to traditional channels such as print media, television, radio, and in-store promotions. Customer behaviour was primarily influenced by physical interactions, word of mouth, and mass media. Brands relied heavily on direct mail, outdoor posters, and face-to-face sales to reach their audience. The customer journey was relatively linear: Awareness, consideration, and purchase often occurred in distinct steps within physical spaces.

The 1970s, 80s, and 90s bought significant technological advancements, with personal computers, the internet, and mobile devices. This transformation was not merely about new tools and technology but a fundamental change in how information can be disseminated and consumed. The internet democratised access to information, enabling customers to research, compare, and interact with brands and each other like never before.

On average, internet users now spend 6 hours and 38 minutes online each day, accessing the web in many ways – smartphones, smart TVs, gaming consoles, wearables, desktops, laptops, and tablets. Yet the reasons for internet use are varied and psychologically motivated, including staying in touch with friends and family, keeping up to date with news and events, schooling, and researching health issues and health care products. Importantly for marketers, 45.2% of users aged 16 and over use the internet to research products and brands (DataReportal. com, 2025).

Social spheres also form online. Social networks and messaging platforms are the most popular destinations on the internet; people have an average of 6.8 different social media accounts, spending 2 hours 21 minutes a day scrolling, sharing and engaging with content (DataReportal.com, 2025). Social media platforms such as Facebook and LinkedIn have redefined how people connect, share, and influence each other. Online video platforms like YouTube and TikTok have become central to how people are educated, entertained and inspired. Peer reviews, influencer endorsements, and online communities also play a crucial role in shaping customer choices.

When people then choose to research a purchase, they no longer need to stroll down the high street. Of course, search engines have existed for decades, but search behaviours are evolving as users turn to a variety of tools including social media, voice assistants, and AI. Online purchasing continues to increase – worth over $7 trillion in 2024 and projected to surpass $10.4 trillion by 2028 (Hedges, 2025).

The tools used for internet access are also continuing to evolve. Mobile-commerce sales accounted for over 80% of all retail-website visits worldwide in 2024 (van Gelder, 2025). Mobile applications have become integral to daily life, facilitating access to services such as food delivery, transportation, and weather updates. Customer spending on mobile apps reached approximately $171 billion in 2024 (Ceci, 2025). A significant portion of internet users – 68.3% – also subscribe to monthly content services, including streaming movies, TV shows, and music, as well as e-books, news, and mobile applications (DataReportal. com, 2025).

What does this mean for marketers? Customer behaviour is now more traceable than ever before. Data provides essential insights about the role the internet plays in everyday life, as well as how customers interact with a brand. Whereas there is little way of knowing who has seen a billboard poster or read a newspaper advert, digital behaviour is measurable. Marketers can now track every online click, like, and purchase. Constant evaluation helps marketers evolve to create relevant and effective activity across websites, mobile apps, social platforms, and email marketing.

More importantly though, what does this mean for marketers who want to utilise psychology? Firstly, through some psychological knowledge, marketers can make sense of all this data to understand the drivers of customer behaviour, social interactions, and decision-making processes. Secondly, it is also now easier than ever to try out new ideas quickly and cost-effectively, putting your psychological knowledge to the test. The digital world is always on, allowing customers to access information, products, and services anytime, anywhere. Reactions are instant and viewable.

However, the internet is a crowded and competitive space, meaning that marketers need to work hard to cut through the noise. As you will learn throughout this book, applying psychological theories helps marketers create content and experiences that stand out, resonate, and drive action. Marketers can plan campaigns that are both creative and effective.

In some ways, whether online or offline, customers react to brand information and make similar purchasing decisions psychologically. We describe people living in a 'digital world' but acknowledge that people still visit shops and still engage with salespeople. In fact, the customer journey often blends digital and physical experiences. For example, some customers 'showroom' (visiting physical stores before making a purchase online) and 'webroom' (researching products online before purchasing in-store). For this reason, our discussion includes both offline and online examples. Many of the theories we present could be applied to either environment.

1.4 THE ROLE OF PSYCHOLOGY IN MARKETING PLANNING

Psychology helps marketers guide people through the customer journey – from the moment they become aware of a brand, through to how they evaluate options, and ultimately, the decisions they make. Whether through organic content, paid advertising, influencer marketing, or search optimisation, marketing is about more than simply being visible. It's about showing up in the right place at the right time – and with the right message. That might mean appearing in a Google search when someone is looking for a solution, being recommended by a trusted voice on social media, or catching attention with a scroll-stopping story. In each case, timing, context, and emotional relevance are key.

Global brands like Coca-Cola, Nike, and Salesforce have long been using psychological theories to help connect with audiences.

Coca-Cola, for example, has consistently tapped into the psychology of happiness and togetherness through its campaigns, often focusing on shared moments of joy, friendship, and positive experiences. One of its most iconic examples is the "Share a Coke" campaign, which personalised bottles with popular names, encouraging customers to associate the product with social connection and shared happiness. Additionally, Coca-Cola has successfully used nostalgia in its holiday campaigns, particularly at Christmas. The brand's festive ads, featuring its signature red trucks and the iconic Santa Claus, evoke feelings of warmth, tradition, and celebration. This emotional appeal fosters nostalgia, reminding customers of childhood memories and family gatherings during the holiday season, deepening their connection with the brand.

Similarly, Nike has mastered the art of aspirational marketing, using the psychology of achievement and empowerment to inspire customers. Its "Just Do It" slogan, for instance, resonates deeply with individuals seeking motivation to push past their limits, whether in sports or in life. By featuring athletes overcoming personal struggles, Nike appeals to the growth mindset – the belief that anyone can achieve greatness through hard work and perseverance. This has not only established Nike as a brand, but as a symbol of empowerment and determination.

Salesforce demonstrates how B2B brands can apply psychological insight just as effectively as their consumer-facing counterparts. Through its "Trailblazer" community, Salesforce fosters a strong sense of belonging and shared purpose, allowing customers to see themselves as part of a wider movement of innovators and problem solvers. The brand regularly showcases success stories, reinforcing social proof and helping potential customers imagine similar achievements. By positioning its CRM and business solutions as tools that empower collaboration, growth, and transformation, Salesforce becomes more than a software provider – it becomes a trusted partner in helping businesses succeed.

Ultimately, understanding psychology should increase conversions (e.g., sales). If you understand psychology, you may apply it to remove friction throughout the customer journey.

Friction is anything that makes it harder for customers to move forward – whether it's unclear copy, long checkout forms, or slow-loading pages. By identifying and smoothing out these bumps, you make it easier for customers to take action.

Identifying friction isn't a bad thing – it's a valuable opportunity to make small, ongoing adjustments that improve the customer experience and help drive conversions. Using psychology insights to gently 'nudge' your customer through their decision-making process should feel natural and seamless, rather than some aggressive persuasion – an approach we strongly advise against. As marketers, our role is to guide and support customers in making informed decisions.

As Alison Hutchinson CBE, CEO of The Pennies Foundation explained to us (see the case study in chapter 8): *"It's always a customer choice; all of our research says put the decision in the hands of customers and they will decide if they want to take action."*

1.5 A NOTE ABOUT ETHICS

We acknowledge that some readers of this book might see the potential to use psychology to manipulate a customer. The reality is that the number of potential variables that affect a purchase decision is huge; there is absolutely no way a brand can control, or even affect, every variable.

However, in a competitive marketplace, using academic research to understand your customer and communicate your brand effectively is perfectly sensible. Some people have legitimate concerns about the market dominance of certain brands and point to the exploitative practices. There are also certain products or services that, personally, you may choose not to promote due to ethical considerations or personal beliefs. In principle though, helping an organisation to grow through effective marketing that focuses on understanding customers is important. We hope this book will help you to achieve this.

CHAPTER 1 REFERENCES

Ceci, L. (2025, January 28). *Global mobile app consumer spending 2016-2023*. Statista. https://www.statista.com/statistics/870642/global-mobile-app-spend-consumer/

DataReportal.com. (2025). *Global Overview 2025*. https://datareportal.com/reports/digital-2025-global-overview-report

Hedges, T. (2025). *AI in search: Charting changing trends in search engines*. GWI. https://www.gwi.com/blog/ai-and-search

James, W. (1890). *The principles of psychology*. Henry Holt.

Statista. (2025). *Advertising and marketing spending worldwide from 2021 to 2025* https://www.statista.com/statistics/1446002/advertising-marketing-spending-worldwide/

Van Gelder, K. (2025, March 4). *E-commerce worldwide – statistics & facts*. Statista. https://www.statista.com/topics/871/online-shopping/#topicOverview

2 Audience: Using Psychology for Segmentation

In this chapter, we explore what makes each customer different and why this knowledge is valuable for you as a marketer. While it's common to segment target audiences based on demographics such as age, gender, or geographic location, these criteria alone don't offer a complete picture of your customers. There are many psychological theories that can help marketers better understand customer behaviour, such as personality traits, cultural influences, and perceived socioeconomic status.

As you read this chapter, please keep in mind the importance of avoiding stereotypes: Those broad, oversimplified assumptions about a set of criteria that can lead to biased thinking.

Ian Murray is the cofounder of Everyday People, but perhaps best known for his provocative thought-leadership pieces for WARC and Marketing Week alongside colleague Andrew Tenzer, challenging the worldview of marketers. The ethos of Everyday People is that marketers should consider psychology when identifying an audience. Psychology is perhaps the most important basis of segmentation. Ian explains more …

YOU ARE NOT YOUR AUDIENCE: WHY MARKETERS NEED PSYCHOLOGY, NOT ASSUMPTIONS, FOR MEANINGFUL SEGMENTATION

Within the marketing industry there is a growing backlash against the use of generational research for the purpose of customer insight. Through their own research and practice, Tenzer and Murray confirm that while demographics and real-world

DOI: 10.4324/9781003541226-3

understanding of generations is useful, more is needed. *"The way marketers define and think about demographic criteria is often too narrow and stereotypical. A more holistic understanding is required."* Murray told us.

Their research, documented in several white papers including Gut Instinct (2018), The Empathy Delusion (2019), and The Aspiration Window (2020), has revealed that psychological 'worldviews' exist across all generations, effectively challenging the marketing industry's tendency to assign assumptions regarding universal traits to age groups.

Drawing from established sources including the World Values Survey, Jonathan Haidt's The Righteous Mind (2012), and cross-cultural psychology research by scholars like Hazel Markus, Tenzer and Murray have created a worldview segmentation model that provides far more predictive power than conventional approaches.

One of Tenzer and Murray's suggestions is that:

"If you want a strategy that truly sets you apart from the competition, you need to start thinking about what people have in common, not what separates them. The marketing and research industries tend to think that understanding people is all about understanding differences."

For example, the 'Everyday People' worldview segmentation shows that, despite all the talk of transformative power of 'Gen Z', young people more or less see and interpret the world the same way as everyone else does. And in their mission to compete on social purpose, *"marketers increasingly overlook so called 'functional' attributes like quality, reliability and service. But they remain the basic building blocks of decision making – for everyone"*. Viewing customers psychologically can challenge received wisdom and stereotypes.

To find out more about Everyday People, visit www.everydaypeopleresearch.com.

2.1 PERSONALITY: FIVE TRAITS

If you're looking for a simple way of understanding how customers differ from one another psychologically, personality traits can be a good place to start.

For example, if we asked you to describe someone you know well, such as your best friend, you might tell us their height or hair colour. More likely, you'd tell us about their character. Perhaps they are kind and caring; perhaps they are full of energy and make you laugh; perhaps they work hard and can always be relied upon. These are all personality characteristics.

People may act differently in different situations, sometimes shouting in anger or expressing love to a partner, for example. However, personality is the term used to describe long-lasting characteristics that typify a person's behaviour and attitudes, rather than situational expressions.

Personality traits affect buying behaviour and responses to marketing. For example, personality traits relate to product choice (Schilling and Bleidorn, 2024).

a) The personality of each customer is based on five traits

Research in this field is dominated by a five-trait theory of personality based on factor analysis. As the name suggests, this theory supports five dimensions, or traits, against which humans can be assessed. Importantly, the five-trait model is widely felt to be far more reliable, and therefore robust, than some other common measures of personality.

This trait-based approach to personality was developed initially by Allport and Odbert (1936), who searched through the English dictionary for all the words that might be used to describe a person. Of the 18,000 words identified, 4,500 were descriptions of character. Later studies used a statistical analysis technique, known as factor analysis, to identify those words with similar meaning, so that the list could eventually be reduced down to five themes (Fiske, 1949) or Big Five personality 'traits' (Goldberg, 1981). These also spell the word *OCEAN* if you rearrange the order in which they are presented (Openness, Conscientiousness, Extraversion, Agreeableness, and Neuroticism).

(Please note that we present the traits below roughly in order of their prominence within psychological literature, rather than in alignment with the acronym. We also discuss them in the following paragraphs, with reference to their definition according to McCrae and Costa (2003). In particular, we discuss sub-characteristics within the traits which are technically called 'facets'.)

Extraversion

People typically have a clear understanding of 'extravert' behaviour. Perhaps you think of somebody loud at a party, keen to express themselves and dominate a conversation. Well, yes, being 'gregarious' and 'assertive' are two aspects, or 'facets', of extraversion. But to score highly in a psychological test of extraversion a person might also seek excitement and generally be shown to experience positive emotion. Each trait is a spectrum, so extraversion is one end of the scale, and the opposite is introversion. For example, Red Bull's extreme-sports sponsorships might appeal to excitement-seeking extraverts.

Neuroticism

Neuroticism is associated with feeling worried. People who feel anxious, vulnerable, and self-conscious are perhaps likely to score high for neuroticism. Depression is also associated with neuroticism. At the other end of the scale is emotional stability, i.e., people who feel pretty contented with life.

Marketers can tailor messaging for customers who score high on the neuroticism scale by addressing their anxieties and concerns. The Calm and Headspace meditation and mindfulness apps, for example, target individuals looking to manage stress and anxiety.

Reassurance and emotional support in marketing can also be effective; a financial services organisation, for instance, might focus on promoting security and peace of mind in their offerings, reassuring potential customers that their investments are safe and well managed.

Agreeableness

People with high scores for agreeableness are likely to be described as being generally friendly. They are likely to be trusting, altruistic, and pretty straightforward people to deal with. They may also be modest, perhaps valuing connection above their own self-expression.

Highly agreeable individuals value empathy and might be more likely to respond to brands that promote community, social causes, and ethical practices. Marketing messages can highlight how products contribute to the greater good; for example, a skincare brand might emphasise its commitment to animal-free product testing. A service-led organisation might become B Corp certified to appeal to people scoring highly for this trait.

Conscientiousness

Conscientious people are generally understood to be hard working. In a personality test therefore, conscientiousness assesses competence and self-discipline. Those scoring highly may also be orderly and dutiful, perhaps described as 'well-organised'. Conscientiousness seems to relate to likelihood of promotion to more senior roles in employment, for example (Kordsmeyer et al., 2024).

Individuals who score high for conscientiousness are often detail-oriented, and appreciate reliability and organisation. Marketers can emphasise product quality, detailed information, and structured offers to attract those with this trait. A brand selling project-management software, for instance, may market key features like organisation tools and productivity tracking.

Openness

Openness might sound like friendliness or being 'open' for others to read and understand. However, in this context the full name of this trait ought to be 'openness to experience', meaning that people with high scores like to experience new feelings, ideas, and aesthetics. Perhaps they fantasise about new possibilities.

Airbnb, the online marketplace for homestays, markets unique, immersive travel experiences to those seeking novelty and adventure, is likely to appeal to those with high openness.

APPLYING THE THEORY: KEY QUESTIONS

Five-factor personality analysis can be used in marketing to tailor plans and campaigns to different personality traits. For example, personality can affect many areas of behaviour, such as diet (Allen et al., 2024) and therefore influence customer choices.

There is lots of evidence that personality traits can be identified through observable behaviours. For example, Sam Gosling showed in his book Snoop (2018) that observers are pretty good at identifying the personality traits of others just by assessing their bedrooms. Online, people leave evidence (known as 'cues') that others can use to assess their personality. On Facebook, for instance, a person's interests can give away their personality. Although most platforms don't currently enable marketers to explicitly target customers based on personality traits, it is perhaps only a matter of time before technology enables personality-based targeting alongside other common segmentation criteria.

Which personality traits – openness, conscientiousness, extraversion, agreeableness, and neuroticism – are likely to characterise your target customers? How can you align your messaging to appeal to those traits?

2.2 PERSONALITY: DARK TRIAD

The five-factor personality model assesses some general aspects of personality that are not necessarily good or bad. Since the establishment of five general factors though, attention has more recently turned to understanding some of the perhaps more undesirable aspects of personality.

a) Some of your customers also have a 'dark' side to their personality

This area of research has resulted in the so-called dark triad of personality, identified by Paulhus and Williams (2002), describing three traits that have the potential to offend others: Machiavellianism, narcissism, and psychopathy. Although these do relate to some five factor traits, these three 'dark' traits are broadly separate traits to those identified in the five-trait model. They are also different to one another.

Machiavellianism

Like the character in Machiavelli's novel *The Prince*, people who score high for Machiavellianism are likely to see people in terms of their benefit to themselves, and then identify ways to encourage (or manipulate) people to achieve these benefits (Christie and Geis, 2013). For example, people who score more highly for Machiavellianism (i.e., manipulativeness) are likely to use fake reviews online (Borghi and Ratcharak, 2025).

Psychopathy

We can all recall psychopathic killers from the movies, but it's crucial to note that not all individuals with psychopathic traits will exhibit violent behaviour or criminal tendencies. Psychopathy is used to describe people who are highly impulsive, yet lack empathy and anxiety (Paulhus and Williams, 2002). They seek thrills without too much worry about the downside.

Narcissism

The famous story of Narcissus, who fell in love with his own reflection in the water, serves as a metaphor for narcissism, highlighting the allure of self admiration and the complexities of self obsession. Narcissism, like psychopathy, is often viewed negatively due to its association with self centeredness and a lack of empathy in interpersonal relationships.

For some time, psychological research has indicated that narcissism is measurable. The Narcissism Personality Inventory for example allows researchers to assess the level of narcissism through a questionnaire. It is then possible to correlate narcissism levels to a range of behaviours – including engagement with social media. For example, research relating to social media (Mehdizadeh, 2010) suggests that those with higher recorded levels of narcissism [and low self-esteem] are likely to use Facebook more [as well as post self-promotional content].

In psychological terms, those scoring highly for narcissism are likely to exhibit grandiosity, believing that they are in some way entitled to more in life and superior to others. These beliefs may lead them to try to dominate others (Raskin and Hall, 1979). Narcissism also affects online communication styles (Gross and Lunardo, 2024) and some narcissists set unrealistic goals for themselves (Finch et al., 2024). A separate study identified that people who focus on their physical appearance (self objectification) are more likely to purchase luxury goods (Sun et al., 2024).

Some campaigns that emphasise personal achievement might appeal to customers with narcissistic traits by relating to their desire for status, individuality, and self promotion.

APPLYING THE THEORY: KEY QUESTIONS

While the 'Dark Triad' traits are often seen in a negative light, they exist on a continuum, and your target customers may display some of these traits to varying degrees. Although we don't advocate targeting people based on dark traits, knowledge of this area of psychology might help you to better understand the behaviour of some customers.

People at the extreme end of the spectrum for each of these traits are likely to have significantly problematic behaviour, perhaps requiring professional support. Yet, many people exhibit some degree of narcissism for example (self focused, status driven, approval seeking). Knowing this might help you understand more about how customers use your product or service, or respond to your marketing:

Do customers use your brand to help enhance their image or be considered successful?

Do customers share content about your brand or perhaps customise your products?

2.3 INTELLIGENCE

Alongside key considerations such as a customer's traits and then demographics, we also want to include consideration of the natural differences between customers according to how they 'acquire knowledge, think and reason effectively, and deal adaptively with the environment' (Holt et al., 2024). This is generally referred to as 'intelligence'.

When people talk of intelligence, it is often as if people have a computer processor or 'random access memory' (RAM) in their head. Those with supposed 'higher' intelligence are sometimes described as having a 'quick mind' or even perhaps 'a bigger brain'. Really, many differences in customer intelligence, or disposition, are more likely to be attributable to *how* the brain is used.

There are many ways of assessing intelligence. Tests that assess one specific ability are often misleading. Somebody may be brilliant at maths for example, but not so good at communicating. General intelligence quotient (IQ) tests are therefore intended to assess a variety of mental abilities, such as mathematics, comprehension, and reasoning. Some people find all sorts of tests or exams tricky, but IQ tests generally exhibit reliability, demonstrating similar results over time, as well some reasonable correlation with other assessment of ability (Sternberg et al., 2001). Yet, cognitive ability, assessed through IQ, is only one perspective on what constitutes intelligence. There are other aspects of intelligence that might affect a customer's choice or use of a product or service, such as an understanding of emotions, language, or music.

a) *Customers can be emotionally intelligent*

Emotional intelligence is the ability to judge and regulate emotion (Salovey and Mayer, 1990), the short-term feeling people experience in a moment. Emotional intelligence includes judgement of a person's own emotions as well as judging others. In their first conceptualisation of emotional intelligence, appraisal of emotion was one of three strands contributing to emotional intelligence.

More recently, the three strands of emotional intelligence have been expanded to four: The ability to perceive emotion, to use emotion to facilitate thought, to understand emotions, and to manage emotions.

Together, the four strands of emotional intelligence framework offer another important perspective on what it means to be 'intelligent'.

b) *There are many other aspects to intelligence*

Howard Gardner (1995) goes further than just assessing cognitive ability and/or emotional intelligence. He originally outlined seven aspects of intelligence (represented in figure 2.1). Emotional intelligence is one so-called modality, all of which are labelled by Gardner as 'interpersonal' intelligence.

As with Salovey and Mayer's (1990) emotional intelligence findings, interpersonal intelligence involves an ability to understand the emotions of other people. This is not to be confused with the similarly named 'intrapersonal' intelligence, associated with a person's capability to assess their own abilities and emotions. Together, inter and intrapersonal intelligence are labelled as personal intelligences.

Cognitive ability (capacity to undertake tasks involving thinking) is assessed through linguistic and logical-mathematical intelligence: Linguistic intelligence is an ability to use language effectively, understanding and selecting appropriate words to convey thought; logical-mathematical intelligence is the ability to understand causes and effects, critically reasoning to make sense of data. For example, a marketer might use linguistic intelligence to craft persuasive ad copy, while

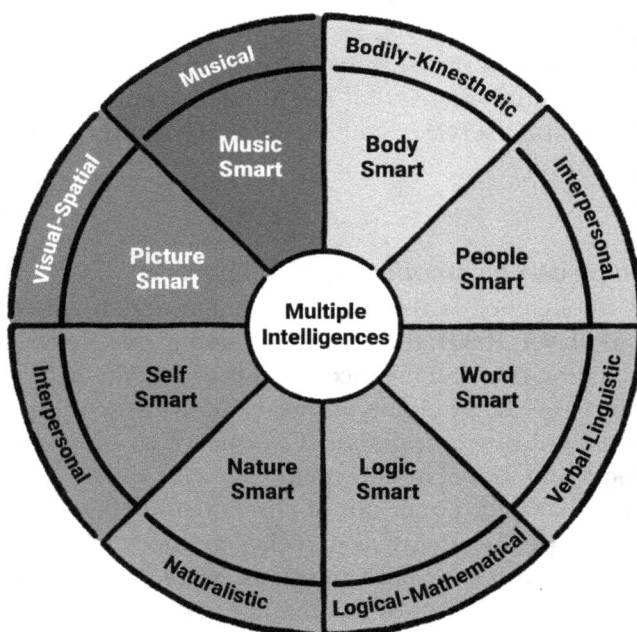

Figure 2.1 Gardner's Theory of Multiple Intelligences

relying on logical-mathematical intelligence to interpret campaign analytics and optimise performance.

Gardner also identified aspects of intelligence that might be associated with artistic tendencies. First, spatial intelligence focuses on visual perception of the world as well as the ability to mentally visualise. Musical intelligence then focuses on sound, with an understanding of pitch (such as melody) as well as rhythm and tone.

Gardner's seventh aspect of intelligence, known as bodily kinaesthetic intelligence, focuses on the ability to control the body. This could be used via interactive in-store demos that encourage customers to physically try products, or through online experiences like virtual try-ons and gamified interfaces that simulate physical interaction.

At a later date, an eighth aspect of intelligence was added, known as 'naturalistic' intelligence. This Gardner described as an identification and understanding of the natural world, such as when individuals show a preference for brands that use natural ingredients or eco-friendly packaging.

APPLYING THE THEORY: KEY QUESTIONS

When considering intelligence, pay attention to how different aspects of intelligence influence how people process marketing messages.

How detailed should the messaging be for your target audience?

How emotionally intelligent is your messaging – are you tuned in to your audience's mood at the time they are consuming your content?

What tone or format helps them best absorb information (e.g. text, visual, audio, interactive)?

2.4 SOCIOECONOMICS

Many attempts have been made to define class. Haralambos and Holborn (2013) generally discuss class based on a person's type of work: Manual labourers are deemed working class, those in professions that do not involve manual labour belong to the middle class, and the upper class is identified according to ownership of significant assets – such as the companies that the working and middle classes work for. However, in modern society, defining class based solely on occupation presents challenges. For example, should a wealthy builder or a reality TV-show prize winner be considered working class or upper class? Are individuals classified by their background, their job, or their wealth?

Discussions about how class influences behaviour are quite common. However, we prefer to refer to the term 'socioeconomics' for several important reasons. Class is a complex notion that is often tied to identity rather than being based on objective data. Individuals may perceive their position within an abstract hierarchy – identifying as lower, middle, or upper class – despite this perception having little connection to their actual economic status. For instance, a famous rock star, who now embodies a life of luxury, might identify as working class due to their starting point in life.

Given these complexities, it is often more effective to examine how income influences thought and behaviour.

Income is more quantifiable and measurable, and in many cultures, it serves as a more significant marker of success. In the U.S., for example, the American Dream is founded on the belief that anyone can rise to the top of society, regardless of their background or social class.

Ethically, it's important to avoid promoting products or services to customers who can't afford them. When thinking about the socioeconomic factors that shape customer behaviour, it's important to recognise that how people feel about their financial situation, compared to others, often matters more than what they actually earn.

How do your customers perceive their own financial situation? You might be surprised that lower income *increases* the likelihood of buying products or services to display wealth, status, or social standing to others – known as conspicuous consumption (Wang et al., 2022; Chowdhury and Swaminathan, 2023).

In her book, *The LUXpreneur* (2024), luxury-brand expert Elizabeth Solaru highlights the importance of marketers at high-end brands understanding which of the eight luxury-client types are driven by psychological 'aspiration' and a desire to display status:

"For 'comfort-first' clients, the emphasis must be on unwavering trust and exclusivity – ensuring they feel secure and valued. For 'aspirational' clients, it's about positioning your brand as a symbol of elite status, and once they're part of your 'club', they must be treated with the utmost care and respect. Effective luxury brand marketing doesn't adopt a one-size-fits-all approach; it speaks directly to the distinct psychological needs of each group, ensuring long-term loyalty and driving sustained engagement."

Socioeconomic status also significantly influences social disparities, which are evident in the unequal distribution of resources, opportunities, and privileges among individuals or groups within society. Inequality often leads to notable differences in well-being, wealth, and education. Plus, there is evidence that people's purchases are judged according to their perceived income level (Hagerty et al., 2022), with wealthier people being perceived as more trustworthy, for example (Boon-Falleur et al., 2024).

This dynamic is particularly relevant for influencers and brands. For example, influencers with a higher social status or appearance of wealth are often perceived as more credible or trustworthy by their audience, regardless of whether their actual financial standing aligns with this perception. Brands sometimes partner with influencers who fit the 'wealthy' or 'successful' image, believing that their endorsement will lend additional credibility to a product or service.

a) Inequality affects how your customers buy products and services

One of the key points about considering socioeconomics is that each of your customers will have a different socioeconomic profile. Society is therefore unavoidably unequal, but there are different extremes of such inequality. Consideration of socioeconomic profile can then have a psychological impact.

The economy and inequality

In 1949, James Duesenberry suggested an economic theory known as the relative income hypothesis. The theory suggests that people judge their income in comparison to others, rather than in absolute terms. This then affects their own spending. If Mr and Mrs Smith's neighbours (the Joneses) get richer, then the Smiths spend more to 'keep up with the Joneses'. Frank, Levine, and Dijk (2010) describe this then creating a 'cascade' situation, where increased expenditure by those higher on the income ladder leads those on the next rung to spend more, and so on.

Relative deprivation

Relative deprivation is a feeling of anger and resentment when one person feels poorly treated in comparison to another (Smith et al., 2012). This is perhaps more likely to occur in an economically unequal society, but it can occur when an individual or group feels unfairly treated (Smith and Pettigrew, 2015). Relative deprivation can also affect customer behaviour, driving a desire for scarce goods for example (Sharma and Alter, 2012).

Living with financial disadvantages can affect a customer's psychological state. Wilkinson and Pickett (2010) demonstrated that the gap between rich and poor matters more than a country's overall wealth, and studies have shown that inequality reduces happiness (Oishi et al., 2011), increases greed (Liu et al., 2024), increases so-called compensatory purchases when people buy products to cope with their perceived deficiencies (Rauber et al., 2024), and even increases a desire for counterfeit goods (Liu et al., 2024).

APPLYING THE THEORY: KEY QUESTIONS

Does your messaging make customers feel included, respected, and understood – regardless of income?

If you're considering working with influencers, how does their perceived socioeconomic status and credibility influence your target audience's trust in your brand?

Is your brand one that others are likely to want to display 'conspicuously'?

2.5 GEOGRAPHY: CULTURE

Often marketers define a population according to geographical boundaries. For example, they might seek to target people within a specific country or region. In reality, it isn't the physical characteristics of a location that affect customer behaviour – it's the culture.

HSBC, known for its tagline 'The World's Local Bank', operates in over 60 countries while adapting its services, marketing, and customer experiences to align with local cultures, financial regulations, and consumer behaviours. This localisation approach is evident in how HSBC tailors its products to regional markets – whether offering Sharia-compliant banking in Muslim-majority countries or SME-focused lending in fast-growing economies. The bank also customises its branding and messaging to resonate with local audiences, as seen in multilingual campaigns and culturally relevant advertising.

Localisation for culture, not just geography, is crucial because customer behaviours, values, and expectations are deeply rooted in cultural contexts.

a) There are ways of classifying the culture of your customers

One of the most-recognised ways of identifying and categorising culture is Geert Hofstede's (1980) 'Dimensions of Cultural Difference'. Hofstede originally used an IBM database of 100,000 questionnaires to analyse cultural differences between countries. Although respondents had answered the same questions, their nationality affected their responses. Subsequent analysis using the World Values Survey has revealed six ways in which cultures can be differentiated between countries.

1 Power Distance is the extent to which there is acceptance and expectation of a large difference in status between authorities and much of the population.
2 Individualism is the extent to which members of the population feel autonomous.
3 Masculinity (now known as Motivation towards Achievement and Success) is the extent to which people are encouraged to be assertive.
4 Uncertainty Avoidance is the extent to which people accept uncertainty, or see ambiguous or unknown situations as a threat to be avoided.
5 Long Term is the extent to which people see a changing world and therefore prepare for the future.
6 Indulgence is the extent to which people enjoy life now.

To understand how your country compares to others around the world, visit the Culture Factor website: www.theculturefactor.com. This will provide a chart as shown in figure 2.2.

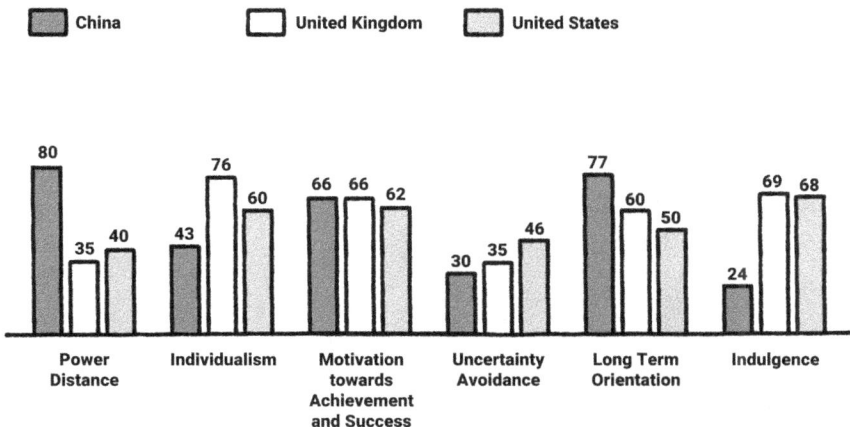

Figure 2.2 Screenshot from www.theculturefactor.com

Hofstede's is not the only list of cultural dimensions available. Schwartz (2012) has proposed a list of ten cultural values that comprise the 'Circular Model of Values', discussed in chapter 3, and Inglehart (2018) maps countries on a grid comprising traditional versus secular (y axis) and survival versus self-expression (x axis). Sweden's emphasis on self-expression and secular views places it the top right for example. There is also evidence of cultural differences in consumption, for example with consumers of luxury goods in Western countries valuing refinement, heritage, and exclusivity more than so-called Eastern countries (Tafani et al., 2024).

Spotify understands cultural differences. It doesn't just promote its platform based on functionality or music variety – it builds emotional connections by aligning with local cultures. From Carnival-themed playlists in Brazil to Bollywood-inspired 'Wrapped' summaries in India, Spotify adapts its content and campaigns to reflect regional tastes and traditions, helping users feel seen and understood.

Tightness and looseness

People often describe cultures as being either tight-knit or loose, reflecting the strength of social norms within a given location. According to Gelfand (2011), cultures can vary significantly in their adherence to established norms. Tight cultures, such as Japan and Singapore, exhibit low tolerance for deviant or unacceptable behaviour, with clearly defined norms that govern social conduct.

For example, Coca-Cola's marketing in Japan often emphasises harmony, respect, and community, aligning with local values and norms.

In contrast, loose cultures, like the United Kingdom and United States, have weaker social norms and a higher tolerance for deviation. These cultures encourage individuality and self-expression, allowing for a wider range of behaviours and lifestyles. Understanding these distinctions helps illuminate how cultural dynamics shape interactions within different locations and influence community relationships.

Nike's 'Just Do It' campaign, which celebrates personal achievement and encourages people to break boundaries, resonates with the individualistic ethos prevalent in loose cultures.

b) The culture of your market affects behaviour

Although we have shown ways of defining the overall culture of a specific society, it is also important to consider how this affects individual customers within that society.

Cultural imprinting

Kevin Simler's (2014) view of advertising is not that individuals each respond when they see an attractive advert, but that adverts can affect the way a whole culture views that product or service. He calls this cultural imprinting. By relating a product to an idea (sometimes an abstract idea), adverts give a product a cultural meaning, which then makes a customer want the product.

For example, does Tom use an Apple iPhone because it has the best operating system (iOS) or because of the brand association with the creativity, innovation, and the tech-forward culture of California?

Sharing attitudes

Social proof is a common marketing tactic when potential customers are shown an example of someone similar who has already made the same decision. Across all cultures people often look to others for validation, guidance, and reassurance when making purchasing decisions.

However, Barnes and Shavitt (2024) suggests that in cultures where self construal is interdependent – meaning individuals define themselves through their relationships with others – customers are more likely to be influenced by how others feel (attitude) about a product, rather than just copying their actions.

Countries such as Japan, India, and Greece are typically seen as having more interdependent self construal. In contrast, the United Kingdom and the United States are generally considered to have more independent self construal, with individuals focusing on personal goals and self-expression.

APPLYING THE THEORY: KEY QUESTIONS

How do cultural norms and values in your target market influence purchasing behaviour, and how can your messaging or product align with these values?

How can you tailor your marketing activities to account for local customs, traditions, or language differences to build stronger connections with your audience? For example, are there specific holidays or events in the region that can be leveraged in your campaigns?

If you're using social proof in your marketing, are you showing potential customers that people like them genuinely value the product?

2.6 AGE

Marketers typically start with demographics as a way of segmenting an audience. Often, for example, a customer's age is included as part of a persona. However, psychologically, there are limits to the usefulness of this criteria. Sometimes marketers might group people into certain age categories or even refer to generations. The categorisation of generations is rather broad though, and also subjective.

It is tricky to say definitively that someone thinks and behaves in a certain way just because of the number of years that they've been alive (their age). However, brains do literally change over time. A child's brain is still growing and developing new neural pathways, whereas an elderly person's brain is probably declining. For example, older brains typically find 'fluid abilities' more difficult, such as processing information quickly and taking on new information (Park et al., 2002). So-called crystallised abilities, such as verbal ability, are less likely to be affected. Your brain is not simply a computer; however, like a computer, processing speed gradually slows down over time (Salthouse, 1996). Such changes are normal.

Aside from physical changes to the brain, which affect its function, there are also age-related changes to behaviour that result from life experience. Several scholars (such as Marcia, 2002) have examined the search for identity during adolescence. For example, as young consumers age, they become more open to learning and opportunities to create (Sun et al., 2025).

Levinson's model of adult development (1986) demonstrates how teenagers form ambitions as they work towards independence, leading to anxiety and experimentation during early adulthood, and eventually identifying a 'niche' as they move towards midlife.

Age may also affect customer reactions to marketing campaigns. For example, older customers believe they are more resistant to celebrity endorsements (Chan and Fan, 2020), yet feeling younger leads to more sustainable consumption (Lee and Kim, 2024). For a great literature review of how aging affects customer behaviour, see Zheng et al. (2024).

In many cultures, there are typical life events that accompany age milestones. Donald Super (1957) studied vocational psychology, demonstrating that people pass through different stages as they establish their work identity, from 'growth' and 'exploration' as they identify preferred careers, to 'establishment' and 'maintenance' stages as careers stabilise in later stages of adulthood. Similarly, romantic partnerships form, often leading to marriage and perhaps the formation of families. Even within just one of these stages, such as marriage, there are different phases; for example, before and after children leave home (Orbuch et al., 1996).

2.7 SEX AND GENDER

Marketers also tend to consider the sex or gender of the customer when preparing their customer personas. To note, sex refers to the biological characteristics, including reproductive organs, chromosomes, and brain structure, which distinguish males from females, while gender is commonly used to refer to the roles, behaviours, and identities shaped by society and culture.

It is difficult to assess the extent to which different behaviours between sexes are due to demonstrable differences in brain activity (rather than how people are 'socialised'). Many psychological theories emphasise that behaviours are shaped not only by biological traits but also by the roles and expectations society associates with gender, such as those discussed in social role theory (Eagly and Wood, 2012).

Gender is a way in which many people establish their identity, and there is a growing body of literature seeking to understand how gender identity affects behaviour and thought. One study, for example (Palomares and Lee, 2010), observed differences in online-communication style according to the apparent gender of a digital avatar. Participants engaged in online conversations while adopting either a male or female avatar. The study found that they started to change the way they communicated to match the gender of the avatar. For example, people using a female avatar used more friendly and expressive language, while those using a male avatar were more direct and focused on tasks.

People view others according to gender stereotypes, especially in economically developed countries according to Napp (2024). If you have ever read *The Turbulent Term of Tyke Tiler*, this will ring true (we apologise if you haven't, as we have just given the game away). Locksley et al. (1980), for example, demonstrated that the name given to a fictional character (male or female) affected perceptions of the character's assertiveness, even when other behavioural information was presented. When only a male name was provided, participants in the study tended to perceive the character as more assertive, even if the character's actions suggested otherwise. Conversely, when only a female name was given, participants tended to perceive the character as less assertive, even when the character's actions were assertive.

Although they have attracted criticism in recent years (Schimmack, 2021), Implicit Association Tests have been used for many years to reveal similar apparent biases (systematic inclinations) through measuring the difference in reaction times when a subject (such a gender category) is labelled positively or negatively. The idea is that people respond more quickly when two concepts are closely associated in their mind – such as 'male' and 'leader' – which can reveal unconscious biases that influence how messages are received or interpreted.

APPLYING THE THEORY: KEY QUESTIONS

How does the age and life stage of your target audience impact their buying decisions? For example, younger customers may focus on personal identity, while older customers with families might value reliability and practicality.

How does your customer's media consumption affect your marketing approach? Younger audiences may prefer social media or video content, while older customers may prefer print or email.

How might the language and imagery you use in your marketing reinforce gender stereotypes – intentionally or not – and what steps can you take to ensure more balanced representation?

Chapter Summary

In this chapter, you've learned the importance of avoiding stereotypes and how to use psychology to help you to understand customers beyond common demographic criteria such as age and sex. You have discovered how you could incorporate factors such as personality traits, socioeconomic status, and cultural influences to ensure that your personas reflect real human experiences rather than generalisations. Apply the key questions when you are next preparing or reviewing your marketing plans.

What's Next?

Having considered broad ways of segmenting customers according to long term psychological and demographic bases, we will now move on in the next chapter to discuss shorter-term dispositional considerations.

CHAPTER 2 REFERENCES

Allen, M.S., Mishra, M., Tashjian, S.M., & Laborde, S. (2024). Linking Big Five personality traits to components of diet: A meta-analytic review. *Journal of Personality and Social Psychology, 128*(4), 905–929.

Allport, G.W., & Odbert, H.S. (1936) *Trait-Names; a Psycho-Lexical Study. A Study from the Harvard Psychological Laboratory.* Harvard Psychological Laboratory.

Barnes, A. J., & Shavitt, S. (2024). Top rated or best seller? Cultural differences in responses to attitudinal versus behavioral consensus cues. *Journal of Consumer Research, 51*(2), 276–297.

Boon-Falleur, M., André, J. B., Baumard, N., & Nettle, D. (2024). Household wealth is associated with perceived trustworthiness in a diverse set of countries. *Social Psychological and Personality Science, 16*(7), 732–742.

Borghi, M., & Ratcharak, P. (2025). Deceptive minds in digital spaces: the influence of the dark triad on posting fake online reviews. *Psychology & Marketing, 42*(7), 1932–1945.

Chan, K., & Fan, F. (2020). Perception of advertisements with celebrity endorsement among mature consumers. *Journal of Marketing Communications, 28*(2), 115–131

Christie, R., & Geis, F.L. (2013). *Studies in Machiavellianism.* Academic Press.

Chowdhury, F., & Swaminathan, S. (2024). Does reference-group comparison impact compensatory consumption for bottom of the pyramid (BOP) consumers? *Journal of Marketing Theory and Practice, 32*(4), 463–485.

Duesenberry, J.S. (1949). *Income, saving and the theory of consumer behavior.* Harvard University Press.

Eagly, A.H., & Wood, W. (2012). Social role theory. In D.T. Gilbert, S.T. Fiske, & G. Lindzey (Eds.), *The Handbook of Social Psychology* (5th ed., pp. 458–476). Wiley.

Finch, E.F., Kalinowski, S.E., Schacter, D.L., & Hooley, J.M. (2024). Aiming (too) high: Narcissism and unrealistic goal setting. *Personality and Individual Differences, 224*, Article 112614.

Fiske, D.W. (1949). Consistency of the factorial structures of personality ratings from different sources. *The Journal of Abnormal and Social Psychology.* 44 (3), 329–344.

Frank, R.H., Levine, A.S. & Dijk, O. (2010). Expenditure cascades. Article 1690612.

Gardner, H. (1995). Reflections on multiple intelligences: Myths and messages. *Phi Delta Kappan, 77*, 200–209.

Gelfand, M.J., Raver, J.L., Nishii, L., Leslie, L.M., Lun, J., Lim, B.C., … & Yamaguchi, S. (2011). Differences between tight and loose cultures: A 33-nation study. *Science, 332*(6033), 1100–1104.

Goldberg, L.R. (1981). Developing a taxonomy of trait-descriptive terms. *New Directions for Methodology of Social & Behavioural Sciences.* 9, 43.

Gosling, S. (2018). *Snoop: What your stuff says about you.* Profile Books.

Gross, J., & Lunardo, R. (2023). Online communication styles of narcissistic content and low versus high social media engagement: Evidence from Instagram. *Marketing Letters*, 1–14.

Hagerty, S.F., Barasz, K., & Norton, M.I. (2022). Economic inequality shapes judgments of consumption. *Journal of Consumer Psychology, 32*(1), 162–164.

Haidt, J. (2012). *The righteous mind: Why good people are divided by politics and religion.* Vintage.

Haralambos, M., Holborn, M., Chapman, S., & Moore, S. (2013). *Sociology Themes and perspectives* (8th ed.). HarperCollins.

Hofstede, G. (1980). Culture and organizations. *International studies of management & organization, 10*(4), 15–41.

Holt, N., Bremner, A., Sutherland, E., Vliek, M., Passer, M., & Smith, R. (2024). *Psychology: The science of mind and behaviour* (9th ed.). McGraw Hill.

Inglehart, R.F. (2018). *Cultural Evolution.* Cambridge University Press.

Kordsmeyer, T.L., Speer, A.B., Wilms, R., & Kurz, R. (2024). Longitudinal effects of employees' Big Five personality traits on internal promotions differentiated by job level in a multinational company. *Journal of Business and Psychology,* 1–17.

Lee, D.C., & Kim, J. (2024). Feeling younger and acting greener: The impact of subjective age on sustainable consumption. *Psychology & Marketing, 41*(10), 2310–2328.

Levinson, D.J. (1986). A conception of adult development. *American psychologist, 41*(1), 3.

Liu, Z., Sun, X., Bao, R., & Ma, R. (2024). Why do people always want more? Perceived economic inequality leads people to be greedy by enhancing relative deprivation. *British Journal of Psychology, 115*(4), 616–640.

Liu, J., Wakeman, S.W., & Norton, M.I. (2024). The egalitarian value of counterfeit goods: Purchasing counterfeit luxury goods to address income inequality. *Journal of Consumer Psychology, 35*(2), 269–280.

Locksley, A., Borgida, E., Brekke, N., & Hepburn, C. (1980). Sex stereotypes and social judgment. *Journal of Personality and Social psychology, 39*(5), 821.

Marcia, J. E. (2002). Adolescence, identity, and the Bernardone family. *Identity: An international journal of theory and research, 2*(3), 199–209.

Mayer, J.D. (2004). *What is Emotional Intelligence?* UNH Personality Lab. 8. https://scholars.unh.edu/personality_lab/8

McCrae, R.R. and Costa, P.T. (2003). *Personality in adulthood: A five-factor theory perspective* (2nd ed.). Guilford Press.

Mehdizadeh, S. (2010). Self-presentation 2.0: Narcissism and self-esteem on Facebook. *Cyberpsychology, Behavior, and Social Networking, 13*(4), 357–364.

Murray, I, and Tenzer, A. (2018). *Why We Shouldn't Trust Our Gut Instinct.* Reach Solutions. https://www.reachsolutions.co.uk/resources/insight/why-we-shouldnt-trust-our-gut-instinct

Murray, I, and Tenzer, A. (2019). *The Empathy Delusion.* Reach Solutions. https://www.reachsolutions.co.uk/resources/insight/the-empathy-delusion

Murray, I, and Tenzer, A. (2025). *The Aspiration Window.* Reach Solutions. https://www.reachsolutions.co.uk/resources/insight/the-aspiration-window

Napp, C. (2024). Gender stereotypes about career and family are stronger in more economically developed countries and can explain the gender equality paradox. *Personality and Social Psychology Bulletin.*

Oishi, S., Kesebir, S., & Diener, E. (2011). Income inequality and happiness. *Psychological Science, 22*(9), 1095–1100.

Orbuch, T.L., House, J.S., Mero, R.P., & Webster, P.S. (1996). Marital quality over the life course. *Social Psychology Quarterly*, 162–171.

Palomares, N.A., & Lee, E.J. (2010). Virtual gender identity: The linguistic assimilation to gendered avatars in computer-mediated communication. *Journal of Language and Social Psychology*, *29*(1), 5–23.

Park, D.C., Lautenschlager, G., Hedden, T., Davidson, N.S., Smith, A.D., & Smith, P.K. (2002). Models of visuospatial and verbal memory across the adult life span. *Psychology and aging*, *17*(2), 299.

Paulhus, D.L., & Williams, K.M. (2002). The dark triad of personality: Narcissism, Machiavellianism, and psychopathy. *Journal of research in personality*, *36*(6), 556–563.

Raskin, R.N., & Hall, C.S. (1979). A narcissistic personality inventory. *Psychological reports*, *45*(2), 590–590.

Rauber, G.N., Barros, L.S.G., Zambaldi, F., & Perin, M.G. (2024). When life throws curveballs: Unpacking consumers' compensatory strategies. *Psychology & Marketing*, *41*(10), 2525–2536.

Salovey, P., & Mayer, J. D. (1990). Emotional intelligence. *Imagination, cognition and personality*, *9*(3), 185–211.

Salthouse, T.A. (1996). The processing-speed theory of adult age differences in cognition. *Psychological Review*, *103*(3), 403.

Schilling, T., & Bleidorn, W. (2024). Personality Traits and Insurance Demand. *Personality and Social Psychology Bulletin*.

Schimmack, U. (2021). The Implicit Association Test: A method in search of a construct. *Perspectives on Psychological Science*, *16*(2), 396–414.

Schwartz, S.H. (2012). An overview of the Schwartz theory of basic values. *Online readings in Psychology and Culture*, *2*(1), 11.

Sharma, E., & Alter, A.L. (2012). Financial deprivation prompts consumers to seek scarce goods. *Journal of Consumer research*, *39*(3), 545–560.

Simler, K. (2014). *Ads don't work that way*. Melting Asphalt. https://meltingasphalt. com/ads-dont-work-that-way/

Smith, H.J., Pettigrew, T.F., Pippin, G.M., & Bialosiewicz, S. (2012). Relative deprivation: A theoretical and meta-analytic *review*. *Personality and social psychology review*, *16*(3), 203–232.

Smith, H.J., & Pettigrew, T.F. (2015). Advances in relative deprivation theory and research. *Social Justice Research*, *28*, 1–6.

Solaru, E. (2024). *The LUXPreneur: How to start and build a successful luxury brand*. ECE Publishing

Sternberg, R.J., Grigorenko, E.L., & Bundy, D.A. (2001). The predictive value of IQ. *Merrill-Palmer Quarterly*, *47* (1), 1–41.

Sun, H., Guo, Z., & Qian, H. (2024). The self on display: The impact of self-objectification on luxury consumption. *Psychology & Marketing*, *41*(10), 2412–2430.

Sun, Z., Chen, S., Wang, K., Yuan, M., & Hou, Y. (2025). Fighting aging with creation: The sense of feeling old enhances young consumers' desire for

experiential creation consumption. *International Journal of Consumer Studies,*
49(1), Article e70016.

Super, D.E. (1957). *The psychology of careers; an introduction to vocational develop-*
ment. Harper & Brothers.

Tafani, E., Vigneron, F., Azoulay, A., Crener, S., & Zahid, A. (2024). The influence of culture and gender in luxury brand consumption: A comparison
across western and eastern culture consumers. *Journal of International*
Marketing, 32(4), 58–80.

Wang, Y., Liu, B., Lin, S., Liu, L., Wu, Y., & Cui, L. (2022). The effects of subjective socioeconomic status on conspicuous consumption. *Journal of Applied*
Social Psychology, 52(7), 522–531.

Wilkinson, R., & Pickett, K. (2010). The spirit level. *Why equality is better for*
everyone.

Zheng, Z., BA M, H.S., Omar Zaki, H., & Tan, Q.L. (2024). Impact of aging on
consumer behaviour: A review and research agenda. *International Journal of*
Consumer Studies, 48(6), Article e70000.

3 Audience: Customer Disposition

In this chapter, we consider how your customers' disposition (their 'outlook' at a particular moment) affects their behaviour. This is often called 'mindset', popularised by Carol Dweck (2006) in her book which focuses on attitudes towards self-development ('growth' or 'fixed' mindset according to whether a person wants to increase their intelligence).

There are a wide range of considerations included within this chapter, such as whether the customer feels positively (attitude) towards the topic of discussion, what they value or believe about the world, and what motivates them. These considerations will help you to understand your customers' point of view, create detailed personas, and effective messaging.

DCUK, based in Devon, England, has been charming customers and collectors alike for over 20 years, but the company's brand awareness and customer engagement has really grown in the last few years – with a lot of the hard work done by embracing the power of psychology. The tone of voice, online presence, and especially the products, are all designed to make you smile, being closely aligned to emotionally charged gifting moments. Head of Marketing, Steve Manser, tells us how his approach to marketing is fuelled by a passion for learning and applying psychology ...

APPLICATION OF PSYCHOLOGY IN MARKETING PRACTICE – MAKING PEOPLE HAPPY

Founded in 2004, DCUK (The Original Wooden Duck Company) is a small but mighty giftware brand known for its charming,

DOI: 10.4324/9781003541226-4

hand-crafted wooden ducks and feathered friends. Inspired by nature and traditional Indonesian craftsmanship, DCUK designs each piece with individuality, creating memorable, thoughtful, and personal gifts.

Emotional connections

The company's core mission is centred on making life a little better by helping as many people as possible to smile. Staff refer to their products as 'characters' to embrace personalities in their products and to create an emotional connection. It's important to DCUK to create positive brand associations, especially as purchasing DCUK products is such an emotional decision. A quick look at the customer reviews on Feefo and video testimonials from trade partners shows they're getting it right!

Surprise and delight (S&D) budget

Steve introduced a specific budget line called 'S&D' (surprise and delight) instead of 'R&D' (research and development) to empower the team to create unexpected positive and personalised experiences for customers. It's not a large budget, but it allows the team to do nice things such as sending free products or other gifts to customers. The 'S&D' approach also creates a positive internal culture while simultaneously building customer loyalty and powerful word-of-mouth marketing for the brand.

Peak-end rule

DCUK's use of emotion also implements the peak-end rule theory, which is where customers evaluate their overall experience based largely on the emotional peak and the final moment, making the purchase process simple, enjoyable, and memorable. The checkout process was apparently a real labour of love to create, especially as it represents part of that final 'end' moment. Using concrete language, reassuringly friction-free phrases, and visual confirmation for peace of mind have all contributed to an industry-busting conversion rate.

When purchasing, customers can also personalise their character with a name or leave it to the DCUK team to include a name, as part of their adoption process. The brochure accompanying the product says, *"Thank you for helping to give one of our characters a new home"* and truly does make you smile. During our conversation with Steve, he shared future plans to encourage sensory reactions such as adding sandalwood essential oil scents to packaging to reinforce the handcrafted approach, and using regional dialect within targeted campaigns for added potency.

Conclusion
DCUK demonstrates how a small company with limited resources can effectively implement psychology theories throughout its marketing activities. The approach is characterised by a deep understanding of emotional triggers, willingness to test theories, understanding of each stage of the customer journey, focus on building positive associations with the brand, and investment in creating authentic emotional connections.

3.1 ATTITUDE

Attitudes are positive or negative reactions to a specific issue. Generally, it is assumed that attitudes lead to behaviours, as demonstrated through models such as the theory of planned behaviour (Ajzen, 1985). This model, for example, shows that intention to behave is partly the result of existing attitudes – as well as an assessment of whether the behaviour is normal (known as subjective norms) and whether the person believes they are able to behave that way (known as perceived control).

Yet, Bem (1967) has also showed that attitudes can develop because of behaviour... A customer who believes sustainable products are important (attitude) may choose to buy eco-friendly items (behaviour). Over time, consistently choosing these products may then strengthen their positive attitude toward sustainability, especially as they begin to see themselves as someone who cares about the environment. Attitudes therefore influence behaviour, but can also *be* influenced by that behaviour.

a) Implicit attitudes
Some attitudes are inherent and involuntary, i.e. 'implicit' (Fazio and Olson, 2003). What do you generally think about pop-up banners on a

website for example? If you're trying to make a quick purchase, a pop-up offering a discount code might be welcomed. If the pop-up is a prompt for a survey, it might be annoying. These instinctive reactions often occur without much conscious thought, yet they shape perception of a brand and influence whether people complete a transaction or bounce off the site altogether.

Expectancy-value model

Attitudes towards online courses are generally positive. Learners begin their studies expecting to obtain a qualification and know that the value of the outcome is high upon completion. This example is an application of the expectancy-value model (Eccles et al., 1983) where people assess the extent to which they expect success and also judge the value of the activity.

The model can help explain why a customer might sign up for a webinar or download a white paper - they believe they'll be able to understand the content (expectancy) and see it as useful or rewarding for their work (value).

b) Explicit attitudes

In contrast to unconscious implicit attitudes, explicit attitudes are conscious viewpoints that people can verbalise. Based on Functional Attitude Theory (FAT), here are some reasons why people might choose to express an attitude explicitly (Katz, 1960) i.e. according to their function:

Adjustment function

Expressing an explicit attitude can be a way to adjust socially in order to maximise opportunities, in other words to 'adjust' to a wider group's attitudes. This is also known as the utilitarian function (Katz, 1960).

In an online-networking group, someone might explicitly express a strong dislike for corporate jargon, perhaps telling others to ditch words like 'reach out' and 'circle back' even if they still use those phrases in client meetings. They're adjusting their stated attitude to fit in with the tone of the group and gain social approval, not necessarily to reflect their real preferences.

Ego-defensive function

Perhaps an attitude is expressed by an individual explicitly to protect their own ego (Katz et al., 1957). Some people show support for a particular sports team, for example, to compensate for their poor self-esteem (Cialdini et al., 1976).

Knowledge function

Explicit attitudes guide the information and 'knowledge' gathered (Locander and Spivey, 1978). For example, people tend to visit blogs to read about topics they know they have an interest in.

Value-expressive function

Explicit attitudes help people to communicate values and beliefs (Kristiansen and Zanna, 1988). When individuals share or display certain attitudes, they also sometimes justify them by relating attitudes to values – known as the value-justification hypothesis (Kristiansen and Zanna, 1988).

APPLYING THE THEORY: KEY QUESTIONS

Understanding attitudes is a key part of customer persona development as you learn more about how they might think and feel about your brand, your products and services.

Can you highlight the value of your products or services in a way that shapes customers' expectations and fosters a positive attitude?

Can you present your products or services as a socially desirable choice for your target audience?

Can you encourage existing customers to share positive feedback within peer communities, influencing potential customers' attitudes and to build trust in your brand?

3.2 BELIEFS

Whereas attitudes describe reactions to a specific issue, beliefs are statements about the way the world is, or the way the world ought to be.

For example, an online shopper might have a positive attitude toward a retailer's website (because of its user-friendly interface and great product selection), but they may also believe that all online stores should offer a clear and easy return policy. This belief influences their decision to shop with the retailer, as they prioritise stores that align with their personal expectations of convenience and customer service.

a) There are many common beliefs

Although people naturally differ slightly in the degree to which they believe certain things, there are nevertheless some themes that group certain beliefs together.

Authoritarianism

People who believe in authoritarianism often believe in conformity and cultural conservatism (Duriez and Van Hiel, 2002).

Just world fallacy

Some believe that humans are generally punished for misbehaviour, i.e., we live in a just world (Rubin and Peplau, 1975). Sometimes this is referred to colloquially as 'karma'. Often people believe that service failures are the result of karma (Li et al., 2024); for example, someone who pays for a product deliberately using an out-of-date gift card might feel a sense of comeuppance when the product stops working.

Locus of control

There are differences in who people think is responsible for their lives. Is success driven internally (by individuals themselves) or externally (by circumstance)? Either option is a different 'locus' of control. How much control, for example, do people have in determining their own online experience? Many people believe that the content they see online is controlled directly by platform owners, rather than shaped by the signals they've given – such as their interests, behaviours, and engagement history.

Consistency

People often try to act consistently according to their beliefs (Gawronski, 2012). Here are three examples:

Coherence

Behaviours are often expected to be 'coherent' or, in other words, in-line with their existing beliefs about themselves (Markus, 1977).

Reinforcement

Current beliefs are often expected to support or 'reinforce' previous or existing beliefs. For example, the mass media reinforces existing beliefs (Schramm and Roberts, 1971).

Self-perception

In some circumstances, beliefs follow behaviour. By behaving in a certain way, beliefs begin to form in order to demonstrate consistency between behaviour and beliefs (Albarracin and Wyer, 2000). People who interact with a global network might be more likely to believe in a multicultural society and value messaging about diversity and inclusivity.

APPLYING THE THEORY: KEY QUESTIONS

What core beliefs do your target audience hold that might influence how they perceive your brand, product or service?

How can you tailor your messaging to resonate with those beliefs and ensure your communication feels authentic and relevant?

3.3 VALUES

Personal values are internal decisions about what is important to an individual, shaping how they interpret messages, make choices, and align themselves with brands that reflect those values – whether that's authenticity, innovation, or social responsibility. Values influence behaviour in both B2C and B2B contexts, affecting everything from everyday purchases to long-term business partnerships.

a) Some common values

There are lots of potential words to describe the guiding principles underpinning behaviour and thoughts at specific moments. Again, many of these can be grouped together into themes.

A summary of the ten values outlined by Schwartz (2012) is shown in figure 3.1 on the next page.

Security

For many, safety or stability is strongly valued. In fact (as you will read later in the chapter), Maslow's hierarchy of needs suggests that this is a basic need for everyone.

Power

Power is really the ability to exert influence over other people. Some people feel that it's important to exert control over other people or

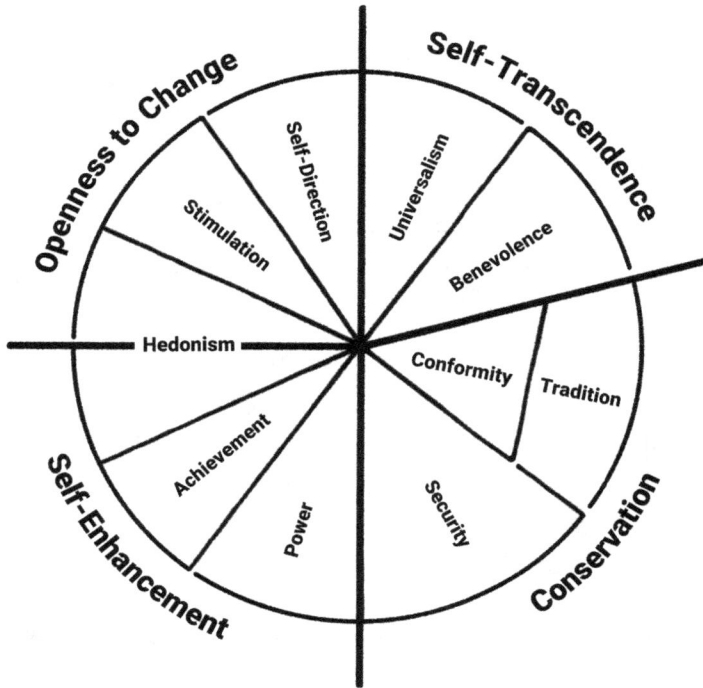

Figure 3.1 Schwarz's Theory of Basic Values

resources, taking a dominant position within society. Power doesn't have to be self-serving; it can also be used to drive positive outcomes, such as empowering a team, shaping ethical campaigns, or advocating for customers' needs.

Achievement

Some people particularly value success in whatever activity they are partaking in, such as online gaming or qualifications.

Hedonism

People with hedonistic values, that is, those who prioritise the pursuit of personal enjoyment, particularly opt for pleasurable pastimes, such as spending money online (Scarpi, 2012).

For marketers, understanding hedonism is useful in creating products or experiences that cater to customers seeking instant gratification, indulgence, or entertainment.

Stimulation (excitement)

People who enjoy new experiences, value stimulation.

Red Bull taps into this by positioning itself as more than just an energy drink, but as a brand that fuels adventurous, high-energy lifestyles, encouraging customers to push their limits and embrace excitement.

Self-direction

Most of us probably value autonomy to some degree (Bandura, 1977); i.e., we want to direct our own actions. A desire for autonomy often influences customer behaviour, as people are more likely to engage with products or services that allow them to make choices, express their individuality, and feel in control of their decisions.

Universalism

Some people value the welfare of everyone in their society.

For marketers, understanding this value is useful because it can guide the development of products, services, and messaging that resonate with customers who prioritise social responsibility, equality, and collective well-being.

Benevolence

Successful networkers value their personal relationships and reward friendship i.e., they are benevolent.

Tradition

In many societies, there are people who value the known customs of their culture (as you learned in chapter 2).

Many English people drink tea for example, as emphasised by the brand Yorkshire Tea, which leans into national identity and cultural pride in its marketing to create a strong connection with its audience.

Conformity

People with high conformity values may be more likely to follow trends, adopt mainstream products, or support brands that are seen as popular or socially accepted. These customers might make purchasing decisions based on what is perceived as 'normal' or expected within their social group, reflecting their desire to align with social norms and expectations. Here are some specific examples:

Availability cascade
'Availability bias' is where people rely on information that is mentally 'available'. Within wider society, the repetition of a stated belief gradually 'cascades' to become accepted and plausible (Kuran and Sunstein, 1998).

Bandwagon effect
Often it is easy for people to adopt views that others already have, by jumping on the 'bandwagon' (Leibenstein, 1950), where the popularity of an action or product influences others to follow suit.

For example, on Valentine's Day you can't walk through the entrance of a supermarket without being greeted by displays of red roses and chocolates – almost daring you not to pick something up for your loved one (as others are doing).

Courtesy bias
It might be socially acceptable, for example in an online group, to be courteous by stating an opinion which reflects present company rather than sharing a person's true feelings (Jones, 1963). This is slightly different to the adjustment function discussed earlier where a person changes their attitude (rather than their values) to fit with a social group.

Groupshift
People like to fit in with their social group and adopt the values of the group to do so. Yet, this can see group members adopting more extreme values than is necessary: Becoming more risk averse in risk averse groups and accommodating more risk in risk-taking groups (Dion et al., 1970).

Truth bias
Information expressed by others (especially acquaintances) tends to be believed (Levine et al., 1999).

APPLYING THE THEORY: KEY QUESTIONS

Which values are the most important to your audience, and which are non-negotiable when choosing a brand, products, or services?

How can you demonstrate how your brand, products or services support the values of your target audience, for example if they value security can you focus on these as key features in your messaging?

How can you demonstrate the popularity of your product to encourage others to purchase?

How do you navigate global campaigns where values may vary significantly across cultures and regions?

Do your content and campaigns reinforce shared values to build loyalty and community around your brand?

3.4 MORALS

Morals are like a 'code of conduct' that is accepted by a majority within a society. For example, many societies uphold the moral belief that honesty is essential in business transactions. This belief influences how customers trust brands and make purchasing decisions, as they are more likely to support companies that they perceive as ethical and transparent in their practices.

a) Six moral foundations

Moral foundations theory (Haidt, 2012) suggests that there are six dimensions against which moral judgements are based. Two are more focused on individual rights (care and fairness), whereas the others are more focused on group behaviour. Attitudes based on broadly accepted morals are known as moral conviction.

Authority

People form a judgement about whether traditional figures of authority ought to be followed.

Care

Should we always care for one another through our actions, or is it acceptable to harm another person?

Fairness
Some form of fairness is usually expected, but some people's moral judgements allow them to cheat.

Liberty
Freedom or autonomy is valued by most people, but to what degree? This is an assessment of liberty.

Loyalty
Are there ever times when it is acceptable to betray another person's trust, or should you always keep a promise? This is an assessment of loyalty.

Purity or sanctity
It is perhaps easier to understand purity by contrasting it to its opposite – disgust. Things are considered pure if they do not disgust.

The view your customer takes of your brand is therefore likely to be based on how they value these underlying moral dimensions.

b) Moral credential effect
When balancing your personal finances, perhaps you sell unwanted clothes or toys in order to allow yourself to buy new ones. The moral credential effect suggests that people do the same with moral behaviour, performing a 'good deed' to give themselves license to then do something 'bad' (Monin and Miller, 2001).

Market research by Hidden Voices Heard indicates that something similar applies to healthy behaviours. People use a healthy choice to justify an unhealthy one. The unhealthy choice is positioned as a reward. As Ruth Dale, the founder of Hidden Voices Heard, summarises: *"It's almost like a mental pass – I went for a run so I can have that extra wine. Looking through the behavioural lens, understanding this behaviour means we can accommodate it and design around it."*

APPLYING THE THEORY: KEY QUESTIONS

How do your customers' moral values influence their perception of your industry or brand?

Do they face any moral dilemmas such as fast fashion or environmental impact? Can you navigate this within your communications?

How can you demonstrate moral conviction and help your customers build moral credentials?

3.5 MOTIVATION

An important consideration affecting the disposition of a customer is the degree to which a person is motivated to adopt a new behaviour, i.e., to buy and use a new product or service. There are several ways to assess motivation.

a) Self-determined behaviour is ideal

Self-determination theory (SDT) describes how people are motivated by either themselves (self-determined motivation) or others (Deci and Ryan, 2012). It distinguishes between two main sources of motivation: External (known as extrinsic motivation) and internal, self-determined (known as intrinsic motivation). Ideally, successful, long-lasting changes should be self-determined (intrinsic) and driven by the person themselves.

For example, many early adopters of technology do so because they want to be ahead of the curve, rather than being told to by others (extrinsic).

Extrinsic

Extrinsic motivation is driven by external pressure. However, there is a spectrum of motivation along which different levels of extrinsic motivation can be mapped. 'External regulation' is driven by a desire for either a reward or to avoid punishment; 'introjection' involves following others' rules; 'identification' involves personally connecting with the rules; and 'integrated motivation' involves accepting the rules completely.

David McClelland (1961) differentiated between three different motivators: Achievement, affiliation, and power. Each seems to relate specifically to extrinsic reasons for adopting a behaviour. Although separate to SDT, we discuss each of them here as they relate to external influences on behaviour:

Achievement

People driven by achievement want to reach recognised goals.

Affiliation

People driven by a need for affiliation, which is the desire to belong or be accepted, want to feel welcomed into a social group.

Power

Those in search of power, want to enjoy a sense of influence over other people.

Intrinsic

Intrinsic motivation is the most effective in affecting long-term behaviour, leading to self-determined behaviour. To lead to intrinsic motivation, people need to firstly feel a sense of autonomy; the decision to adopt the behaviour needs to be their own. They also need to recognise their competence to adopt the behaviour, and they need to see how their efforts have a purpose in relation to other people.

Customers are intrinsically motivated to purchase organic food for example (Buil and Mata, 2024), through consideration of health, and sustainability.

Overjustification effect

It's interesting to consider how motivation can shift from one to another when a reward is offered for an activity which otherwise would be driven intrinsically (Lepper et al., 1973). You might assume that being paid to do something you love is the dream – a professional online gamer, for example – but this is overjustification. Research shows, in fact, that intrinsic motivation decreases when a reward is then offered for the same activity (Promberger and Marteau, 2013). This might explain why turning a hobby into a business doesn't always feel as fulfilling as expected – what once felt joyful and effortless can start to feel like hard work.

b) *Consider the 'hierarchy' of your customers' needs*

In one of the most famous theories relating to motivation, Abraham Maslow (1943) suggested that humans satisfy specific needs in order of priority, as shown in figure 3.2. Firstly, people consider their basic physiological needs. Once fulfilled, safety needs must be met, followed by love and belonging, then esteem. Only once these are met do people seek to meet self-actualisation needs.

Maslow's theory applies to both B2C and B2B marketing by guiding how organisations can address customers' core needs – whether it's providing essential products, creating a sense of security, fostering relationships, building brand reputation, or enabling customers to achieve their full potential.

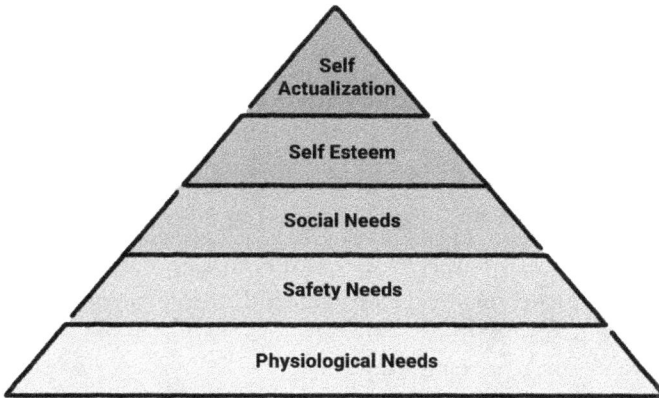

Figure 3.2 Maslow's Hierarchy of Needs

c) *Close goals are more motivating*

Goal gradient theory (Hull, 1932) suggests that motivation has a slope-like effect, with motivation increasing as the goal gets nearer, like reaching the end of a slide at a children's playground: Speed increases the further down the slide you travel. Perhaps you can recall a school project for example, or a tender/pitch, where most of the work was undertaken in the final 24 hours, i.e., as the deadline loomed the motivation to get it done increased.

d) *Mental contrasting*

When people have a goal in mind, they also weigh up the potential obstacles. For example, Tom would love to become an international rockstar, but the money and practice required make this unachievable (for now)! Luan would love to embrace van life, traveling the world in a campervan and working from picturesque locations – but the reality is that she also needs home office space with reliable Wi-Fi. This is known as 'mental contrasting' (Oettingen, 2000). A marketer's role is to reduce the perceived obstacles and help customers envisage success.

APPLYING THE THEORY: KEY QUESTIONS

Motivation is at the heart of marketing and psychology – understanding what drives people to act (or not act) is essential. By understanding motivations (intrinsic and extrinsic), and applying theories such as Maslow's Hierarchy of Needs, marketers can move customers through the buying journey.

What motivates your audience to engage with your brand?

How can you appeal to intrinsic motivations such as purpose and enjoyment?

How can you appeal to extrinsic motivations and show your customers that they are close to achieving a goal or reward?

What obstacles can you remove (and communicate) to help your customer achieve success? For example, can your calls to action (CTAs) help guide them through different barriers, e.g., 'get started here' or 'get certified today'?

3.6 EXECUTIVE FUNCTIONS

There is plenty of evidence to suggest that humans are essentially a brain, and the neurons in a person's brain send signals that create thoughts and behaviours. In other words, many thoughts and behaviours are automatic or responses to stimuli – hence all the research on biases which we explore throughout the book. In contrast, there are times when a person takes control of their own mind and controls or directs attention. This ability to 'execute' decisions in order to achieve certain goals is referred to as 'executive function' (Diamond, 2013).

a) Customers can be cognitively flexible

Unlike a machine, striving to achieve a specific goal to the desired specifications, humans can change their approach when needed. People may start searching online for a specific product or service but change direction when new information comes to light. Humans can process new stimuli and are therefore cognitively flexible.

As marketers, we need to be aware that customer decision-making can shift. We need to incorporate curiosity, comparison, and reconsideration into our marketing planning and campaign messaging.

Different perspectives

One of the most difficult, but most important, steps in an argument or debate is to think about what another person is feeling. Why are they arguing a point that seems so wrong? Being able to change perspective is an important example of cognitive flexibility – perhaps one that is unique to humans.

Adaptation
Because humans can process new information, they can set new priorities and change behaviour when the environment changes. Since 2020 for example, when COVID-19 forced many people to work from home, many businesses have incorporated remote working tools and adapted communication practices for virtual rather than face-to-face meetings.

Creative thinking
People commonly refer to those with new ideas as 'thinking outside the box'. This ability to think about a problem is highly prized in competitive situations where new products or designs make a real difference. Everyone has this ability to a degree. Yet, customers don't like new products being presented too creatively (Jiang et al., 2024) because it's difficult to then relate the product to themselves.

Marketers, therefore, must strike a balance between innovation and familiarity to ensure customers can easily connect with the messaging.

b) Inhibitions prevent behaviours
Another example of executive function is the ability to exert control over our behaviour. If people acted purely on instinctive impulse all the time for example, the world would be chaotic and probably anarchic! Fortunately, humans can consider and control their behaviour.

Interference control
Despite whatever a child or partner may tell you at home ("I didn't hear you asking for help with the laundry."), people do have some ability to direct their attention. Television and background noise for example may be a distraction, but with some willpower (executive function), it is still possible to focus on a different source of information (Colás et al., 2017) such as a mobile phone screen.

Response inhibition
Self-control can also be exercised in emotional situations. Whereas animals might act on instinct to 'fight' or take 'flight', humans have far

more developed brains that are capable of taking control of behaviour. Humans are also capable of recognising inappropriate reactions and acting to change them (Mostofsky and Simmonds, 2008). For example, if a certain topic causes them to feel anger, many people will simply scroll past the content.

c) Consider 'front of mind' information

At this point it's useful to refer to the concept of 'working memory', which is the information temporarily held in the mind when applying executive functions (Baddeley and Hitch, 1974). For example, someone might immediately search online for a new product they see advertised on TV, but in the long-term the product will be forgotten. In *Why We Remember*, Charan Ranganath (2024) focuses on memory as a resource to understand the present and navigate the future.

This brings us to the idea of 'mental availability' – the likelihood that a brand or product will come to mind when a customer is ready to make a purchase. For B2B marketers, this is even more important due to longer buying cycles and the '95:5 rule' (Sharp and Romaniuk, 2016), which suggests that 95% of potential customers are not actively in the market at any given time. The key to success therefore is to remain front of mind so that when the 5% of buyers enter the decision-making process, your brand is the first they think of. This is a key principle behind positioning (Ries and Trout, 1981) and is central to effective marketing: Staying visible and memorable to customers, even when they're not actively buying.

APPLYING THE THEORY: KEY QUESTIONS

Are you creating clear, engaging messaging that help customer focus on what's important and make it easy for them to process information?

Are you guiding your customer towards specific goals and helping them to stay focused during the decision-making process?

When environmental changes occur, are you communicating to your customers how you can help them adapt effectively?

Are you communicating consistently so that you stay front of mind?

3.7 SELF-EVALUATION

Self-evaluation refers to the process by which individuals assess their own abilities, performance, and overall value, often comparing themselves to personal standards or external benchmarks.

'Self-efficacy' refers to an individual's belief in their ability to successfully complete a task or achieve a goal. For example, while many people recognise the need to limit their screen time, their confidence in their ability to follow through on this goal can vary significantly.

'Esteem' is a judgement about status and can be positive or negative. For example, people who are valued are held in high esteem. Similarly, people hold a judgement of themselves, known as self-esteem, which affects their self-identity. In this section, we discuss various theories relating to self-evaluation.

a) Customers are overconfident in their abilities

People are constantly making judgements about their ability to undertake specific tasks, from cooking a nutritious meal to learning a new skill. Often, people tend to overestimate how capable they really are.

Illusory superiority

It's very easy to apply for jobs online. Applicants may feel well-qualified to undertake the roles they scroll through and find it hard to imagine others with better experience and ability. Yet, this overconfidence (and failure to consider problems) is often an illusion (Hoorens, 1993).

Dunning-Kruger Effect

When people visit a website, they probably feel reasonably confident about their requirements – perhaps even sure about the product or service they want. How much do most of us really know about the products we buy? Does a customer really know, for example, which product would best suit their needs? Confidence in decisions can often be deluded. Similarly, experts frequently underestimate their own expertise. This mistaken estimation – upwards and downwards – is known as the Dunning-Kruger Effect, as shown in figure 3.3 (Dunning, 2011).

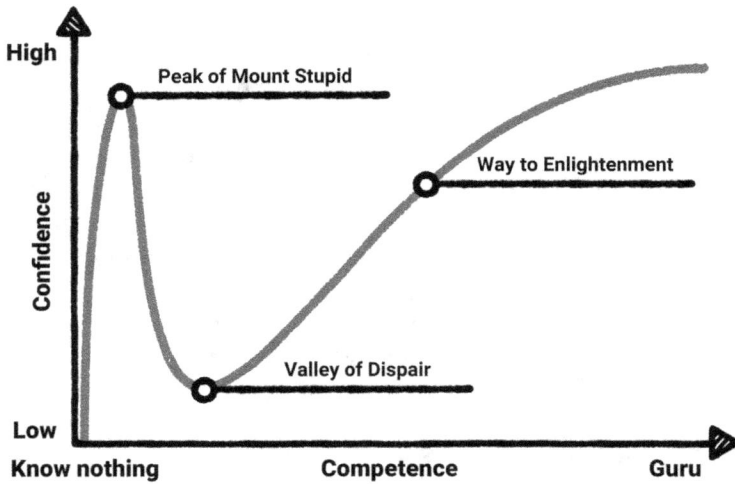

Figure 3.3 Dunning-Kruger Effect

Bias blind spot

If you ask many customers how they make decisions, few will recognise the biases that led them to a purchase. For example, they may not realise that they selectively sought out information that confirmed their initial preference for a product (confirmation bias). Ironically, they probably do recognise biases in others (Pronin et al., 2002).

Objectivity illusion

People fail to recognise their own biases. Similarly, in comparison to others, people believe themselves to be basing decisions on objective information, such as data (Berger and Berry, 1988). You may own one brand of laptop for example, and your friend another. Both of you believe you have acted objectively, based on rational assessment of factual information. But if that were true, wouldn't you have both purchased the same brand (assuming you had the same budget)?

False uniqueness bias

In the film *Fight Club*, Tyler Durden says, "You are not special. You are not a beautiful or unique snowflake". Yet, people falsely assume that they *are* unique (Chambers, 2008) and are willing to pay more for 'cool' brands that make them appear unique (Koskie and Locander, 2023).

Illusion of validity

Wouldn't it be odd if someone in a passionate online discussion suddenly admitted their view had been an error? This doesn't usually happen (Einhorn and Hogarth, 1978) because people tend to feel extremely confident (perhaps overconfident) that their judgement is valid.

Naive cynicism

If you've ever mislaid an important item somewhere, perhaps your wallet or set of keys, you probably dashed back to retrieve it. The fear is that, if left for long, someone will take it. In reality, how many selfish thieves are there lurking among the public? In an online environment, many are similarly nervous about online payment, even when this is perfectly secure. The expectation that others are more self-centred than you (and are therefore likely to steal your money) is probably misplaced. We call this 'naive cynicism' (Kruger and Golivich, 1999).

Naive realism

If everyone believed the same facts and shared the same values, the world would be a wonderfully harmonious place. Yet the reason that disagreements occur, sometimes on a large scale, is that both sides believe they are viewing the problem more rationally and clearly than the other. Neither understands that their sense of reality is subjective.

Marketers too may feel their message is clear and objective, whilst customers interpret it differently, based on their own unique perspective. Understanding this can help to create more empathetic, targeted messaging that resonates with customers' viewpoints and values, rather than assuming a one-size-fits-all approach.

Illusion of explanatory depth

Many people think they know how a car works. Obviously, something to do with the engine and gears, but do you really know how the brakes or suspension, or even the engine itself, works? When you start asking more questions, you might realise that the depth of your knowledge is shallower than you thought (Rozenblit and Keil, 2002).

Illusion of asymmetric insight

Sharing idle talk about other people is common. Have you ever considered that other people are probably chatting about you in equal measure? Oddly, many assume that their knowledge of others outweighs other people's knowledge of them (Pronin et al., 2001). If you're thinking about your clients or customers, they're probably also thinking about you!

Restraint bias

People make a commitment to change behaviour, often knowing that doing so will require ceasing another – reading more books for example, rather than online gaming, or cycling rather than driving to work. However, this confidence that temptation can be 'restrained' is overconfident (Nordgren et al., 2009).

b) Assumed differences

People often assume that others are very different from themselves, but these assumptions can lead to misunderstandings. For marketers, recognising this tendency is essential – effective marketing relies on understanding your audience through evidence and insight, not assumption.

Third-person effect

People often talk about 'the general public' as if a such a 'mass' exists as a separate entity to their own social groups (Davison, 1983). Of course, no third-party 'public' exists. This is a 'third person effect' (Davison, 1983): Most of us are just as susceptible to media messages as anyone else.

Trait ascription bias

Nobody likes to think of themselves as a certain 'type' of person. Yet, in others, they identify characters with well-defined traits (Kammer, 1982). Don't forget that, as unique as you might feel, in someone else's mind (such as your customer) you are probably being categorised, i.e., labelled in line with brand or personality traits.

c) Judgement of emotion

Emotion often guides behaviour, yet when a person is in a specific emotional state it can be difficult to acknowledge the effect that that state is having.

Misattribution of arousal

Sometimes people make mistakes when interpreting the reason for their feelings (Schachter and Singer, 1962). This is known as the misattribution of arousal. Consider an online romance for example. Two people meet one another while discussing an area of common interest. Both assume that the positivity they feel whilst in each other's company is entirely due to their attraction to one another. But what role did the topic of discussion play? Was that feeling really love for the person or the situation?

In a marketing context, someone might feel a rush of excitement while attending a high-energy product launch or scrolling through a beautifully designed website – and misattribute that excitement to the brand itself. Some marketers pair product messages with emotionally stimulating environments, music, or visuals to transfer the positive feelings generated to the brand.

Empathy gap

"Pull yourself together!" or "Get a grip!" is a refrain familiar to many who grew up in the twentieth century, reflecting a time when emotional struggles were often dismissed. Thankfully, society today is more attuned to emotional well-being, although people still frequently underestimate the emotions of others. They may see a person online, emotionally affected by a specific situation, perhaps even crying, and yet still lack empathy. This error in judgement of another person's feelings, for example in commercial exchanges, is called an empathy gap (Van Boven et al., 2000).

If you're a long-term user of LinkedIn, you might recall a CEO of a marketing agency posting a tearful selfie after laying off employees. He intended to show vulnerability and emotional leadership, but the reaction was deeply divided. Some praised his openness, while many criticised him for making the layoffs about himself rather than those affected. The response of critics highlighted an empathy gap – others who were not in the CEO's emotional state (grieving a tough decision) found it difficult to empathise and instead judged his reaction through their own perspective.

Hot-cold empathy gap

We all get irritated with other people – sometimes we might even argue with them. While the reason for disagreement might seem logical, probably it is, at least in part, affected by other factors such as tiredness or hunger. Often, when people are emotional (hot state) they fail to acknowledge that this is different to how they will feel when not emotional (cold state) and vice-versa. Some readers may recall the famous Snickers campaign, underlining that "you're not you when you're hungry". Failure to acknowledge the impact of emotion on a person's own behaviour is a separate mental 'gap' (Loewenstein, 2005).

Compassion fade
Most people will feel horror at news of a fatality in a house fire. When local-news media report the name and personal story of the person who died, the sense of compassion increases. Sadly, even when a comparable incident claims more, but unnamed, victims, compassion remains greater for the smaller incident with a named victim. Compassion appears to fade as the number of victims increases (Slovic, 2007). Yet, believing that compassion is limited, is a self-fulfilling prophecy (Gainsburg and Lee Cunningham, 2023).

Introspection illusion
It's very easy for people to make mistakes about themselves, such as the origins of a particular mood (Pronin, 2009). Perhaps they lost out on a product they wanted in an online auction, or they missed a Snapchat streak, and suddenly feel very grumpy. They blame the website or perhaps a broadband glitch. Was the result really the cause though, or just the tipping point after a more fundamental problem beneath the surface? People overweight their own 'introspective' assessment, rather than objectively assessing the situation (Pronin, 2009).

d) Predicting future selves
People don't realise that they will change or that emotion is a short-term feeling.

Projection bias
When people look or 'project' ahead they often make errors of judgement. Think about how much you have changed during your lifetime so far. Are you really the same person that you were as a child or teenager? In biological terms you are literally made up of different cells. In psychological terms too, the way you think and feel about certain issues has probably also changed. The odd thing is that when people

look ahead, they don't necessarily expect their future selves to differ from today. When people consider future decisions they will make, they assume that their feelings will remain the same – which is perhaps unlikely (Loewenstein et al., 2003).

End of history illusion

When you look back at your life so far, you can probably notice all the ways in which you've changed. You've changed physically, but emotional events will also have affected you psychologically. When many people look ahead, they fail to acknowledge the possibility that they will continue to change. To borrow a line from the famous Francis Fukuyama book (1992), people assume that now is the 'end of history' (Quoidbach, Gilbert and Wilson, 2013).

Impact bias

The 'end of history' illusion suggests that people don't predict their future selves. The impact bias similarly suggests that people don't accurately predict the feelings that they will feel in the future (Gilbert et al., 2002), sometimes overestimating emotional impact.

APPLYING THE THEORY: KEY QUESTIONS

How can you ensure that your messaging highlights the true value of your product or service, helping customers avoid overestimating its benefits based on initial impressions?

How can you empower your customers to feel confident in their understanding of your product or service?

How do you ensure your marketing doesn't just appeal to how customers see themselves but also accounts for the ways they might misjudge their own abilities, preferences, or uniqueness? For example, are you communicating with your audience in a way that reinforces their self-image, helping them feel confident, capable, and seen, or might you be unintentionally prompting self-doubt or overconfidence by assuming too much about their knowledge, values, or preferences?

Have you considered your audience's emotional state at the moment of receiving your message and how it might differ from your intention?

Chapter Summary

In this chapter, we've explored the key elements that influence your target audience's decision-making process, including customer disposition and intelligence, as well as attitudes, values, morals, and motivation. You've learned how intelligence and executive function influence cognitive processes. As you review your customer personas, ask yourself: Do they go beyond demographics to capture the value-based motivations and emotional drivers that truly impact your audience? Remember to apply the key questions from this chapter as you plan and refine your marketing approach to ensure you're addressing the full complexity of your target audience.

What's Next?

In the next chapter ('Audience'), we turn to the dynamics our customers face in terms of understanding their own reference points and the influence of those around them.

CHAPTER 3 REFERENCES

Ajzen, I. (1985). From intentions to action: A theory of planned behavior. In J. Kuhl & J. Beckman (Eds.), *Action control: From cognitions to behaviors* (pp. 11–39). Springer.

Albarracin, D., & Wyer Jr, R.S. (2000). The cognitive impact of past behaviour: influences on beliefs, attitudes, and future behavioural decisions. *Journal of Personality and Social Psychology, 79*(1), 5.

Baddeley, A.D., & Hitch, G.J. (1974). Working memory. In G. H. Bower (Ed.), *The psychology of learning and motivation* (vol. 8, pp. 47–89). Academic Press.

Bandura, A. (1977). Self-efficacy: Toward a unifying theory of behavioural change. *Psychological Review.*

Bem, D. J. (1967). Self-perception: The dependent variable of human performance. *Organizational Behavior and Human Performance, 2*(2), 105–121.

Berger, J.O., & Berry, D.A. (1988). Statistical analysis and the illusion of objectivity. *American scientist, 76*(2), 159–165.

Buil, T., & Mata, P. (2024). Intrinsic motivation and its influence in eco shopping basket. *Journal of Consumer Behaviour, 23*(6), 2812–2825.

Chambers, J.R. (2008). Explaining false uniqueness: Why we are both better and worse than others. *Social and Personality Psychology Compass, 2*(2), 878–894.

Cialdini, R. B., Borden, R. J., Thorne, A., Walker, M. R., Freeman, S., & Sloan, L. R. (1976). Basking in reflected glory: Three (football) field studies. *Journal of Personality and Social Psychology, 34*(3), 366.

Colás, I., Triviño, M., & Chica, A.B. (2017). Interference control modulations over conscious perception. *Frontiers in Psychology, 8,* 712.

Davison, W.P. (1983). The third-person effect in communication. *Public Opinion Quarterly, 47*(1), 1–15.

Deci, E.L., & Ryan, R.M. (2012). Self-determination theory. *Handbook of Theories of Social Psychology, 1*(20), 416–436.

Diamond, A. (2013). Executive functions. *Annual review of psychology, 64*(1), 135–168.

Dion, K.L., Baron, R.S., & Miller, N. (1970). Why do groups make riskier decisions than individuals?. *Advances in Experimental Social Psychology, 5,* 305–377.

Dunning, D. (2011). The Dunning–Kruger effect: On being ignorant of one's own ignorance. In *Advances in experimental social psychology* (vol. 44, pp. 247–296). Academic Press.

Duriez, B., & Van Hiel, A. (2002). The march of modern fascism. A comparison of social dominance orientation and authoritarianism. *Personality and Individual Differences, 32*(7), 1199–1213.

Dweck, C.S. (2006). *Mindset: The new psychology of success.* Random house.

Eccles, J. (1983). Expectancies, values and academic behaviours. In J. T. Spence (Ed.), *Achievement and achievement motives: Psychological and sociological approaches* (pp. 75–146). W.H. Freeman.

Einhorn, H.J., & Hogarth, R.M. (1978). Confidence in judgment: Persistence of the illusion of validity. *Psychological review, 85*(5), 395.

Fazio, R.H., & Olson, M.A. (2003). Implicit measures in social cognition research: Their meaning and use. *Annual Review of Psychology, 54*(1), 297–327.

Fishbein, M., & Ajzen, I. (1975). *Belief, attitude, intention and behavior: An introduction to theory and research.* Addison-Wesley.

Fukuyama, F. (1992). *The end of history and the last man.* Free Press

Gainsburg, I., & Lee Cunningham, J. (2023). Compassion fatigue as a self-fulfilling prophecy: Believing compassion is limited increases fatigue and decreases compassion. *Psychological Science, 34*(11), 1206–1219.

Gawronski, B. (2012). Back to the future of dissonance theory: Cognitive consistency as a core motive. *Social Cognition, 30*(6), 652–668.

Gilbert, D.T., Driver-Linn, E., & Wilson, T.D. (2002). The trouble with Vronsky: Impact bias in the forecasting of future affective states. In L. F. Barrett & P. Salovey (Eds.), *The wisdom in feeling: Psychological processes in emotional intelligence* (pp. 114–143). Guilford Press.

Haidt, J. (2012). *The righteous mind: Why good people are divided by politics and religion.* Pantheon

Hull, C.L. (1932). The goal-gradient hypothesis and maze learning. *Psychological review, 39*(1), 25.

Jiang, H., Messinger, P.R., Liu, Y., Lu, Z., Yang, S., & Li, G. (2024). Divergent versus relevant ads: How creative ads affect purchase intention for new products. *Journal of Marketing Research, 61*(2), 271–289.

Jones, E.L. (1963). The courtesy bias in South-East Asian surveys. *International Social Science Journal, 15*(1).

Kammer, D. (1982). Differences in trait ascriptions to self and friend: Unconfounding intensity from variability. *Psychological Reports, 51*(1), 99–102.

Katz, D., McClintock, C., & Sarnoff, I. (1957). The measurement of ego defense as related to attitude change. *Journal of Personality.*

Katz, D. (1960). The functional approach to the study of attitudes. *Public Opinion Quarterly, 24*(2), 163–204.

Koskie, M. M., & Locander, W. B. (2023). Cool brands and hot attachments: their effect on consumers' willingness to pay more. *European Journal of Marketing, 57*(4), 905–929.

Kristiansen, C.M., & Zanna, M.P. (1988). Justifying attitudes by appealing to values: A functional perspective. *British Journal of Social Psychology, 27*(3), 247–256.

Kruger, J., & Gilovich, T. (1999). "Naive cynicism" in everyday theories of responsibility assessment: On biased assumptions of bias. *Journal of Personality and Social Psychology, 76*(5), 743.

Kuran, T., & Sunstein, C. R. (1998). Availability cascades and risk regulation. *Stanford Law Review, 51*, 683.

Lepper, M.R., Greene, D., & Nisbett, R.E. (1973). Undermining children's intrinsic interest with extrinsic reward: A test of the" overjustification" hypothesis. *Journal of Personality and Social Psychology, 28*(1), 129.

Leibenstein, H. (1950). Bandwagon, snob, and Veblen effects in the theory of consumers' demand. *The Quarterly Journal of Economics, 64*(2), 183–207.

Levine, T.R., Park, H.S., & McCornack, S.A. (1999). Accuracy in detecting truths and lies: Documenting the 'veracity effect'. *Communications Monographs*, 66(2), 125–144.

Li, R., Zhang, M., & Aggarwal, P. (2024). Retail karma: How our shopping sins influence evaluation of service failures. *Journal of Consumer Research*, ucae027.

Locander, W. B., & Spivey, W. A. (1978). A functional approach to attitude measurement. *Journal of Marketing Research, 15*(4), 576–587.

Loewenstein, G. (2005). Hot-cold empathy gaps and medical decision making. *Health Psychology, 24*(4S), S49.

Loewenstein, G., O'Donoghue, T., & Rabin, M. (2003). Projection bias in predicting future utility. *Quarterly Journal of economics*, 1209–1248.

Markus, H. (1977). Self-schemata and processing information about the self. *Journal of Personality and Social Psychology, 35*(2), 63.

Maslow, A.H. (1943). A theory of human motivation. *Psychological Review, 2*, 21–28.

McClelland, D.C. (1961). *The achieving society. Van Nostrand.*

Monin, B., & Miller, D.T. (2001). Moral credentials and the expression of prejudice. *Journal of personality and social psychology, 81*(1), 33.

Mostofsky, S.H., & Simmonds, D.J. (2008). Response inhibition and response selection: two sides of the same coin. *Journal of Cognitive Neuroscience, 20*(5), 751–761.

Nordgren, L.F., Harreveld, F. V., & Pligt, J.V.D. (2009). The restraint bias: How the illusion of self-restraint promotes impulsive behaviour. *Psychological Science, 20*(12), 1523–1528.

Oettingen, G. (2000). Expectancy effects on behavior depend on self-regulatory thought. *Social Cognition, 18*(2), 101–129.

Promberger, M., & Marteau, T.M. (2013). When do financial incentives reduce intrinsic motivation? comparing behaviors studied in psychological and economic literatures. *Health Psychology, 32*(9), 950.

Pronin, E., Kruger, J., Savtisky, K., & Ross, L. (2001). You don't know me, but I know you: The illusion of asymmetric insight. *Journal of Personality and Social Psychology, 81*(4), 639.

Pronin, E., Lin, D.Y., & Ross, L. (2002). The bias blind spot: Perceptions of bias in self versus others. *Personality and Social Psychology Bulletin, 28*(3), 369–381.

Pronin, E. (2009). The introspection illusion. *Advances in Experimental Social Psychology, 41*, 1–67.

Quoidbach, J., Gilbert, D.T., & Wilson, T.D. (2013). The end of history illusion. *Science, 339*(6115), 96–98.

Ranganath, C. (2024). *Why We Remember: Revealing the Hidden Power of Memory.* Faber & Faber.

Ries, A., & Trout, J. (1981). *Positioning: The Battle for Your Mind.* McGraw-Hill.

Rozenblit, L., & Keil, F. (2002). The misunderstood limits of folk science: An illusion of explanatory depth. *Cognitive science, 26*(5), 521–562.

Rubin, Z., & Peplau, L.A. (1975). Who believes in a just world?. *Journal of Social Issues, 31*(3), 65–89.

Scarpi, D. (2012). Work and fun on the internet: the effects of utilitarianism and hedonism online. *Journal of Interactive Marketing, 26*(1), 53–67.

Schachter, S., & Singer, J. (1962). Cognitive, social, and physiological determinants of emotional state. *Psychological Review, 69*(5), 379.

Schramm, W. and Roberts, D.F., (Eds.) (1971). *The Process and Effects of Mass Communication* (revised edition). University of Illinois Press

Schwartz, S.H. (2012). An overview of the Schwartz theory of basic values. *Online Readings in Psychology and Culture, 2*(1), 11.

Sharp, B., & Romaniuk, J. (2016). *How brands grow.* Oxford University Press.

Slovic, P. (2007). When compassion fails. *New Scientist, 194*(2598), 18.

Van Boven, L., Dunning, D., & Loewenstein, G. (2000). Egocentric empathy gaps between owners and buyers: Misperceptions of the endowment effect. *Journal of Personality and Social Psychology, 79*(1), 66.

Van Hoorens, V. (1993). Self-enhancement and superiority biases in social comparison. *European Review of Social Psychology, 4.*

4 Audience: Navigating Social Dynamics

In this chapter, we consider the role of social dynamics and how they influence customer behaviour. Understanding how customers view themselves – how they develop relationships, compare themselves to others, and assess their place within social groups – will help you develop marketing that truly resonates. Brains are wired to interpret and respond to the actions of others, meaning that customer decisions are often shaped by subtle cues, group norms, and social comparisons. By recognising these patterns, marketers can better understand audience behaviour in real-world contexts.

Orlo is a social digital-engagement platform that allows organisations to listen, monitor, and interact with conversations taking place across their online communities. Orlo specialises in serving public-sector organisations including local councils, central government bodies, higher education institutions, housing associations, and emergency services. We spoke to Managing Director, Phil Evans, and Head of Marketing and Communications, Helena Hornby, about the importance of understanding online communities ...

BUILDING TRUST THROUGH COMMUNITY-CENTRED SOCIAL MEDIA MANAGEMENT

Public sector organisations face unprecedented challenges. There's declining trust in institutions, increasing mistrust of traditional media, the ever-changing digital landscape, alongside the rapid spread of misinformation and disinformation, to name but a few. Right now,

DOI: 10.4324/9781003541226-5

many organisations are also operating with reduced budgets, forcing them to accomplish more with fewer resources. This environment often leads to reactive thinking that prioritises immediate action over sustainable, outcome-focused engagement.

As well as managing their social presence, the Orlo platform gives organisations valuable insight into how their audiences view and discuss relevant issues across the digital environment.

ORLO'S COMMUNITY-CENTRED PHILOSOPHY

Orlo's approach is built on the understanding that effective engagement doesn't come from just broadcasting messages across social media – it comes from fostering genuine community connections and building trust. Through using Orlo's tools, teams can understand the behaviours of online communities and use this knowledge to build effective relationships within groups. As Phil Evans, explains:

> *"What we want to do is help organisations to create active communities, not just lists of people, so that they are really focused on their purpose and having meaningful two-way conversations. So, we're not just helping public sector organisations to broadcast: citizens can engage, and we can be involved in a proper community where there's a good two-way dialogue going on and we all then learn from it."*

This philosophy stems from research showing that trust emerges from genuine community engagement. When public institutions foster authentic connections with citizens, they build credibility that enables them to accomplish their strategic objectives more effectively.

THE POWER OF COMMUNITY ADVOCATES

Orlo recognises that the most powerful voices in any community aren't institutional ones but trusted fellow community members. Helena Hornby explains:

> *"Nothing speaks to trust like voices who become advocates for you and amplify your message. Focusing on a small community that can act as your advocates will really improve trust exponentially …*

*Having them tell your story is more powerful than a comms team
pushing out the same message repeatedly. "*

By helping organisations identify and nurture community advocates, Orlo enables public sector organisations to extend their
reach and build deeper connections with the communities they
serve.

NAVIGATING THE COMPLEXITIES OF COMMUNITY DYNAMICS

Social media creates both opportunities and challenges for
community building. The same dynamics that make communities
powerful can, however, also create 'echo chambers' where people
only interact with like-minded individuals. This can potentially
reinforce divisions and amplify mis- and disinformation in the
digital spaces.

Orlo helps clients navigate these complexities by promoting
inclusive community-building practices that connect diverse
groups while maintaining safety and trust. This balanced approach
recognises both the "potential for good and potential for harm" in
community spaces.

BEYOND SHORT-TERM THINKING

Building meaningful community engagement requires investment and patience. Phil said:

*"If organisations can spend the time investing in building trust with
communities, then citizens are more likely to trust messages from the
institution when they are shared. You'll have that slack in the rope ...
They're more likely to be invested in the big picture if the organisation
has been able to invest in trust over time."*

Helena added:

*"It's really important for public sector organisations to have a strategic
approach for the long-term, which has clear objectives. These desired*

outcomes will give focus for the organisation's communications and engagement, helping the teams engaging with communities to have a purpose. They'll be able to show progress towards goals and the impact their work is having on those communities. This is great for the organisation, but also for citizens to see how their lives are being improved over time, helping build more trust."

This approach emphasises the value of consistent, authentic engagement over quick wins or short-term metrics.

CONCLUSION: THE ENDURING POWER OF COMMUNITY

These insights from Orlo highlight the importance of observing and understanding group dynamics, and their impact on human behaviour. Pairing data gathered within the Orlo platform, with knowledge of the fundamental principles of social psychology, can be deeply insightful. In an era when physical community connections are diminishing, digital communities have emerged as powerful forces shaping how people receive information, form opinions, and make decisions.

Communities provide their members with a sense of belonging, trust, and shared purpose. They amplify messages through trusted voices and personal stories that resonate far more deeply than institutional communications. These community dynamics explain why messages spread rapidly through social networks, why people often trust peer recommendations over official sources, and why community-based social proof remains one of the most potent influences on human behaviour.

What makes the Orlo approach significant from a psychological perspective is its recognition that digital communities operate according to the same fundamental principles as traditional communities. People still seek connection, still respond to trusted voices, and still make decisions influenced by their social groups – even in digital spaces. By applying core psychological principles to modern digital communication, organisations can create more meaningful engagement and positive social impact in an increasingly fragmented world.

4.1 RELATIONSHIPS WITH OTHERS

This chapter is all about how people behave when they are not alone, i.e., in a social setting. A sensible starting point is to understand some different ways in which humans engage with one another.

a) Types of relationship

The word 'relationship' can mean different things to different people. In fact, some psychologists have even identified that, from an early age, people differ in the degree to which they seek or avoid relationships, known as attachment theory (Shaver and Mikulincer, 2009). There are many general reasons why people connect with others, and quite a few theories to explain these reasons. Here are a few:

Social exchange theory

Many relationships are based on some form of social exchange (Cook et al., 2013), whether the exchange is physical or emotional. Social behaviours therefore involve creating relationships that offer benefits to all parties involved.

Ben Franklin effect

When new neighbours move in next door, your instinct might be to go and offer them your assistance, for example offering refreshments or carrying boxes. You want to start the relationship off on a good footing. You might not realise that by helping someone else you increase your affection for them (Jecker and Landy, 1969) – as well as them appreciating you (hopefully). Sharing helpful hints and tips through social media content and direct messages is also likely to lead to a similar effect.

Social-dependency norm

Humans have evolved to live side-by-side, and to form communities and societies where they rely on one another. Imagine a world for example where you had to produce and cook all food yourself, make all your own tools, find your own clean water and create your own energy. Today, people in most cultures depend on others to live comfortably. Online tools and mobile apps make this even easier. For example, many services can be advertised and perhaps even delivered online. Plus, there is informative and useful content on just about any topic you can think of.

Social facilitation

Social facilitation is the tendency for people to perform tasks better when they are in the presence of others – especially if the task is simple or well practiced. Zajonc (1965) suggests that this is due to increased drive when in the presence of others.

Shared experience

When people share an experience, enjoyment of the experience is increased (Boothby et al., 2014). Imagine watching a great music concert alone for example. The music sounds good, but isn't the whole experience more enjoyable when you can discuss it, and reflect on it afterwards, perhaps in an online community alongside other fans?

Game theory

There are lots of examples of games, demonstrating different social principles. The general principle of game theory (Fudenberg, 1991) is that people make decisions as if playing a game, considering other players, but taking into account cognitive biases and previous experiences. Think about limited-time offers or competitive bidding – customers don't just weigh up the product, they also think about what others might do. For example, during an online sale or auction, shoppers may speed up decision-making or overpay, influenced by the behaviour (or anticipated behaviour) of other customers.

Parasocial relationships

Parasocial relationships are one-sided feelings for media personnae (Tukachinsky and Stever, 2019) and are, strictly speaking, not really relationships at all. How many of Taylor Swift's 280-plus million Instagram followers has she actually interacted with personally? The connection her followers feel is real to them, but it's largely one-way or, at best, unequal (apologies if you are a Swiftie).

People viewing YouTube can also develop a sense of parasocial relationship (Penttinen et al., 2022), feeling like they know the video host even though most don't.

Matching hypothesis

Isn't it odd when you see a couple who look completely different; perhaps one person very glamourous and the other far more demure. Many couples just look like a natural fit. The 'matching hypothesis' psychological theory suggests that this isn't coincidence: people appear to naturally match themselves with those who have a similar level of attractiveness (Berscheid et al., 1971). In an online world, this matching is probably occurring virtually when people choose which way to swipe on dating apps!

b) Understanding how others think

People focus on and assess different things – there isn't a single, universal way of seeing and interpreting the world. Yet some people don't realise that others may perceive things very differently.

Objectivity versus subjectivity

You might assume that a pretty pattern is a pretty pattern. Your interpretation of a pretty pattern may well be shared by many other people, but don't assume this is universal. Aesthetic preferences are not objective (Pandir and Knight, 2006). Taste (by which we mean artistic taste rather than the literal 'olfactory' senses) is subjective. Otherwise, everyone would prefer Nine Inch Nails to ABBA (like Tom)!

Attitude polarisation

When members of a group share views, research indicates that the prevailing group attitude can be more extreme than many individuals within the group (Myers and Lamm, 1975). Rather than balancing alternative viewpoints, the outcome of discussion is polarisation towards one side. In an era where controversial topics are debated daily online, this feels particularly apt to consider. You may recognise this as similar to the attitude adjustment function or courtesy bias within values.

Theory of mind

Theory of mind is likely to be a uniquely human characteristic. It is the ability to consider how other people feel (Leslie et al., 2004). Many people have a rough idea of what is likely to be going through the mind of a close associate.

The best negotiators use this skill to the maximum, deliberately presenting information in a way that considers the potential interpretations. Marketers do this too – when crafting messages that anticipate customer concerns or objections, they're using theory of mind to frame communications in a way that feels understood and persuasive from the customer's perspective.

Curse of knowledge

When you know your product inside out, it's easy to forget that your audience may be encountering it for the first time. This is the 'curse of knowledge': holding, and being affected by, information that others don't have (Camerer and Loewenstein, 1989). Good marketing means stepping outside your own perspective and meeting people where they are – culturally, emotionally, and intellectually.

c) Customers value fairness

Most people believe in the concept of fairness. A fundamental question for most societies is what constitutes 'fair': A uniform share of resources, or a differential reward based on effort or outcome? Many seem to believe that 'first come first served' is fair for example (Park and Kwon, 2024).

Reciprocity

There is a long-established theory of expected reciprocity between people. In fact, expectations of reciprocity drive evaluation of behaviour (Bogdan et al., 2023). This was first established in a restaurant setting where good service was rewarded monetarily (Tidd and Lockard, 1978). The theory appears to apply to both punishment and reward, with Hackel (2018) demonstrating that effort is proportional (or reciprocal) to the reward offered.

For example, when a brand offers something of value – like helpful content or a free trial – customers often feel inclined to reciprocate, perhaps by signing up to a mailing list or making a future purchase.

Door in the face

If a customer is asked to pay or donate a large amount of money, their immediate reaction may well be negative. If this is followed up by a much smaller request though this suddenly seems much more palatable. The salesperson has reduced their request, so the customer reciprocates (Cialdini et al., 1975).

Inequity aversion

The desire to act with fairness seems to run so deep that some people will even give up a reward in order to act with propriety (Fehr and Schmidt, 1999). This is an aversion to inequity.

For example, customers might boycott a brand they previously liked – even if it means missing out on discounts or rewards – if they perceive that the organisation treats its employees unfairly. This willingness to give up a personal benefit in protest reflects inequity aversion: People are prepared to incur a cost to avoid being part of, or supporting, what they see as an unjust system.

Altruism

Giving is pleasurable, regardless of fairness. Buying presents for others and anticipating their positive reaction is a nice experience and seems to support a natural desire to share resources (Fehr and Fischbacher, 2003). Pro-environmental behaviour, for example, also makes people feel happy (Prinzing, 2024).

Moral luck

The former England football manager, Gareth Southgate, will forever be remembered (by Tom) for his failure to win an international trophy. Yet, twice his teams made international finals. On one of those occasions, failure was determined by a penalty shootout that he could not have determined. This is an example of moral luck – being blamed or praised on the basis of luck (Nagel, 1979).

Similarly, social media content can sometimes go viral, leading to relative fame for the creator, based on the fortunate timing of the post, rather than perhaps the quality of content regularly posted on the account (and it's worth noting that going viral isn't always positive, as it can sometimes bring unintended attention or backlash)!

Honesty

There appears to be a universal expectation that people should be honest with one another. Honesty leads to trust (Bellucci et al., 2019) and self-disclosure helps customers bond with influencers (Zhang and Mac, 2023), leading to an intention to purchase (Leite and Baptista, 2022). Where people are not honest with one another, relationships break down. Too much self-disclosure though (known as 'oversharing') can damage credibility for influencers (Leite et al., 2022).

Trust and honesty

In order to put faith in another person and mentally feel at ease in their company, a relationship must be created to enable social closeness. Salespeople who self-disclose, for example, increase trust (Park and Yi, 2023). You might assume that honesty is a prerequisite in order to establish trust. Strangely, the evidence is in the opposite direction: Trusting people makes them more honest (Zhao et al., 2024).

d) Social interaction errors

As with other biases, there are common ways in which people make errors when assessing other people in a social group.

Fundamental attribution error

Imagine you are scrolling on social media and come across a post containing an obvious mistake. Your immediate reaction may be that this is a person who doesn't pay attention to detail. In truth, maybe they were just in a rush to post. Maybe they were juggling multiple important tasks at the same time and were distracted. The immediate judgement of this person could therefore be a fundamental error in how you initially attribute cause (Ross, 1977). Marketers need to be careful when jumping to conclusions but should also be mindful that others may quickly form opinions about our work.

Spontaneous trait inference

It's tempting to make quick judgements about people (Winter et al., 1985). Perhaps Gabriel seems very quiet in an online chat, or Dee seems grumpy. We all have quiet or grumpy moments. Making a spontaneous judgement about personality traits is unlikely to be accurate.

Group attribution error

If you haven't met many people from a specific geographic location, there is a temptation to make assumptions about people from that location, based on the first person you meet. Perhaps they were particularly friendly, or funny for example. This might sound odd, especially for places with millions of inhabitants, yet this assumption that a group (especially a group decision) is representative of its members' attitudes is so common it has its own name – 'group attribution error' (Allison and Messick, 1985).

Stereotyping

There are many examples of stereotyping, based on legally-protected personal characteristics such as ethnicity, and age for example. To avoid offence, we won't give examples here but suffice to say stereotyping is unfortunately a bias that affects most people in some way (McGarty, Yzerbyt, Spears, 2002).

Ad Hominem fallacy

When you discuss your views about a hot topic with your friends, you might be tempted to describe those who oppose your views in disparaging terms (please be kind and avoid this temptation). This is an example of the ad hominem fallacy. Logically, arguments should argue against a rational point, rather than making personal comments about who is involved in the discussion (Van Eemeren et al., 2000).

To avoid the ad hominem fallacy, a brand campaign might highlight how their product outperforms competitors by focusing on specific features, such as superior battery life or faster processing speed, using evidence-based messages to position it as the smarter choice for customers.

e) Searching for reasons

When people observe behaviour, they assume a cause which is either dispositional or situational (Heider, 1958). This is attribution theory. Commuters rushing from the train station must be late for work (situational). A man shouting must be an angry person (dispositional), for example.

However, there are several biases that do affect judgement, presenting both challenges and opportunities for marketers. By understanding these biases, marketers can better shape perceptions and avoid misinterpretations.

Intentionality bias

It's not unusual for children to play with sticks. But when one complains that the other has hit them with a stick, a parent or teacher may automatically scold the other child. Yet, perhaps they were simply twirling the sticks and accidentally hit the other. The belief that accidents have a deliberate cause is an intentionality bias (Rosset, 2008). Similarly, people often jump to conclusions based on only snippets of information they see online.

Self-serving bias

The self-serving bias is a tendency towards accepting responsibility only when the outcome is successful (Miller and Ross, 1975). For instance, a sports team that wins a game might credit their victory to superior team-work and preparation. However, if they lose, they may be more inclined to blame the referee's decisions or unexpected weather conditions rather than acknowledging areas where they could have performed better.

Defensive attribution hypothesis

Accidentally leaving a computer unlocked could have little consequence. However, when the outcome is severe (someone hacks your personal files), the blame attributed for the same mistake increases (Walster, 1966). This is a defensive tactic as people want to attribute blame to a specific reason to reassure themselves that the problem is preventable in future.

Extrinsic incentives bias

Motivation to behave can be driven by intrinsic (internal) or extrinsic (external) causes, as discussed earlier in relation to self-determination theory. There is a human tendency to assume other people are more likely to be driven by extrinsic factors, such as money, when they them-selves are driven only by pleasure (Heath, 1999).

Hostile attribution bias

Imagine the scenario. You're about to launch a new product, and the excitement builds as the launch date approaches. As buzz spreads on social media and early reviews start circulating, customers feel a sense of urgency to act quickly, eager not to miss out on the latest must-have item. The anticipation and growing demand encourages them to purchase the product as soon as it becomes available, sensing that others are just as eager to get their hands on it. This attribution of the hostile intent (competition) of others is again a common bias (Tuente et al., 2019).

APPLYING THE THEORY: KEY QUESTIONS

How can you ensure that your brand's actions, from pricing to employee treatment, are perceived as fair, so customers feel confi-dent in their choice to buy from you?

How can you share helpful tips or advice that adds value to your customers but also encourages them to engage with your brand in return?

Can you foster a sense of community among your customers, where they feel connected and supported by one another? Will you create your own community?

How can you inspire customers to share their own experiences with your brand, so others can see the results and impact?

Do you assume an audience has the same level of knowledge about our product or service as you do? How can you communicate effectively without overwhelming them with jargon or information they might not be so familiar with?

How might your audience's biases influence how they interpret your message, and what steps can you take to guide their judgements in a fair and positive way?

4.2 USING OTHERS AS REFERENCE POINTS

In both offline and online social settings, people observe others to judge how they fit within a group and assess their relative social standing. Whether in person or on social media, individuals use the actions, behaviours, and opinions of others as a benchmark to navigate the group dynamics.

a) Customers compare themselves to others

In a social system people inevitably pay attention to others – and to some people in particular. There are several concepts and theories to consider, relating to such assessment of others.

Social comparison

Judgement of value is formed through comparison; for example, most people would think that £100 for a new laptop is very good value (because we know that laptops often cost £1,000 or more). Similarly, comparison occurs in social situations. People understand their status in a social network through comparison to others.

In a hierarchical social system, this comparison can occur upwards and downwards. For example, people sometimes share the 'cringeworthy' moments of others, allowing the sharer to compare themselves favourably to the person who caused the 'cringe' (Escoe et al., 2024). On the other hand, sometimes people aspire to be like those who have a higher social standing: comparing upwards to fitter people can encourage more physical activity (Kim, 2022) and comparison with respected influencers can drive impulse purchasing (Mundel et al., 2024).

Social comparison can also be either self-enhancing (identifying dimensions on which a person compares themselves favourably to others) or self-protective (focusing on dimensions on which a person is 'not poor') (Buunk and Brenninkmeijer, 2025).

Social comparison bias
Because people know that assessment of their own status (by others) is formed through comparison, they sometimes steer comparisons with others against whom they will compare favourably (Garcia et al., 2010).

Reference groups
Reference groups (Sherif, 1953) are groups against which people can compare themselves, whether online or offline. We refer to these when we mention 'in group bias' for example. Often there are perceived in-groups to which membership is desirable, and out-groups that are not attractive (Tajfel and Turner, 1979).

Primary groups are those that people are closest to, such as immediate family; secondary groups are wider associates, such as work colleagues; aspirational groups are those that people would like to join (Cooley, 2017); and dissociative groups are those that they definitely don't want to join.

Hard-easy effect
If you watch gymnasts on YouTube, standing on your hands might start to look easy. It isn't! On the other hand (no pun intended), many magic illusions look impossible to replicate, but with a bit of practice most people could probably perform a basic card trick. Estimating what is hard or easy is not straightforward (Lichtenstein and Fischoff, 1977).

Imposter syndrome
When connected with other similar people, it's sometimes difficult not to feel inferior in some way. The extreme of this is a feeling of being an imposter, compared to others who are better qualified (Langford and Clance, 1993). Yet, people often have a more positive impression of us than we do (Elsaadawy and Carlson, 2022).

b) The effect of being observed

As well as observing and assessing others, customers are themselves observed and judged within a social situation. Knowledge of this also affects behaviour.

Hawthorne effect

The term 'Hawthorne effect' (French, 1950) was used many years after the original research at Western Electric Company's Hawthorne Works, to describe the apparent effect of participants being observed. Although the original intention of the research was to demonstrate the effect of lighting, it appears that the participants were more productive just because they were being observed.

Social desirability

People like to please, which can be a problem when trying to gather accurate data by undertaking social science research (Zerbe and Paulhus, 1987). However, it does mean that, in a social setting (such as a visible social media environment for example), asking people to adopt socially desirable behaviour increases the likelihood of behaviour change.

Pygmalion effect

This is also known as the Rosenthal effect after an influential paper by Rosenthal and Jacobson (1968). The effect describes how people increase their performance level when they know others have high expectations. This can be seen in how brands frame their messaging to inspire confidence in their customers or communities. For example, professional development platforms or software companies often describe their users as 'leaders', 'innovators', or 'changemakers'. This kind of language doesn't just flatter, it sets a positive expectation that encourages people to rise to the occasion, engage more deeply, and see themselves as capable of achieving more.

Liking gap

It's difficult to judge what other people think of us. On average, it's reassuring to know that people tend to be liked more than they realise (Boothby, 2018)! This phenomenon is known as the 'liking gap' – the tendency to underestimate how positively others perceive us. People often feel more self-conscious than they need to, believing that others are less favourable toward them than they actually are. This can be valuable for marketers to understand, as it means customers may be more receptive to their brand than they might expect, especially when trust and rapport are built over time.

Spotlight effect

Have you ever awoken on the day of a big presentation to find a big spot on your cheek – perhaps caused by the stress of preparing over recent days? You're sure that this will be the first thing people see when you join the meeting. In reality, they may be so consumed by their own thoughts (perhaps some of them also have a spot on their cheek), or focused on your presentation, that they don't even notice. You feel metaphorically 'under the spotlight' (Gilovich, 2000).

Customers feel the spotlight effect, but so can marketers! Be reassured, if you're planning a launch campaign, carefully crafting every detail – your visuals, the tone of voice, and the timing of your posts – your audience is far less focused on those details than you might think. They're more likely to be focusing on how your product or service meets their needs or how it adds value to their lives. Seth Godin's advice to 'Just Ship It' emphasises the importance of taking action and putting your work out into the world over getting bogged down in overthinking or perfection.

Illusion of transparency

Just as people worry about others assessing their appearance, individuals also tend to overestimate how well others understand their own thoughts and feelings. The mistaken belief that people show their feelings and emotions 'transparently' is an illusion (Gilovich et al., 1998).

Invisibility cloak illusion

No, this isn't about Harry Potter! While the spotlight effect suggests that people feel more vulnerable than they ought to, what about the tendency to 'people watch'? Many assume that although they gaze at (and judge) others, few people actually do the same of them (Boothby, 2017).

Feedback

It's not nice to receive criticism. However, evidence shows that people generally respond to negative feedback quickly. This is sometimes called the 'boomerang effect' (Herzing and Jacobsson, 2019). As a marketer, receiving uncomfortable feedback can actually be a helpful prompt for marketing content.

Research by Hall (2024) highlights how individuals often adjust their self-presentation on social media based on the feedback they receive. This feedback loop, whether positive or negative, can lead people to refine how they communicate or present themselves in future interactions.

For marketers, feedback offers valuable insight into customer behaviour. Negative feedback can provide an opportunity to make improvements, build better connections with the audience, and demonstrate responsiveness. By actively listening to customer concerns and using their feedback to make changes, marketers not only address immediate issues but also create a more engaging and supportive environment, where customers feel heard and valued. This kind of responsiveness can enhance customer loyalty and positively shape how the brand is perceived.

APPLYING THE THEORY: KEY QUESTIONS

How can you use social comparison to encourage your audience to engage with your brand, for example by showing them relatable success stories or progress made by others like them?

Who are the reference groups or individuals that influence your target audience's decisions? How can you align your brand to create stronger connections?

How can you make your brand, product, or service more socially desirable by aligning with the values, trends, or lifestyles that resonate with your target audience?

Can you help your customers overcome feelings of imposter syndrome? Can you provide evidence that they belong or can succeed with your product or service?

How can you use the understanding of the liking gap and the spotlight effect to make your customers feel more confident and appreciated when interacting with your brand?

Can you use feedback, both positive and negative, to refine your brand's approach and build stronger connections with your audience?

4.3 IMPRESSION MANAGEMENT

Because most people observe others all the time, sometimes comparing their relative social status, many also understand that others observe and compare them too. Therefore, they try to 'manage' the impression they give to others.

Peer effect (Bramoullé et al., 2009) is the academic way of describing the effect of a person's friends and family (peers) on their behaviour. Social proof, for example, is a way of benefiting from the expected peer effect. Peer effects particularly seem to affect sales of eco-friendly products for example (Chen et al., 2024), and teenagers are influenced by peers when selecting food brands (Zhang et al., 2022). Even online purchases are affected by peers (Jin and Youn, 2022).

a) *Improving status*

Self-monitoring

To judge whether they fit in with a social circle, people often self-monitor (Snyder, 1974). This really means that they try to observe their own behaviour (by judging the reactions of others) and exert self-control where needed.

Signalling

People send both intentional and non-intentional signals about their status. Accents are (mostly) non-intentional, whereas clothing is likely to be more intentional (Aghaei et al., 2017).

Conspicuous consumption

We touched on this briefly when considering the economic profile of an audience. There is lots of specific research on the drivers of this phenomenon, but the core concept of conspicuous consumption is the showing off of purchases to increase social standing (Veblen, 1899). People choose brands to send a signal to a social group (Raimondo et al., 2022). For example, why order a new item of clothing to be discreetly delivered, when you can post a photo of it on social media? Or perhaps you even take a selfie of yourself 'conspicuously consuming' delicious food at a top-end restaurant! People also give conspicuously branded gifts to others when they feel guilty (Chang and Lin, 2024) and people in lower social classes prefer gifts with conspicuous brand logos (Lee et al., 2024).

Sharing

It might feel tempting sometimes to lurk in the background of a group to gain acceptance, but actually contributing makes a difference.

Sharing, such as sharing knowledge, increases the status of the people who share (Cheng, 2013). Giving a financial gift also makes people feel good (Dunn et al., 2008).

Competence

Warmth' and 'competence' are fundamental ways to judge human character. Competence in particular is also linked to increased perceived status (Fiske et al., 2018).

Social currency

People tend to share things that help to improve their social status. The conversation therefore needs to have a value, or a social 'currency', sometimes referred to as social capital (Bourdieu, 1977).

Word usage

As well as just 'accommodating' another person's communication styles in conversation, a more conspicuous signal can be the deliberate choice of words used in conversation. Whether you call an evening meal 'tea', 'dinner', or 'supper' for example, may give a very clear impression of your desired social class. Academic research in this area over many years shows that people use language that reflects their social status (Ross, 1954).

Humblebragging

In many societies it's considered vulgar to promote yourself, or to talk about money. The solution? Slip clues about your wealth into conversation. Humblebragging is an extreme example of this where an apparently modest comment or complaint ("It was too hot on the private beach in the South of France...") actually conveys a promotional message (Sezer et al., 2018).

Jargon

Status compensation is a term used to describe situations where a person recognises their inferiority and tries to 'compensate'. One way to try and feign importance is to drop jargon into conversation (Brown et al., (2020). A supposed expert might try to impress you with their apparent knowledge for example, to mask the fact that they don't currently know how to solve your problem. However, using slang when customers don't expect it can be perceived as inauthentic (Pyrah et al., 2025).

Communication accommodation

When people want to fit in with a social group, they often try to adopt its behaviours. Perhaps they wear similar clothes. The same occurs with language (Giles and Ogay, 2007): People adjust their language according to the social situation. For example, in 2024 this might have included using the word 'brat' (a word adopted by the singer Charli XCX and used for her 2024 album of the same name).

Agency communion

The agency communion (Abele et al., 2014) model of influence, is a continuum along which people can be plotted. Either they intend to impose themselves on their surroundings (agency) or they want to form a communion with others. In this context, agency refers to traits such as assertiveness, independence, and goal-orientation – focused on acting upon the world to achieve outcomes – whereas communion reflects a desire for connection, empathy, and collaboration. For example, in B2B marketing, a high-agency brand like Salesforce often positions itself as an enabler of business growth and innovation, emphasising leadership and transformation, while a communion-oriented brand like HubSpot leans into themes of partnership, support, and building relationships with its customers.

APPLYING THE THEORY: KEY QUESTIONS

How visible is your social proof – are testimonials, reviews, and user content easy to find and relatable?

What does using your product allow someone to signal about their identity?

How clearly does your messaging support the image your audience wants to project?

Does your content offer value, emotion, or conversation starters that are worth sharing?

Does your use of jargon strike the balance between belonging and clarity? Are customers likely to use the same phrases?

4.4 THE INFLUENCE OF CROWDS

Simply having relationships with others is one aspect of social dynamics, but often a person's relationships are with other people as part of a large group.

a) *Being in a crowd affects behaviour*

As well as smaller networks of families and friends, sometimes people are affected by far larger groups. In fact, Chenoweth and Stephan (2011) have shown that a group representing just 3.5% of a population, protesting together, can influence national change.

Later, in chapter 6, we will look at the role of influential individuals, but here we focus on the effect of groups of people.

Herd behaviour

Just like cattle tend to follow one another when moving, humans often also stick together (Bannerjee, 1992), whether online or offline. This may be an instinctive behaviour, learned through evolution, but it can also spark unnecessary mass panic when crowds of people act together. Sometimes this is referred to as groupthink (Janis, 1972). If you have ever heard of William Golding's novel *Lord of the Flies*, you may know that the basic premise is that the boys alone on a desert island end up hunting an imaginary 'beast' and killing two children. The frenzy generated is irrational, but unchecked: a classic example of group members failing to act independently and reducing group conflict by suppressing individual dissent.

Social norm

Societies, and even small groups, typically have specific behaviours that are considered 'normal'. Even signalling growth of a trend can make the trend appear to be a 'norm' (Costello et al., 2024). These norms often link to cultures of regions for example. Norms don't need to be geographically defined though. In fact, many people become so attached to the norms and values of their society that they become defensive when they are challenged. This can lead to the justification of familiar systems, even when those systems are not necessarily in the best interests of the person defending them (Jost and Banaji, 1994).

Ritual

When communities of people repeat a specific sequence of behaviours for particular occasions, we refer to these as rituals (Rook, 1985). There is also evidence that partaking in a ritual helps customers to appreciate consumption (Vohs et al., 2013).

Unboxing videos on YouTube and TikTok represent a modern online ritualised consumption behaviour. Viewers and creators alike follow a specific sequence – presenting the box, slowly revealing contents, commenting on packaging, and offering first impressions. Brands like Apple and luxury-beauty companies intentionally design packaging to support this ritual, knowing it contributes to both satisfaction and social sharing.

Social proof

Social proof points are people who have adopted the 'normal' behaviour of the wider society or group (social norms). This 'proof' is then referred to when others have uncertainty about how to behave in a new situation (Cialdini, 1984). The views of others affect a customer's perception of quality, even after consumption (Colliander et al., 2023). Online 'likes' and social media comments can also affect purchase intention for social media adverts (Pittman and Haley, 2023).

Deindividuation

People communicating around live sport events sometimes do things that they would never do in any other environment, such as posting abusive words. In a group situation, surrounded by fans, people sometimes lose their sense of 'self', becoming absorbed into the crowd and copying the behaviour of others. This is known as deindividuation (Diener, 1979).

Bystander effect

If you were to ask group members for help, you might find that the larger the group, the less likely each individual is to offer assistance. This is known as the bystander effect (Fischer et al., 2011), as individuals become bystanders when in group situations.

Social loafing

With the bystander effect, people are less inclined to offer help within a group. Similarly, when given a whole group task, individuals have more opportunity to 'keep their head down' and 'shirk responsibilities' compared to when they are alone (Simms and Nichols, 2014).

False consensus

Sometimes, in a social situation, people say something controversial that most group members individually would disagree with. Yet, not wanting to speak up, in a social situation the comment passes unchecked leading to a false impression of consensus (Ross et al., 1977). This is a problem, for example, when undertaking focus group research.

In-group bias
People generally favour the 'in-group' that they are part of (Mullen et al., 1992), rather than others who form the out-group. For example, the power of in-groups is such that when resources are scarce, people even prefer to share these limited resources with members of an in-group (Cui et al., 2023).

Dissent
Groupthink can be problematic when the dominating thoughts are potentially harmful to others in society. However, research suggests (Packer, 2008) that just one dissenting voice, opposing the majority, can be sufficient to break the consensus.

Threshold model
Nobody likes taking part in activities that make them feel uncomfortable. For many people just a few years ago, the idea of making a phone call would have been preferable to a video call. Yet, there comes a point (or a threshold; Granovetter, 1978) at which the need to fit in with the group overcomes embarrassment or reluctance.

Fear of missing out (FOMO)
You may have experienced the feeling that, by logging out of social media for a period of time (perhaps for a holiday), you will somehow miss something important. This concern about missing opportunities is the basis of FOMO (Przybylski et al., 2013). FOMO is particularly strong for experiences that offer the opportunity to bond socially, and when the activity involves valued social groups (Rifkin et al., 2024). People who wait in queues also increase their purchase intention as curiosity increases (Wang, Liang and Sun, 2023).

Events, such as concerts, festivals, or even business conferences, are prime examples of FOMO, where people fear being excluded from a shared experience. The buzz around these events often grows on social media, with attendees posting about their experiences in real-time. This creates a sense of urgency for those not attending, as they feel left out of the collective excitement and connection others are enjoying. This social aspect of FOMO can push people to act more quickly in securing tickets for future events or to make sure they don't miss the next big thing, driven by the desire to be part of the shared group experience.

Contact hypothesis

In our experience, universities are wonderful examples of people from a range of cultures and backgrounds studying alongside one another – both online and offline. The contact hypothesis theory (Pettigrew, 1998) suggests that the more 'contact' such people have with others, perhaps online, the more they begin to understand and accept them.

Consensus-building conversation

Conversations change people's brains. Beau Sievers (2024) found that where conversations lead to consensus, people within the group have similar brain activity – known as 'neural alignment'.

Robbers Cave

In the 1950s, Sherif (1961) undertook an experiment which demonstrated that when two groups are expected to compete, they naturally become hostile to one another. Yet, they reconcile when given tasks that encourage cooperation. Similar effects are seen in the modern world. People from all walks of life come together online, for example to discuss their favourite sports team, music, or pastime – regardless of their other differences.

b) Observing crowds affects judgement

Being in a crowd has a range of potential psychological effects, but sometimes people observe groups of others to which we are not yet related. Online, for example, customers see many other people engaging with one another. Observing such groups also has an effect on thoughts and behaviour.

Assumed similarity

It can be a bit daunting when you join a new online group. You may have noticed that often there are similarities between group members – topics of conversation and language used. In fact, reflecting what

Cialdini (2021) calls 'unity' when social bonding occurs (see discussion of this in chapter 6), group members tend to identify 'assumed similarities' (Cronbach, 1955) between members and perhaps forget clear differences such as social background or employment.

Marketers can use this insight, encouraging a sense of community by ensuring individuals who represent their brand online adopt a group's tone, language, and shared values. For instance, when a B2B professional joins a LinkedIn group, they can build rapport and trust by contributing to discussions using familiar terminology, aligning with group norms, and focusing on shared industry challenges – positioning themselves as part of the community rather than an outsider promoting a brand.

Cheerleader effect

You can probably recall the group of 'cool' kids at school. They hosted and attended parties, perhaps played sports or music together. Perhaps you were in the 'it' crowd yourself? What you will probably remember is that people found the cool kids attractive – in part just because each of them was associated with a wider group (Walker and Vul, 2014). Following this theory, seeing groups of people online is also likely to make each person within that group slightly more attractive – apparently like a cheerleader appearing more attractive when with their cheerleading team (hence the theory's name).

Marketers can tap into this by showcasing teams, communities, or groups in their social content – rather than individuals alone – to create a stronger sense of appeal and belonging. For example, a technology organisation might highlight its employee team at an industry event or show customers collaborating in a webinar screenshot, signalling credibility and social appeal through group association.

Warranting theory

Warranting theory shows that information about a person is more valuable when it can't be manipulated by that person themselves (Walther and Parks, 2002). Positive reviews of a brand are therefore also likely to be perceived more positively than an advert, because the brand shouldn't be able to manipulate a review, i.e., reviewers are generally expected to be unbiased. There is a wealth of research exploring how reviews specifically influence readers' perceptions and decision-making. For example, photos make reviews more helpful to a reader (Ceylan et al., 2024). Reviews that relate to product quality have a particularly strong effect (Sun et al., 2023), and comparing products also results in better sales for the favoured product (Zhang et al., 2024).

Shared information bias

When people are among friends, they tend to talk about things that they know their friends are interested in – even when this might not be top of mind when they are alone. For example, if you met an old friend online tomorrow, you'd probably talk about memories of your fun times together. This is a bias towards focusing on 'shared information' (Forsyth and Burnette, 2010). If you want to bond with someone, try to find topics that you already share experience of.

c) Networks are structured

Academics tend to talk about networks as being a set of 'nodes' (people) joined by 'ties' (relationships).

Below are some specific theories relating to networks, discussing aspects such as how many relationships people can manage, how networks permit sharing, and why people choose to join certain networks.

Uses and Gratifications

There is a large body of literature explaining the media people choose to consume according to the 'use' of the media and the need that it 'gratifies' (Katz et al., 1973). This is known as uses and gratifications theory. Most recently, research has focused on uses and gratification provided by social media. The guiding principle underpinning this research is that people choose to consume media that serves social and individual needs.

Dunbar's number

Robin Dunbar is known for his work on network size (Hill and Dunbar, 2003). In particular, he found that although people might 'know' a huge number of people, on average people can actually sustain an active network of between 100 and 250 people – or more specifically 250 'relationships'. Generally, 150 is stated as a reasonably 'comfortable' number as shown in figure 4.1.

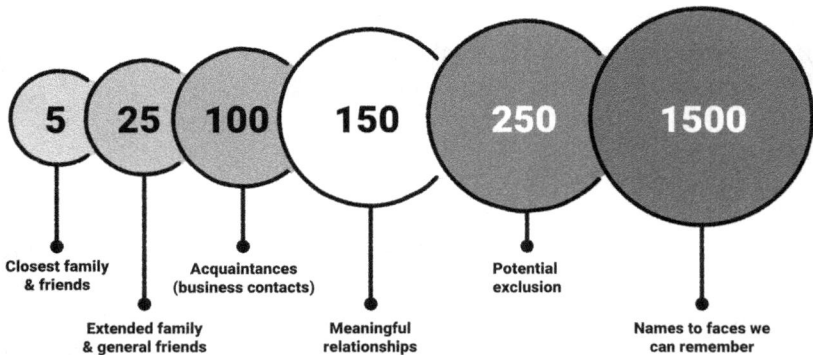

Figure 4.1 Dunbar's Number

While it's common for professionals to have thousands of connections on LinkedIn, many users are only actively engaging with a smaller subset. These are the individuals they interact with regularly, whether through direct messaging, commenting on posts, or sharing content. The rest of their connections may simply be "known" in a more distant sense, where they recognise names or positions but don't engage in consistent, personal communication.

Network effect

Networks are useful because they allow people to share resources. In fact, there is a chicken/egg debate about networks only being useful when they have lots of other people in them. Metcalfe's Law (1995) suggests that the benefit of a network is the number of members squared (n^2).

Six degrees of separation

In 1967 Stanley Milgram (also famed for his 'obedience' study) published research involving a parcel being sent across America to a random 'target' civilian via word of mouth. The first participant was asked to send the addressed parcel to someone likely to know the target, and so on. On average it took around five intermediaries for the parcel to reach its intended target, showing that Americans appear to be connected to one another within just a few 'steps' (known as the six degrees of separation). Nowadays of course, social media would enable this to occur virtually – in fact, LinkedIn tells us how many steps are between us and other people we search for.

Privacy

Although large numbers of people join social networks, there are differences in the degree to which people engage with networks and disclose personal information. Concern for privacy is affected by gender for example (women are less likely to reveal information) (Tufekci, 2008), and as adults age they also seem to have a higher concern for privacy (Van den Broeck et al., 2015).

APPLYING THE THEORY: KEY QUESTIONS

How are you leveraging herd behaviour to encourage participation by showcasing the actions of others, like highlighting product popularity, social proof, or trending activity?

How visible is your social proof, and how can you show that others trust or use your brand?

How are you tapping into FOMO (fear of missing out)?

Can you use Dunbar's Number to build deeper, more personalised connections with a targeted audience instead of focusing on large network size?

Can you make your product or service more valuable by encouraging people to join groups that lead to a vibrant community experience?

Chapter Summary

In this chapter, we've examined the complex social dynamics that shape how people behave and make decisions. From understanding how individuals relate to others and interpret social cues, to recognising common interaction errors and the powerful effects of social comparison, being observed, and group influence – we've covered a broad spectrum of interpersonal factors. We've also explored the concept of impression management and how people consciously (and unconsciously) present themselves to others. As you refine your marketing strategies, ask yourself: are you considering the social environment your audience operates within? Use the insights and key questions from this chapter to ensure your messaging aligns with the social context, norms, and group influences that impact your audience's perceptions and choices.

What's Next?

We now move on to the second part of our ABC Approach: Brand.

CHAPTER 4 REFERENCES

Abele, A.E., & Wojciszke, B. (2014). Communal and agentic content in social cognition: A dual perspective model. *Advances in Experimental Social Psychology* (vol. 50, pp. 195–255). Academic Press.

Aghaei, M., Parezzan, F., Dimiccoli, M., Radeva, P., & Cristani, M. (2017, May). *Clothing and people-a social signal processing perspective* [Conference presentation]. 2017 12th IEEE International Conference on Automatic Face & Gesture Recognition.

Allison, S.T., & Messick, D.M. (1985). The group attribution error. *Journal of Experimental Social Psychology, 21*(6), 563–579.

Aronson, E. (2008). *The social animal* (10th ed.). Worth.

Banerjee, A. V. (1992). A simple model of herd behaviour. *Quarterly Journal of Economics, 107*(3), 797–817.

Bellucci, G., Molter, F., & Park, S.Q. (2019). Neural representations of honesty predict future trust behaviour. *Nature Communications, 10*(1), 5184.

Berscheid, E., Dion, K., Walster, E., & Walster, G.W. (1971). Physical attractiveness and dating choice: A test of the matching hypothesis. *Journal of Experimental Social Psychology, 7*(2), 173–189.

Bogdan, P.C., Dolcos, F., Moore, M., Kuznietsov, I., Culpepper, S.A., & Dolcos, S. (2023). Social expectations are primarily rooted in reciprocity: an investigation of fairness, cooperation, and trustworthiness. *Cognitive Science, 47*(8), Article e13326.

Boothby, E.J., Clark, M.S., & Bargh, J.A. (2014). Shared experiences are amplified. *Psychological Science, 25*(12), 2209–2216.

Boothby, E.J., Clark, M.S., & Bargh, J.A. (2017). The invisibility cloak illusion: People (incorrectly) believe they observe others more than others observe them. *Journal of Personality and Social Psychology, 112*(4), 589.

Boothby, E.J., Cooney, G., Sandstrom, G.M., & Clark, M.S. (2018). The liking gap in conversations: Do people like us more than we think?. *Psychological science, 29*(11), 1742–1756.

Bourdieu, P. (1977). *Outline of a Theory of Practice.* Cambridge University Press.

Bramoullé, Y., Djebbari, H., & Fortin, B. (2009). Identification of peer effects through social networks. *Journal of Econometrics, 150*(1), 41–55.

Brown, Z.C., Anicich, E.M., & Galinsky, A.D. (2020). Compensatory conspicuous communication: Low status increases jargon use. *Organizational Behavior and Human Decision Processes, 161*, 274–290.

Buunk, A. P., & Brenninkmeijer, V. (2025). Raising Satisfaction When Burned-Out Through Cognitive Social Comparison. Journal of Applied Social Psychology, 55(11), 847–854

Camerer, C., Loewenstein, G., & Weber, M. (1989). The curse of knowledge in economic settings: An experimental analysis. *Journal of Political Economy, 97*(5), 1232–1254.

Ceylan, G., Diehl, K., & Proserpio, D. (2024). Words meet photos: When and why photos increase review helpfulness. *Journal of Marketing Research, 61*(1), 5–26.

Chang, C.C.A., & Lin, Y.C. (2024). Giving a conspicuously branded gift: The role of guilt. *International Journal of Consumer Studies, 48*(5), Article e13090.

Chen, C., Li, Z., Yang, S., & Cao, D. (2024). Driving eco-friendly product purchases through social media: How does peer influence work?. *Journal of Consumer Behaviour.*

Cheng, J. T., Tracy, J. L., Foulsham, T., Kingstone, A., & Henrich, J. (2013). Two ways to the top: evidence that dominance and prestige are distinct yet viable avenues to social rank and influence. *Journal of Personality and Social Psychology, 104*(1), 103.

Chenoweth, E. & Stephan, M.J. (2011). *Why Civil Resistance Works: The Strategic Logic of Nonviolent Conflict.* Columbia University Press.

Cialdini, R. (1984). *Influence: The psychology of persuasion.* William Morrow

Cialdini, R. B. (2021). *Influence: The psychology of persuasion.* Harper Business.

Cialdini, R.B., Vincent, J.E., Lewis, S.K., Catalan, J., Wheeler, D., & Darby, B.L. (1975). Reciprocal concessions procedure for inducing compliance: The door-in-the-face technique. *Journal of Personality and Social Psychology, 31*(2), 206.

Colliander, J., Dahlen, M., & Thorbjørnsen, H. (2023). Do customer ratings influence consumers who have already experienced a product?: how memory reconstruction and conformity can reshape product evaluations and perceptions. *Journal of Advertising Research, 63*(1), 17–29.

Cook, K.S., Cheshire, C., Rice, E.R., & Nakagawa, S. (2013). Social exchange theory. *Handbook of Social Psychology,* 61–88.

Cooley, C.H. (2017). *Human nature and the social order.* Routledge.

Costello, J. P., Garvey, A. M., Germann, F., & Wilkie, J. E. (2024). The uptrend effect: Encouraging healthy behaviours through greater inferred normativity. *Journal of Marketing Research, 61*(1), 110–127.

Cronbach, L.J. (1955). Processes affecting scores on" understanding of others" and" assumed similarity.". *Psychological Bulletin, 52*(3), 177.

Cozolino, L. (2013). *The social neuroscience of education: Optimizing attachment and learning in the classroom.* W. W. Norton.

Cui, F., Deng, K., Liu, J., Huang, X., Yang, J., Luo, Y. J., ... & Gu, R. (2023). Resource scarcity aggravates ingroup bias: Neural mechanisms and cross-scenario validation. *British Journal of Psychology, 114*(4), 778–796.

Dagogo-Jack, S.W. (2024). The moral superiority of temporal (vs. social) comparisons. *Journal of Consumer Psychology, 34*(4), 650–659.

Diener, E. (1979). Deindividuation, self-awareness, and disinhibition. *Journal of Personality and Social Psychology, 37*(7), 1160.

Dunn, E.W., Aknin, L.B., & Norton, M.I. (2008). Spending money on others promotes happiness. *Science, 319*(5870), 1687–1688.

Elsaadawy, N., & Carlson, E. N. (2022). Do you make a better or worse impression than you think?. *Journal of Personality and Social Psychology, 123*(6), 1407.

Escoe, B., Martin, N. S., & Salerno, A. (2024). That's so cringeworthy! Understanding what cringe is and why we want to share it. *Journal of Marketing Research, 62*(4), 664–683.

Fehr, E., & Fischbacher, U. (2003). The nature of human altruism. *Nature*, *425*(6960), 785–791.

Fehr, E. and Schmidt, K.M. 1999. A theory of fairness, competition, and cooperation. *Quarterly Journal of Economics*, 114 (3): 817–868

Fischer, P., Krueger, J. I., Greitemeyer, T., Vogrincic, C., Kastenmüller, A., Frey, D., ... & Kainbacher, M. (2011). The bystander-effect: a meta-analytic review on bystander intervention in dangerous and non-dangerous emergencies. *Psychological Bulletin*, *137*(4), 517.

Fiske, S.T., Cuddy, A.J., Glick, P., & Xu, J. (2018). A model of (often mixed) stereotype content: Competence and warmth respectively follow from perceived status and competition. In *Social cognition* (pp. 162–214). Routledge.

Forsyth, D.R., & Burnette, J. (2010). Group processes. In R. F. Baumeister & E. J. Finkel (Eds.), *Advanced social psychology: The state of the science* (pp. 495–534). Oxford University Press.

French, J.R.P. (1950). Field experiments: Changing group productivity. In J. G. Miller (Ed.), *Experiments in social process: A symposium on social psychology* (pp. 81–96). McGraw-Hill.

Fudenberg, D. (1991). *Game theory*. MIT press.

Garcia, S.M., Song, H., & Tesser, A. (2010). Tainted recommendations: The social comparison bias. *Organizational Behaviour and Human Decision Processes*, *113*(2), 97–101.

Giles, H., & Ogay, T. (2007). Communication accommodation theory. *Explaining Communication: Contemporary Theories and Exemplars*, 293–310.

Gilovich, T., Savitsky, K., & Medvec, V.H. (1998). The illusion of transparency: biased assessments of others' ability to read one's emotional states. *Journal of Personality and Social Psychology*, *75*(2), 332.

Gilovich, T., Medvec, V.H., & Savitsky, K. (2000). The spotlight effect in social judgment: an egocentric bias in estimates of the salience of one's own actions and appearance. *Journal of Personality and Social Psychology*, *78*(2), 211.

Granovetter, M. (1978). Threshold models of collective behaviour. *American Journal of Sociology*, *83*(6), 1420–1443.

Hackel, L.M., & Zaki, J. (2018). Propagation of economic inequality through reciprocity and reputation. *Psychological Science*, *29*(4), 604–613.

Hall, M.J. (2024). Embracing the spotlight (effect): how attention received online influences consumers' offline spotlight biases. *Marketing Letters*, *35*(1), 45–57.

Heath, C. (1999). On the social psychology of agency relationships: Lay theories of motivation overemphasize extrinsic incentives. *Organizational Behaviour and Human Decision Processes*, *78*(1), 25–62.

Heider, F. (1958). *The Psychology of Interpersonal Relations*. Wiley

Herzing, M., & Jacobsson, A. (2019). Measuring the effects of feedback from inspections on cleanliness in Swedish pre-schools–A field experiment. *Journal of Behavioural and Experimental Economics*, *78*, 1–9.

Hill, R.A., & Dunbar, R.I. (2003). Social network size in humans. *Human nature,* *14*(1), 53–72.

Janis, I.L. (1972). *Victims of Groupthink: A Psychological Study of Foreign-Policy Decisions and Fiascoes.* Houghton Mifflin.

Jecker, J., & Landy, D. (1969). Liking a person as a function of doing him a favour. *Human Relations, 22*(4), 371–378.

Jin, S.V., & Youn, S. (2022). "They bought it, therefore I will buy it": The effects of peer users' conversion as sales performance and entrepreneurial sellers' number of followers as relationship performance in mobile social commerce. *Computers in Human Behaviour,* 131, Article 107212.

Jost, J.T., & Banaji, M.R. (1994). The role of stereotyping in system-justification and the production of false consciousness. *British Journal of Social Psychology, 33*(1), 1–27.

Kahneman, D., Krueger, A.B., Schkade, D., Schwarz, N., & Stone, A.A. (2006). Would you be happier if you were richer? A focusing illusion. *Science, 312*(5782), 1908–1910.

Katz, E., Blumler, J.G., & Gurevitch, M. (1973). Uses and gratifications research. *The Public Opinion Quarterly, 37*(4), 509–523.

Kim, H. M. (2022). Social comparison of fitness social media postings by fitness app users. *Computers in Human Behaviour, 131.*

Langford, J., & Clance, P.R. (1993). The imposter phenomenon: Recent research findings regarding dynamics, personality and family patterns and their implications for treatment. *Psychotherapy: Theory, Research, Practice, Training, 30*(3), 495.

Lee, J., Haderlie, T.C., Miyazaki, A.D., & Lee, Y. (2024). Social class and conspicuous brand logo in gift choice. *Journal of Consumer Behaviour.*

Leite, F.P., & Baptista, P.D.P. (2022). The effects of social media influencers' self-disclosure on behavioural intentions: The role of source credibility, parasocial relationships, and brand trust. *Journal of Marketing Theory and Practice, 30*(3), 295–311.

Leite, F.P., Pontes, N., & de Paula Baptista, P. (2022). Oops, I've overshared! When social media influencers' self-disclosure damage perceptions of source credibility. *Computers in Human Behaviour, 133,* Article 107274.

Leslie, A.M., Friedman, O., & German, T.P. (2004). Core mechanisms in 'theory of mind'. *Trends in Cognitive Sciences, 8*(12), 528–533.

Lichtenstein, S., & Fischhoff, B. (1977). Do those who know more also know more about how much they know?. *Organizational Behaviour and Human Performance, 20*(2), 159–183.

McGarty, C., Yzerbyt, V.Y., & Spears, R. (2002). Social, cultural and cognitive factors in stereotype formation. *Stereotypes as explanations: The formation of meaningful beliefs about social groups, 1,* 1–16.

Metcalfe, R.M. (1995). Metcalfe's law: A network becomes more valuable as it reaches more users. *Infoworld, 17*(40), 53–54.

Milgram, S. (1967). The small world problem. *Psychology Today, 2*(1), 60–67.

Miller, D.T., & Ross, M. (1975). Self-serving biases in the attribution of causality: Fact or fiction?. *Psychological Bulletin*, 82(2), 213.

Mullen, B., Brown, R., & Smith, C. (1992). Ingroup bias as a function of salience, relevance, and status: An integration. *European Journal of Social Psychology*, 22(2), 103–122.

Mundel, J., Wan, A., & Yang, J. (2024). Processes underlying social comparison with influencers and subsequent impulsive buying: The roles of social anxiety and social media addiction. *Journal of Marketing Communications*, 30(7), 834–851.

Myers, D.G., & Lamm, H. (1975). The polarizing effect of group discussion: The discovery that discussion tends to enhance the average prediscussion tendency has stimulated new insights about the nature of group influence. *American Scientist*, 63(3), 297–303.

Nagel, T. (1979). Moral luck. *Mortal Questions*. Cambridge University Press, 1979.

Ng, J.C., Lin, E.S., & Lee, V.K. (2023). Does Instagram make you speak ill of others or improve yourself? A daily diary study on the moderating role of malicious and benign envy. *Computers in Human Behaviour*, 148, Article 107873.

Packer, D.J. (2008). On being both with us and against us: A normative conflict model of dissent in social groups. *Personality and Social Psychology Review*, 12(1), 50–72.

Pandir, M., & Knight, J. (2006). Homepage aesthetics: The search for preference factors and the challenges of subjectivity. *Interacting with Computers*, 18(6), 1351–1370.

Park, J., & Yi, Y. (2023). The influence of frontline employee self-disclosure about products in a retail store on customer trust in the retailer in the context of service encounters. *Psychology & Marketing*, 40(7), 1417–1430.

Park, J., & Kwon, H. (2024). First come, first served versus the draw: Perceived fairness in the new product purchase competition. *Psychology & Marketing*.

Penttinen, V., Ciuchita, R., & Čaić, M. (2022). YouTube it before you buy it: The role of parasocial interaction in consumer-to-consumer video reviews. *Journal of Interactive Marketing*, 57(4), 561–582.

Pettigrew, T. F. (1998). Intergroup contact theory. *Annual Review of Psychology*, 49(1), 65–85.

Pittman, M., & Haley, E. (2023). Cognitive load and social media advertising. *Journal of Interactive Advertising*, 23(1), 33–54.

Prinzing, M. (2024). Proenvironmental Behaviour Increases Subjective Well-Being: Evidence From an Experience-Sampling Study and a Randomized Experiment. *Psychological Science*, 35(9), 951–961.

Przybylski, A.K., Murayama, K., DeHaan, C.R., & Gladwell, V. (2013). Motivational, emotional, and behavioural correlates of fear of missing out. *Computers in Human Behaviour*, 29(4), 1841–1848.

Pyrah, B., Wang, J., Li, Y., & Xie, Y. (2025). Express: The slang paradox: Connecting or disconnecting with consumers?. *Journal of Marketing Research*.

Raimondo, M.A., Cardamone, E., Miceli, G.N., & Bagozzi, R.P. (2022). Consumers' identity signalling towards social groups: The effects of dissociative desire on brand prominence preferences. *Psychology & Marketing*, *39*(10), 1964–1978.

Rifkin, J. R., Chan, C., & Kahn, B.E. (2024). Anxiety about the social consequences of missed group experiences intensifies fear of missing out (FOMO). *Journal of Personality and Social Psychology.*

Rook, D. W. (1985). The ritual dimension of consumer behavior. *Journal of Consumer Research*, *12*(3), 251–264.

Rosenthal, R., & Jacobson, L. (1968). Pygmalion in the classroom. *The Urban Review*, *3*(1), 16–20.

Ross, A.S. (1954). Linguistic class-indicators in present-day English. *Neuphilologische Mitteilungen*, *55*(1), 20–56.

Ross, L., Greene, D., & House, P. (1977). The "false consensus effect": An egocentric bias in social perception and attribution processes. *Journal of Experimental Social Psychology*, *13*(3), 279–301.

Ross, L. (1977). The intuitive psychologist and his shortcomings: Distortions in the attribution process. In *Advances in experimental social psychology* (vol. 10, pp. 173–220). Academic Press.

Rosset, E. (2008). It's no accident: Our bias for intentional explanations. *Cognition*, *108*(3), 771–780.

Sezer, O., Gino, F., & Norton, M.I. (2018). Humblebragging: A distinct—and ineffective—self-presentation strategy. *Journal of Personality and Social Psychology*, *114*(1), 52.

Shaver, P.R., & Mikulincer, M. (2009). An overview of adult attachment theory. *Attachment theory and research in clinical work with adults*, 17–45. Guilford Press.

Sherif, M. (1953). The concept of reference groups in human relations. In M. Sherif & M. O. Wilson, *Group relations at the crossroads* (pp. 203–231). Harper.

Sherif, M. (1961). *Intergroup conflict and cooperation: The Robbers Cave experiment* (vol. 10, pp. 150–198). University Book Exchange.

Sievers, B., Welker, C., Hasson, U., Kleinbaum, A. M., & Wheatley, T. (2024). Consensus-building conversation leads to neural alignment. *Nature Communications*, *15*(1), 3936.

Simms, A., & Nichols, T. (2014). Social loafing: A review of the literature. *Journal of Management*, *15*(1), 58–67.

Snyder, M. (1974). Self-monitoring of expressive behaviour. *Journal of Personality and Social Psychology*, *30*(4), 526.

Sun, B., Kang, M., & Zhao, S. (2023). How online reviews with different influencing factors affect the diffusion of new products. *International Journal of Consumer Studies*, *47*(4), 1377–1396.

Tajfel, H., & Turner, J.C. (1979). An integrative theory of intergroup conflict. In W.G. Austin, & S. Worchel (Eds.), *The social psychology of intergroup relations* (pp. 33–37). Brooks/Cole.

Tidd, K.L., & Lockard, J.S. (1978). Monetary significance of the affiliative smile: A case for reciprocal altruism. *Bulletin of the Psychonomic Society, 11*(6), 344–346.

Tuente, S.K., Bogaerts, S., & Veling, W. (2019). Hostile attribution bias and aggression in adults-a systematic review. *Aggression and Violent Behaviour, 46,* 66–81.

Tufekci, Z. (2008). Can you see me now? Audience and disclosure regulation in online social network sites. *Bulletin of Science, Technology & Society, 28*(1), 20–36.

Tukachinsky, R., & Stever, G. (2019). Theorizing development of parasocial engagement. *Communication Theory, 29*(3), 297–318.

Van den Broeck, E., Poels, K., & Walrave, M. (2015). Older and wiser? Facebook use, privacy concern, and privacy protection in the life stages of emerging, young, and middle adulthood. *Social Media+ Society, 1*(2).

Van Eemeren, F.H., Meuffels, B., & Verburg, M. (2000). The (un) reasonableness of ad hominem fallacies. *Journal of Language and Social Psychology, 19*(4), 416–435.

Veblen, Thorstein. (1899). *The theory of the leisure class: An economic study of institutions.* Unwin Books; reprinted Dover Publications, 1994.

Vohs, K. D., Wang, Y., Gino, F., & Norton, M. I. (2013). Rituals enhance consumption. *Psychological Science, 24*(9), 1714–1721.

Wang, T., Liang, S., & Sun, Y. (2023). So curious that I want to buy it: the positive effect of queue wait on consumers' purchase intentions. *Journal of Consumer Behaviour, 22*(4), 848–866.

Walker, D., & Vul, E. (2014). Hierarchical encoding makes individuals in a group seem more attractive. *Psychological Science, 25*(1), 230–235.

Walster, E. (1966). Assignment of responsibility for an accident. *Journal of Personality and Social Psychology, 3*(1), 73.

Walther, J. B. & Parks, M. (2002). Cues filtered out, cues filtered in: Computer mediated communication and relationships. *Handbook of interpersonal communication, 3,* 529.

Winter, L., Uleman, J.S., & Cunniff, C. (1985). How automatic are social judgments?. *Journal of Personality and Social Psychology, 49*(4), 904.

Zajonc, R.B. (1965). Social Facilitation: A solution is suggested for an old unresolved social psychological problem. *Science, 149*(3681), 269–274.

Zerbe, W.J., & Paulhus, D.L. (1987). Socially desirable responding in organizational behaviour: A reconception. *Academy of management review, 12*(2), 250–264.

Zhang, H., Li, R., Veeck, A., & Yu, H. (2022). Peer influence on teenagers' preference for brand name food products: The mediation effect of peer identity. *International Journal of Consumer Studies, 46*(4), 1099–1112.

Zhang, Y., & Mac, L. (2023). Social media influencers: The formation and effects of affective factors during online interactions. *International Journal of Consumer Studies, 47*(5), 1824–1837.

Zhang, M., Li, Y., Sun, L., Wang, G A., & Du, J. (2024). The effects of comparative reviews on product sales. *Journal of Interactive Marketing, 59*(2), 167–182.

Zhang, L., Li, Y., & Zheng, C. (2024). Better and richer than me? The joint effect of performance and performance-related social comparison on goal-pursuit motivation. *Psychology & Marketing, 42*(2), 311–331.

Zhao, L., Mao, H., Harris, P.L., & Lee, K. (2024). Trusting young children to help causes them to cheat less. *Nature Human Behaviour, 8*(4), 668–678.

5 Brand: Shaping Brand Perception

A brand is "a name that influences buyers" (Kapferer, 2008). In this chapter, we want you to consider what customers will think when they learn about your brand, and how you can affect this.

First, you need them to know that your brand exists, so how will you generate that awareness? What do you want customers to then think and feel? Perhaps this can be encapsulated through stories and language that engages them. In a digital environment, sound and pictures will be key to this, but what will customers recall about your brand? All of this will lay the groundwork for making product or service-based choices.

Daryl Fielding has created new brand strategies across many categories, is a recognised speaker on brands and marketing leadership and recently published a practical guide to brands called The Brand Book *(2022). As well as time working on the New Labour General Election Campaign in 1997, her work has since included commercial brands including Vodafone, Milka, Cadbury and Ford. Most notably, Daryl played a leading role in the rejuvenation of Dove during the 2000's and beyond.*

Daryl explains how psychology insights led to such effective messaging and the establishment of a new direction for the brand …

DOVE'S REAL BEAUTY CAMPAIGN: UNDERSTANDING CUSTOMER PSYCHOLOGY TO DEFINE BRAND PURPOSE

Dove's Real Beauty campaign stands as one of the most influential and enduring brand purpose initiatives in marketing history.

DOI: 10.4324/9781003541226-6

Launched in 2004, what began as a strategy to revitalise a brand has evolved into a two-decade movement that has fundamentally changed how beauty is represented in advertising.

THE BUSINESS CHALLENGE

In 2001, Unilever's biggest Home and Personal Care brand, Dove, identified that future growth would need to come from existing categories and markets – through increasing customer loyalty and cross-category usage. At the time, people tended to only buy individual products, rather than multiple products across the range, and the Dove brand was not perceived to be relevant or interesting.

The consensus from multicountry research could be captured as follows: *"If Dove were a person, it would be like a girl at a party who is very nice, but she'll only have one drink. Although she's nice, you'll be glad when she's gone so the fun can begin"*.

RESEARCH INSIGHTS

Led by Daryl Fielding in her role as Managing Partner at Ogilvy, the team developed a hypothesis based, in part, on a competitive review of existing beauty industry advertising that highlighted pivotal insights: *"These ads made us feel like crap"* and *"they seemed to be designed to leverage feelings of insecurity"*.

The initial hypothesis proposed that a more positive approach to beauty was necessary. But was it possible? There were so few previous examples to draw inspiration from.

The team consulted psychologists with expertise in women's self-esteem, body image, and the psychological impact of beauty standards. They theorised that exposure to conventional advertising and idealised beauty imagery was detrimental to women's self-perception. This hypothesis was validated by the psychologists, ultimately leading to the development of the iconic Real Beauty campaign to reposition the brand.

THE BRAND PURPOSE EVOLUTION

Dove's brand purpose became clear: To create a world where more women felt more beautiful every day by inspiring them to take great care of themselves and to present a more inclusive vision of beauty.

Since 2004, the Dove Self-Esteem Project has become the world's largest provider of body confidence and self-esteem education. Visually, Dove immediately attracted massive media attention for their use of adverts featuring women with a wide range of body shapes and skin tones – quite unlike many other adverts at the time.

The Real Beauty campaign therefore built a unifying brand reputation that transcends category boundaries and has transformed Dove from a functional personal-care brand to one with emotional significance. It appeals to self-esteem and self-actualisation needs by challenging unrealistic beauty standards.

THE AI EVOLUTION

Twenty years after the Real Beauty campaign, Dove became the first beauty brand to commit to never using artificial intelligence (AI) to represent women in its advertising. As AI-generated and altered images become more prevalent, Dove has positioned itself against the potential harm these technologies can cause when they perpetuate unrealistic beauty standards.

The brand now advocates for transparency in AI-modified images, diverse representation in AI training data, and ethical guidelines for beauty depictions in digital spaces. This evolution demonstrates how the fundamental insight – *"beauty images make me feel ugly"* – remains relevant even as technology changes.

CONCLUSION

Dove's Real Beauty campaign demonstrates how a powerful brand purpose grounded in deep human insights can transform a brand's perception and business performance. By addressing a fundamental tension in women's lives and maintaining consistency while evolving with culture, Dove created not just a successful marketing campaign, but a movement that has influenced how beauty is portrayed in advertising globally.

5.1 ATTENTION

This chapter is all about how people initially perceive a brand, before they even start to consider which specific products or services to choose.

To raise customer awareness of your brand, first you need to identify where to engage with them (the marketing channel) and then grab their attention, i.e., get them to focus on your message. Before we present a range of specific theories relating to attracting attention, let's review some more general psychology theories relating to attention.

Although we referenced the theory of planned behaviour (Ajzen, 1991) earlier, very often humans do not carefully plan their behaviour. There are several psychological 'dual process' models which suggest that there is more than one way in which the brain processes information received (as shown in figure 5.1). For example, Daniel Kahneman's book, *Thinking Fast and Slow* was based on this premise, i.e., that sometimes humans 'think fast' (using so-called system 1), and others when they 'think slow' (called system 2).

Les Binet and Peter Field (2013) published an influential book (called *The Long And The Short Of It*) showing that emotion-based advertising, appealing to system 1, is particularly effective for longer-term brand-building, priming later reactions to rational messages that appeal to system 2 and result in sales.

Other academics also describe dual processes in decision making. One of the most-cited dual-process theories is the Elaboration Likelihood Model (Petty and Cacioppo, 1986). This says that there are times when people absorb information into the 'core' of their mind and cognitively elaborate on the points being made when they feel heavily 'involved' with the issue being presented. Higher involvement products, such as a holiday or IT system for example, lead to greater 'central' processing (Palla et al., 2022). However, there are also times when people accept information at face value, only really processing it in the 'periphery' of

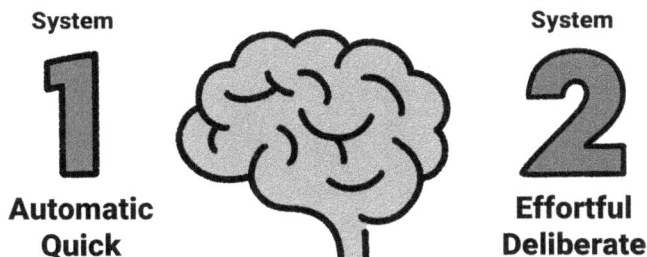

System 1 Automatic Quick

System 2 Effortful Deliberate

Figure 5.1 Two Systems of Cognition

their mind (central and periphery are metaphors rather than specific parts of the brain).

However, simply making a small change to your brand won't necessarily lead to processing through either route. For example, Ernst Heinrich Weber (1948) established Weber's Law, finding that changes perceived through the senses are assessed proportionally. For example, the extent of difference between two objects (e.g. in weight) is assessed as a percentage. Small changes are not notable.

a) *How to attract the attention of a potential customer*

Distinctive, new, surprising or even shocking information is more likely to grab attention, probably without careful thought, i.e., relating to System 1.

Novelty

Your customers' brains respond to new information. Whilst personality traits indicate that some people seek new information more readily than others, in general, new information seems to generate blood flow to certain areas of the brain – the left premotor area, left anterior cingulate, and right ventral striatum (Berns et al., 1997), perhaps even without conscious realisation. Novelty therefore attracts attention.

Surprise

Aside from whether the observed stimulus is different or distinctive, people also pay more attention to unusual information. In other words, events that we're not expecting attract attention and direct it away from an intended task (Meyer et al., 1991). For example, unexpected adverts get more attention (Cherif and Baccino, 2022). Such events are referred to as being 'schema-discrepant' as they differ from a usual or expected experience. However, telling people to expect a surprise reduces enjoyment (Schumacher et al., 2024).

Adverts that stand out also lead to better attitudes and purchase intention (Zhu et al., 2023) and using unconventional packaging can increase impulse purchasing (Das et al., 2023).

Shock

Much has been written about the salience of campaigns that deliberately shock customers or induce fear. You've probably seen online campaigns demonstrating the health risks of smoking, or dangers of drink driving, for example. Fear has been shown to both increase and decrease persuasion (Boster and Mongeau, 1984), but the Extended Parallel Process Model (Witte, 1992) suggests that the messenger needs to consider the severity of the threat, the susceptibility of the recipient, whether this threat can be countered, and whether the recipient can counter the threat themselves. Fear is also particularly effective when there is 'congruence' (such as similar ethnicity) between the audience and actor (Talebi et al., 2024).

b) What do you do once you've grabbed attention?

How you follow up the attention-grabbing activity might need some careful strategic planning. One approach after providing information to 'disrupt', is then to add a rational argument:

Disrupt then reframe (DTR)

Davis and Knowles (1999) discuss confusion as a technique for grabbing attention, describing a process labelled 'Disrupt Then Reframe'. Providing some odd-sounding information to a customer (such as use of verbose language) might sound counter-intuitive, but following this up with a rational argument (a plain English summary of the information) is the principle of this technique. Disrupt the established flow of thought, then provide the real substance once the customer is paying attention.

c) Make information relevant to your customers

People also pay particular attention when the information provided to attract attention is relevant to them in some way, even in a noisy environment:

Relevance

New information is not treated impartially by your customers. Common features of a product or service for example are evaluated in relation to existing preferences. In other words, customers assess features whilst considering whether those aspects are relevant to them. This is a theory very similar to confirmation bias, but known as 'confirmatory reasoning' (Chernev, 2001).

When evaluating a new smartphone, for example, customers often focus on features that align with their current preferences, such as the camera quality, while overlooking other features like battery life or pro-cessing speed unless those are also relevant to their needs.

Broadbent's theory of attention (cocktail party effect)

Have you ever noticed when, in a crowded room, you hear someone mention your name in the background? Similarly, when you get a message from a brand that addresses you personally. Suddenly, you find yourself paying far more attention to this information than other content. This is often referred to as the 'cocktail party' effect, but the true name for this situation is a 'filter theory' as described by Broadbent (1958). Essentially, despite being bombarded with information (such as at a noisy party), people are able to filter the stimuli and direct their attention.

d) The effect of attention on customers

The benefit of grabbing attention is sometimes then an increase in the frequency with which people notice whatever has grabbed their atten-tion, but also consider how your attention grabbing might affect what is expected:

Frequency illusion

Last month Tom noticed a musician wearing a brand he'd never heard of. Naturally, he googled it and discovered it was affordable and looked pretty cool. Since then, whether walking through town, or scrolling social media, Tom has seen countless different designs all carrying the same brand logo that first grabbed his attention on Facebook. This is the frequency illusion (Zwicky, 2006), in effect, also known as Baader-Meinhof. Something held in conscious thought, appears noticeable far more frequently.

Expectancy

You've probably heard the phrase 'perception is reality' before. In marketing terms, this means that your customer's perception is not entirely based on their experience. Very often, customers' percep-tions are actually guided by the experience they expect. Advertise a restaurant as five-star, provide quality packaging (Wansink, 2006), or perhaps update a high-spec website to make a product feel high-end.

APPLYING THE THEORY: KEY QUESTIONS

How can you grab attention by tapping into system 1 (fast, intuitive thinking) or system 2 (slower, more deliberate thinking)?

How are you tailoring your messaging to engage people who want all the details (central processing)?

What steps can you take to keep your message relevant and reframe it in a way that resonates with your audience once you've grabbed their attention?

How are you managing expectations to ensure that your audience's anticipation matches the reality of what your product or service delivers?

5.2 COGNITION

Grabbing attention is helpful, but it is unlikely to be meaningful without a customer understanding some details about your brand. You will want your customer to know about your brand, and in psychological terms this is referred to as cognition. Before we look at specific theories, there are a few terms relating to cognition that we need to introduce.

Firstly, human language requires the use of nouns to describe both physical and metaphysical 'things'. If you have ever read or been told about the semiotic work of Ferdinand de Saussure (1989) for example, you will know that he referred to 'the signifier' (e.g., a written word) and 'the signified', i.e., whatever the word refers to. In psychological terms a 'concept' is a similar idea, involving placing things into categories (Jarvis and Okami, 2019). Concepts also help us succinctly describe abstract ideas such as 'happiness'. In fact, using a 'proper noun' can lead to higher product evaluation (Rathee et al., 2023).

A 'schema' (Piaget, 1952) is a mental framework for understanding how cues (or concepts) in our environment tend to be found together. For example, when you see a distant animal with four legs and a wagging tail, you might assume it is a dog. A similar creature with a bushy tail might be a fox. People naturally draw conclusions from the clues in front of them.

Through experience, people also expect to find certain stimuli grouped together (Jarvis and Okami, 2019) in what is known as a 'perceptual set'. For example, when we glance at a sports crowd, we expect to see many adults' faces. You might have to look very carefully to notice an alien for example. This then leads to inattentional blindness, such as the famous 'gorilla among the basketball players'.

In this well-known experiment conducted by Daniel Simons and Christopher Chabris (1999), participants were asked to count the number of passes made by players in white shirts while a person in a gorilla suit walked through the scene. Surprisingly, many observers failed to notice the gorilla at all, illustrating how focusing on a specific task can cause individuals to miss unexpected stimuli in their environment. This phenomenon highlights the limitations of human attention and suggests that when we concentrate on certain aspects of a scene, we may overlook other significant details, even when they are conspicuously presented. This research has broader implications for fields such as advertising and safety, as it emphasises the importance of drawing attention to critical information in visually complex environments.

a) Everyday use of concepts and schema among your customers

People use shorthand to describe concepts or schema succinctly. The language guides perception.

Sapir-Whorf hypothesis

The basis of the Sapir Whorf hypothesis (Koerner, 1992) is that language affects perception of the world. This is also known as 'linguistic determinism'. Imagine someone using social media in their lunch break for example (perhaps the person we described in chapter 1). Whether you describe them as 'doomscrolling' or 'relaxing' would change how others perceive the person in your description. Similarly, when someone browses the internet are they 'surfing' or 'researching'? Language is also sometimes used to name and simplify complex processes. More recently, a study has also shown that naming a behaviour makes it more likely to be adopted (Fritze et al., 2024).

b) Guiding the cognition of customers

Whether processing concepts, schema, or perceptual sets, when people digest information, very often their attention needs to be guided to this information in order to cognitively acknowledge and process it. Yet, the depth of cognition (length of thinking time) doesn't necessarily relate to the scale of the issue.

Attentional bias

Put simply, attention is guided rather than objective (such as Pool et al., 2016). Nobody could possibly stand on the top floor of a skyscraper and observe everything happening in a city or observe every online message when they are scrolling social media. People are more likely to cognitively process stimuli that relate to existing thoughts.

Scope insensitivity

You might expect people to be doubly concerned to solve a problem affecting two million people, compared to one million people for example. In fact, it appears that humans are insensitive to the scope or size of the issue (Dickert et al., 2015). When cognitively processing, the issue itself triggers a reaction, and the scale then makes little difference.

c) Customers see the world through 'human' eyes

One of the ways of guiding attention is to focus on the effect of the news to human life, including themselves:

Anthropocentric thinking

Think about the news headlines today. If you follow politics, perhaps also consider the current debates in the political world. Most likely, top of the agenda is a topic involving humans and the way they live their lives. Many humans assume that humans are more important than non-humans, or even that the non-human world (plants and animals) ought to serve the human world (Mylius, 2018).

Anthropomorphism

Sometimes humans observe things in the natural world that are then understood and described using human analogies (Strongman, 2007). Does your cat really feel cross that you are considering a holiday, or are you projecting the emotions that you imagine a cat might experience if it could understand words and feel disappointment? During the COVID-19 pandemic, reporters sometimes described the virus as being 'clever' for example. Brand perceptions increase for brands that have anthropomorphised logos (Daryanto, Alexander and Kartika, 2022),

and anthropomorphising can even help to sell irregular fruit and vege-
tables (Kim et al., 2024)!

Examples of anthropomorphism include Freddie, the Mailchimp
monkey, and 'Duo' the Duolingo owl mascot where brands are using
animal characters with humanlike traits to make their services feel more
approachable and relatable. These playful, memorable mascots help
create an emotional connection with users, enhancing brand recognition and engagement through their personality-driven personas.

Interestingly, in 2025 Duolingo staged the "death" of Duo as part of a
viral marketing campaign to boost user engagement. Fans mourned the
loss, and Duo was brought back to life after the community reached a
goal of 50 billion experience points, generating widespread attention
and interaction.

Identifiable victim effect

You might assume that people react to campaigns where the data
appears persuasive, such as focusing on the scale of a problem. Actually,
humans tend to cognitively respond to examples of other humans
(Jenni and Loewenstein, 1997), i.e. when there is an 'identifiable victim'
to be helped. Such knowledge might help raise money for charity
campaigns, or support other cause-related marketing.

Second-person pronouns

Addressing the recipient makes a message more persuasive.
Personalisation is ideal, such as using a name in emails (Sahni et al.,
2018), or when placing an order as Starbucks does (Lim et al., 2024).
Using a customer's first name can also boost perceived ethicality
(Septianto et al., 2023). Yet, just referring to the recipient as 'you' also
makes a difference. Cruz, Leonhardt, and Pezzuti (2017) found that
customers feel greater involvement when addressed on social media as
'you' and develop more positive brand attitude. Recent research also
suggests that as more brands adopt personalisation, brands need to be
more creative, such as using a customer's surname instead of first name
(Defau and Zauner, 2023).

Labels

As well as cognitively processing external information according to
schema, people also process information according to how it relates to
their self-schema, i.e., a perception of information about themselves. In

other words, people create labels for themselves and look for information relating to their label (such as Farrington, 1978).

For example, fitness brands often target individuals who identify as 'runners'. When someone labels themselves as a runner, they are more likely to engage with marketing messages, products, or content that aligns with that identity – perhaps running shoes, athletic wear, or marathon-training plans. In B2B marketing, companies that identify as 'innovative' or 'sustainable' are more likely to engage with products or services that align with these self-schemas, such as cutting-edge technology or eco-friendly solutions.

d) The effect of time on cognition

Time is a specific area of research, with several studies indicating that there are ways in which time affects cognitive processing. Here are a few:

Special days

Discounts make a difference to sales. The same product sold with a 10% discount is widely expected to sell more. Danny Zane (2022) discovered that this effect is amplified even further when a reason is given for that product to be discounted on that specific day. Common examples include Independence Day, Mothers' Day, and Black Friday.

Temporal landmarks

The fresh start effect (Dai et al, 2014) occurs when people choose a specific date to make a change. New Year's Day for example is a common point for people to make resolutions for a change in behaviour. Other obvious temporal landmarks might be a significant birthday or a national event.

People also feel more optimistic and therefore take more financial risks at the end of a specific time period, such as a week or month (Li and Shah, 2020). If you are encouraging behaviour change among your customers, these dates change the likelihood of your message being considered.

Well-travelled road effect

Do you ever drive to work and not remember the journey? Research indicates that perception of time can change based on how familiar someone is with a task (Avni-Babad, 2003). People often perceive regular journeys as shorter than new ones, making 'well-travelled roads' seem to pass by more quickly. A similar phenomenon occurs in other routine activities, such as exercising: Many people report that familiar workouts seem to take less time than new routines, likely because they are less mentally engaged in the familiar tasks. Although the novelty might have decreased, the acceptance of a routine is helpful for a brand trying to establish a new habit.

Mortality reminders

Being reminded that our time on this earth is limited (known as mortality salience), can alter the way people behave. This is often referred to as terror management theory. However, the effect is different for different people. For example, when reminded of human mortality, some judges become more punitive (punishing those who don't obey the legal system), whereas others become more lenient (Arndt et al., 2005). Some people even spend more money on themselves (for a review, see Gobrecht and Marchand, 2023) and some donate more (Dunn, White and Dahl, 2020). So, before issuing a 'mortality reminder', consider why you are doing so.

APPLYING THE THEORY: KEY QUESTIONS

How are you using established concepts and schemas to guide your audience's thinking and shape their understanding of your product or service?

How can you leverage second-person pronouns ("you") to make your messaging feel more personal and engaging for your audience?

Perhaps identify a specific moment for customers to begin a 'fresh start' with your product.

5.3 EMOTION

Emotion is the short-term feeling people experience in a moment. Experiencing patterns of feeling over the longer-term might be described as mood, but emotions are immediate and automatic reactions to a specific stimulus or stimuli. In marketing terms, for example, this might be a response to watching an advert on a social media platform or perhaps a feeling when viewing a website.

Perhaps brands can also communicate emotion through an association. Why would a financial services organisation sponsor a sport for example? Aside from some relevant spectators potentially spotting the logo, what benefit could there be for the sponsor? Well, Zillman (1996) explains that excitement can actually be misattributed between stimuli. Spotting a sponsor logo after watching your team win, for example, might make you feel excitement towards the sponsor.

Emotions, then, guide both cognition and behaviour. Valence is a broad way of categorising the experience of emotion as either positive or negative. This is just one way of assessing emotion.

Positive feelings release dopamine within our brains which is extremely pleasurable (Lembke, 2021). Offering an experience that makes a customer feel good (as opposed to warding off a threat) could be a very good strategy. Positive words are easier to recall than negative (Tse and Altarriba, 2022), but customers like adverts that show both happiness and sadness (Jones and Hamby, 2023). In fact, customers seem to pay more attention to negative news (Melumad and Meyer, 2024) and negative social media comments (Kohout et al., 2023).

Professor Paul Ekman used facial expressions to identify seven basic emotions that humans display. Whilst humans can contort their faces into huge range of expressions, for example combining movements of the mouth and eyebrows, these indicate broad groups (he calls them 'families') of emotions that are universal. There is some debate about the distinction between each, but Ekman describes these as anger, happiness, sadness, surprise, fear, disgust, and contempt. Most will be familiar to you, although it is worth explaining that contempt means a feeling of superiority (Ekman, 2004).

Although Ekman suggests that basic emotions are universal, Lisa Feldman Barrett (2017) disputes this. She points out that much of the early work on emotion used English words used to differentiate feelings, whereas some of these concepts don't exist in other cultures. Instead, Feldman Barrett prefers that we consider 'constructed emotion' whereby the human brain perceives emotion as it predicts sensory inputs.

a) Emotion guides cognition

Whether emotions are universal or not, there are a range of ways in which emotions guide cognition:

PAD model

The pleasure arousal dominance (PAD) emotional state model is a way of generally understanding how all the emotions affect behaviour. The idea is that people react emotionally by feeling a degree of pleasure, excitement, and a drive to take action – each of which is measurable. For example, all three have been linked to the sharing of viral videos (Wen et al., 2021).

Affect heuristic

The effect of emotion on a person is referred to by psychologists as 'affect'. Broadly, affect can be positive or negative, but also high or low stimulation (known as 'arousal'). As much as your customers like to think that every decision they take is a carefully considered balance of the available information, very often people are guided by emotion. This is referred to as the affect heuristic (Slovic et al., 2007).

Appraisal-tendency framework

Imagine you are at work when a message pops up on your phone that, sadly, your pet has been hit by a car. Your immediate reaction might be anger. You know nothing about the details, but why didn't the driver steer out of the way? Were they driving too fast? Were they distracted? Lerner and Keltner (2000) explored how emotions guide appraisal through a model called the Appraisal Tendency Framework. Essentially, emotions affect the tendency to appraise information in different ways. This in turn affects the depth of thought given to the information.

Mood congruence

Messages are generally more affective when they are congruent with a person's mood. Happy people are more likely to accept the likelihood of good weather and vice-versa for example (Mayer et al., 1992).

Spotify's annual 'Wrapped' campaign exemplifies mood congruence through personalised year-in-review summaries. At the end of each year, Spotify shares users' listening habits, highlighting their favourite songs, artists, and genres. This campaign taps into users' nostalgic and happy memories associated with their most-listened-to tracks, creating a positive emotional response. By aligning their messaging with the celebratory mood that often accompanies the new year, Spotify enhances user engagement and loyalty.

Fear

Tom has owned two cats in his life. The first would scuttle away at the first sign of danger. The second loves a scrap. Whether you choose to 'fight' or take 'flight', fear is an emotion that marketers often use to drive a response in online campaigns.

Yet, while lab studies demonstrate the effect of fear (Rogers, 1983), field studies cast doubt on the benefit due to inequity between those affected, and the risk of creating anxiety (Hastings, Stead, and Webb, 2004). However, Please do think carefully before scaring your customers!

Loewenstein et al. (2001) also demonstrated many years ago that emotion (or 'feeling) plays a prominent role in assessing risk. In particular, fear can play a big role in steering people away from a decision that seems to pose a risk. In this way, some might say that we 'feel' risk through the emotion generated, known as 'risk as feelings'. For example, the prospect of getting a large purchase wrong at work might seem daunting, hence the well-known saying "No one ever got fired for buying IBM".

Empathy

It is painful to see other people in discomfort. Rizzolatti and Sinigaglia (2016) describe this as a mirror mechanism whereby sensory representations of an observed behaviour are experienced in the brain of the observer. In other words, people represent the feelings other others. The purpose appears to be a way of helping people to understand others' emotions and the reason for their actions.

Licensing effect

Sometimes, at the end of a busy day or a hard week, you might allow yourself a treat. A glass of wine or a Friday night takeout as a reward; an emotional boost. Perhaps ahead of a holiday you work extra hard at the gym to burn off the calories that you know you'll be ingesting. This is known as the licensing effect. People adopt virtuous behaviour in advance, to give themselves a notional 'license' to indulge (Khan and Dhar, 2006).

b) Emotions change over time

By their very nature (they are not long-term traits), emotions are short-term and therefore people can feel different emotions at different moments.

Emotional adaptation

During life, positive and negative changes occur that require a re-evaluation of the way people see the world. This includes changes to the physical environment as people literally move around, as well as changes that affect them psychologically. We might refer to these as 'life transitions'. These can be emotionally destabilising, perhaps even distressing. The result of emotional discomfort is the cognitive construction of new schemas as we learn to cope and adapt to a new reality (Healy, 1989).

Hedonic adaptation

Living in a warzone is horrific, but you may have heard stories of people trying to continue their lives as normally as possible. Similarly, there are cases of lottery winners who have continued their day job despite no longer needing the income. Phrases such as 'money can't buy you happiness' and 'wartime spirit' might spring to mind. Essentially, whilst events inevitably affect emotion and mood, many people return to their own 'normal' in time. People accept change and hedonically adapt (Diener et al., 2006).

Being asked to think creatively avoids boredom created by hedonic adaptation (You et al., 2024), for example inviting customers to enjoy different aspects of a product or service they regularly buy and use.

c) Customers anticipate emotion

It is sometimes possible to anticipate the effect of emotions in advance and take appropriate anticipatory action.

Information avoidance

Because people know that negative information can affect their emotions, some people deliberately avoid this. Perhaps they switch off viewing news on social media for a while. With reference to the 'ostrich effect' (Galai and Sade, 2006), they bury their head in metaphorical sand by finding distractions.

Regret aversion

You can probably recall a time when you received a negative comment on a social media post. You remember the emotion you felt. This experience causes people to avoid the same situation. They want to avoid feeling regret and people avoid risks that might lead to regret (Loomes and Sugden, 1982).

APPLYING THE THEORY: KEY QUESTIONS

What emotion does your brand trigger for your target audience. Fear of a threat? Joy?

How are you using empathy to connect with your audience's feelings and show that you understand their needs and desires?

How can you help your audience feel justified in their decision to buy your product or service?

How are you making your product or service feel more relatable by addressing the emotional journey your audience goes through when solving their problems?

Consider using trigger warnings when posting about sensitive content.

5.4 BRANDING

An important consideration when attracting a potential customer's attention is the brand that you intend to convey. Whatever content you use to communicate will probably need to feature some reference to your organisation and will therefore start to position your brand against competitors.

Orlando Wood (2019) from System 1 Group describes the instantly recognisable properties of a brand as 'fluent devices'. These include features such as logo, slogans, packaging and colours which make it easy to identify a brand. Use of fluent devices has been shown to lead to more customers, market share, and increase in profits.

This is a big topic, but we suggest a few key psychological considerations.

a) A brand is more than a logo

There are many aspects of a brand that have an influence on customers, such as the personality of the brand, memories of the brand, plus the brand name itself.

Brand names

Some brands use singular nouns (Apple) whereas others (Starbucks) use plural names. Interestingly, research by Gupta et al. (2024) found that some brands with plural names are associated with better brand attitude due to the perception of the name representing a group (entitativity). Using scientific names for specific ingredients also boosts utilitarian products in particular (Tok et al., 2024), unusual spelling improves memory of brand names (Lowrey et al., 2003), and using a name that conveys the benefit of the product also improves recall (Keller et al., 1998).

Brand personality

As with human personality, brands have a personality. If asked, you would probably describe a brand to your friends using human characteristics. Jennifer Aaker's (1997) research found that these descriptors fit within five themes (or factors) which are sincerity, excitement, competence, sophistication, and ruggedness, as shown in figure 5.2. Customers assess brands against each theme. Brands don't need to focus on one theme exclusively, but it might help to consider these themes when planning brand communication. For example, logos are one factor in assessing brand personality (Eyni et al., 2023), including audio logos (Melzner and Raghubir, 2023).

Brand simplicity

Recent research has identified that customers judge the simplicity or complexity of a brand according to the mental representation of the brand (Light and Fernbach, 2024). Simple brands are those that keep communication and advertising visually sparse and therefore do not encourage thoughts beyond the materials presented – such as the product range or people involved. The communication work of some of the

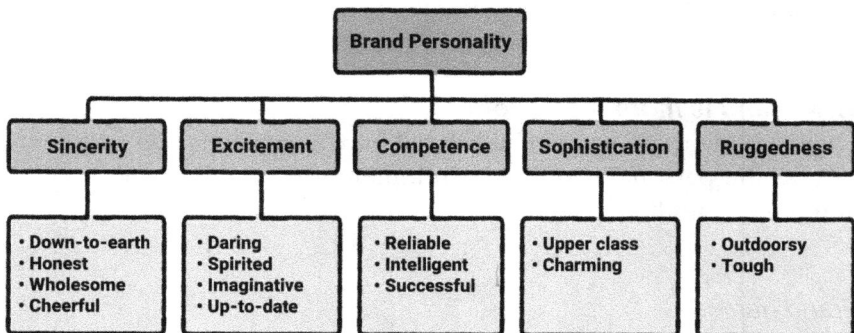

Figure 5.2 Aaker's Five Brand Personality Traits

world's most famous brands, such as Apple for example, is generally pretty straightforward to grasp or explain to others (its design is clean and technology intuitive to use). In fact, this also seems to reduce the perception that the brand's products or service might fail (Light and Fernbach, 2024). Complex brands on the other hand take more effort to cognitively process. IBM, for example, offers a range of products and services required more nuanced communications to its diverse audiences.

APPLYING THE THEORY: KEY QUESTIONS

What name will you choose for a new brand?

How can you apply the Aaker Brand Personality Model to identify your brand's identity?

5.5 MESSAGING

Whatever you want to communicate, how you say it matters just as much as what you say. Ask yourself: What do you want people to know, feel, or do with this information? In a commercial context, your message is competing with those from your rivals – so you need to clearly articulate why your product or service stands out and offers greater value.

a) Effective ways to construct your message

There are several theories that might guide how you structure your points.

Inoculation theory

If you know that another brand or critic is likely to oppose your point of view, tell your customer. This might seem counterintuitive, but providing a sample of another viewpoint will help to protect against the alternative viewpoint becoming accepted at a later date, just like a vaccine can inoculate against disease (Compton, 2024). Research even suggests referring to a direct rival (Berendt et al., 2024). Yes, you should provide all the reasons why that viewpoint is wrong but be bold and address it up front. This is sometimes called two-sided messaging, i.e., giving the alternative view as well as your own. In fact, two-sided messages seem particularly effective on sceptical customers (Hernandez et al., 2023).

For example, Monzo, a digital-first bank, preempts concerns about trust and security by openly addressing worries such as safety features, transparency, and customer service upfront. Monzo acknowledges concerns but reinforces its image as a modern, trustworthy alternative.

Argument dilution effect

When evaluating an argument being made, people summarise and average the points made. You might naturally try to include as many reasons as possible for a customer to purchase your product or service, but if some of your points are perceived to be weaker than others your overall argument will actually be less persuasive. This is called the argument dilution effect (Sivanathan and Kakkar, 2017). Similarly, Shu and Carlson (2014) have shown that making too many claims about a product or service seems to have a negative effect; three claims appears to be optimal.

Truth sandwich

Like inoculation theory, another approach to addressing opposition is to create a 'truth sandwich' (König, 2023). Present misinformation but ensure that there is correct information on either side of this.

b) Helping customers to accept a message

Before your customer can respond to your message, they need to actually absorb and understand it. There are various theories that relate to this:

Because

Adding the word 'because' increases the persuasiveness of an argument – even when the following reason is irrelevant. In an experiment by Langer et al., (1978), people asked to push to the front of the queue for a photocopier. Whilst some gave a logical reason ("because I'm in a rush") others gave a so-called placebo reason, i.e., no reason ("because I have to make copies"). The results revealed that while giving a reason helps, it doesn't seem to matter what the reason is after using the word 'because'!

Lowball technique

Sometimes brands deliberately offer you a product at an attractive offer price, only to later withdraw the offer. Yet, customers who have already committed to the purchase decide to continue with the new deal, i.e., increased price. This is known as the lowball technique (Cialdini et al., 1978).

Goal dilution

Trying to tell a customer that a particular product or service can solve many problems is unlikely to be effective. Zhang et al., (2007) demonstrated that it is more effective to communicate that taking a specific action (such as exercising) solves a specific goal, rather than 'diluting' the message with a claim to solve several goals (such as building muscle as well as losing weight).

c) Encouraging new behaviours

What about encouraging people to adopt new behaviour? Again, there are several suggestions from academic literature about how to encourage new information to be recalled and acted upon:

Regulatory focus theory

There are two ways in which people can regulate their behaviour (Higgins, 1997). When seeking to prevent harmful behaviour, people focus on safety and responsibilities. When seeking to promote a new beneficial behaviour, people instead focus on the opportunity for growth and development (accomplishment and aspirations).

This theory gives marketers two ways to present a message in different ways to reach either 'promotion-focused' or 'prevention-focused' people.

Habit stacking

If you are asking customers to adopt a new behaviour, it might help to attach this behaviour to an existing behaviour. Maybe you could point out when the customer should use the product or service you are offering. For example, perhaps they should take their daily vitamin tablet with their breakfast. It might not really matter, but most customers eat breakfast. Adding a new habit to an exisiting one should be simple. This is called habit stacking (Clear, 2020).

Chunking

How do you eat an elephant? In small chunks apparently (we've never eaten an elephant). Similarly, several studies have shown that it helps to divide information for customers. This includes helping customers to remember information – ideally three or four distinct chunks say Mathy and Feldman (2012) – as well as breaking up a task into smaller actions (Wijland et al., 2016).

APPLYING THE THEORY: KEY QUESTIONS

How clear is your messaging when it comes to what your audience should do next – and why it matters to them?

How are you breaking down your messaging into manageable chunks to make it easier for your audience to absorb and act on?

Can you encourage new behaviour by linking your product or service to habits your audience already has?

5.6 STORYTELLING

Whether you intend to explain the history of your organisation or use case studies to show the effectiveness of your product or service, both will involve creating a narrative to engage your audience. Stories help customers relate to and contextualise factual information, making it more engaging and memorable.

a) *Stories engage customers*

Stories are an age-old way of engaging an audience and conveying a clear message. Stories also link cognitive information together in a way that makes it memorable (Schank and Abelson, 1995). Creating a fictional story about a brand can increase the brand's value (Ganassali and Matysiewicz, 2021), whether offline or online.

Here are some considerations for effective storytelling:

Transportation theory

Fictional books and films are fantastic forms of escapism, sometimes helping the reader or viewer to visualise themselves in another place and time. This experience is known as narrative transportation (Gerrig,

2018). In fact, the experience can be so deep that the reader or viewer shares some of the feelings apparently experienced by the characters – a potentially powerful form of persuasion.

In *Harry Potter and the Philosopher's Stone*, readers are introduced to Harry, an ordinary boy who learns he's a wizard. As he enters the magical world of Hogwarts, readers are transported into this new world alongside him. The vivid descriptions of Diagon Alley, the magical spells, and the characters' awe-inspiring encounters help readers experience a world beyond their own, immersing them fully in the narrative. Readers don't just observe Harry's story: They feel his emotions. Narrative transportation, in this way, doesn't just make Harry's world feel real; it influences how readers relate to their own, potentially inspiring them to face challenges with similar courage and resilience.

Speer et al. (2009) have shown that when readers experience a story their brains react as if the story is happening to them. Depicting movement can also increase narrative transportation (Grigsby et al., 2023). However, there are times when setting realistic expectations (rather than helping a customer to fantasise) is more effective because customers are then able to focus on taking action (Koukova, 2025).

Seven types of story

In a book which took 34 years to write, Christopher Booker (2007) analysed the plot lines of many, many stories and identified seven key plot lines to stories. Given that we've told you that fictional stories improve brand value, you might want to consider which of these stories best enables you to communicate your brand. 'Overcoming a monster' involves defeating a threatening force, 'rags to riches' sees a character lose everything then gain it all back, 'the quest' focuses on a journey, 'voyage and return' involves a journey followed by a return, a 'comedy' is light-hearted with a happy ending, a 'tragedy' sees a hero make a mistake, and a 'rebirth' is when a character improves themselves somehow. However, aside from following a rigid structure, introducing serendipity can increases interest in a product within a story (Kuai and Wei, 2025).

APPLYING THE THEORY: KEY QUESTIONS

What type of story best allows you to explain the benefits of your product?

How can you convey your factual information using captivating narrative?

5.7 LANGUAGE

Any language, whether spoken or otherwise, is a code (Jarvis and Okami, 2019). Therefore, marketers need to adopt a code for communicating their message to the customer. Language enables a communicator to use words that convey intent. The receiver then decodes this to understand intended meaning. Obviously, a good linguist is better than a poor one at using language to convey the intended points efficiently and effectively. There are also some odd effects of language, such as people liking words that begin with a consonant and end with a vowel (Maschmann et al., 2024).

a) *Using language for your product or service*
A good starting point is to think about the words you will use to describe your own product or service.

Concreteness
Many years ago, a journalist complained to Tom that various businesses would describe themselves as providing 'solutions' in whichever industry sector they operated in. Such an abstract word didn't really explain the exact widget they made or the practical service they offered. Theory supports this: Concrete language (illustrated in figure 5.3), relating to objects, is far more effective than abstract. Customers prefer concrete language (Packard and Berger, 2021), but not technical language (Liu et al., 2024). Don't tell them a new factory is 'huge' (abstract language) or even a certain number of metres. Tell them how many

Figure 5.3 Concrete Language

football pitches or double-decker buses you could fit inside. Begg (1972) has also shown that people are better at remembering concrete rather than abstract phrases. It's important for people to visualise information. However, using abstract language seems to be effective for describing services rather than products (Tang and Hou, 2024).

Cognitive semiotics

Cognitive semiotics is a whole field of psychology, with its own journal of peer-reviewed academic research (called *Cognitive Semiotics*). For the purposes of this book, think of it as the way people understand meaning from absorbing 'signs' (such as words). Very often marketers use metaphors to convey such meaning, such as 'as strong as iron'. In fact, adverts with metaphors are easier to remember (Beard et al., 2022). Customers also use metaphors, such as describing a person as either a 'good egg' or a 'bad apple'. Zaltman (2003) outlines a technique called the 'metaphor elicitation process' to understand how customers use metaphors to convey meaning, for example when describing your product or service.

Tense

When you message others to describe a holiday destination, do you say the country 'was a great place to visit' or 'is a great place to visit'? It turns out that your decision to use either present or past tense makes a difference. Research by Packard, Berger and Boghrati (2023) showed that using the present tense is more persuasive, and use of verbs (action words) as well as concrete language then makes language in turn feel more action-oriented (Formanowicz et al., 2023).

Concise

As a young marketer learning the ropes, Tom was once told that some of the best writers work for the tabloid press. Many celebrities would question the ethical practices of some of the journalism, but summarising the news they present succinctly is a great skill. In fact, research also shows that summarising the point being made concisely is also more persuasive to the reader (Macintosh and Gentry, 1999), and readers prefer 'simple' headlines (for example using common words) in articles (Shulman, Markowitz & Rogers, 2024). Daniel Oppenheimer (2006) demonstrated that use of complex vocabulary can actually reduce perceived intelligence.

b) Using language to generate feelings

As well as describing the product or service factually, you should also consider how you want your customers to feel when you communicate about your brand.

Actual and desired state

If you want your customers to recognise their current deficiencies (for which your product or service will compensate), try using words like 'could' and 'should' in your messaging. Show how your customers' lives 'could' or 'should' be improved with your assistance (Pezzuti, 2023).

Arousal

You might also want to reconsider arousal when choosing the language you use to explain your brand. Being too emotional on social media might sometimes feel a bit uncomfortable, but the feelings evoked by emotional words affect reading comprehension (Smith et al., 2022).

Sensory language

An intriguing study by Cascio-Rizzo et al. (2023) found that when influencers use language that mimics the senses, such as 'crumble' and 'juicy', they increase both engagement and the willingness of customers to purchase their products.

Curiosity effect

Customers are curious. They read gossip and they search for celebrity news online. They are also enticed to click on news headlines that grab their attention. Whilst 'clickbait' (catchy headlines) is often seen for what it is, authoritative news websites can attract customers to a story with a well-crafted summary of the news in a headline (Scacco and Muddiman, 2020). In fact, evoking curiosity, then providing information, can increase attitudes and purchase intention (Hüttl-Mack et al., 2024).

APPLYING THE THEORY: KEY QUESTIONS

Can you use metaphors to simplify complex ideas and create a memorable image in your audience's mind?

Are you using the present tense in your messaging to create a sense of urgency or immediacy around your product or service?

5.8 HUMOUR

As Dr Richard Wiseman found in his search for the 'world's funniest joke' (2008), humour affects people in different ways. Many people enjoy 'clever' jokes (Howe et al., 2023), but people laugh at different things and differ in the degree to which they find certain jokes funny. Laughter can be contagious (Provine, 1992), but that would be tricky to emulate online. In any case, what makes the first person laugh?

a) *Humour benefits brands*

Humour can increase perceptions of competence or warmth (Hoang et al., 2023), generating positive emotions, and purchase intention (Eisend, 2009). Even chatbots using humour increase service satisfaction (Shin et al., 2023).

Dollar Shave Club's viral launch video "Our Blades Are F***ing Great" used humour to disrupt the shaving industry. By being irreverent and humorous, the brand connected with its audience and built an image of being bold and unpretentious.

Although there is no simple equation for producing a universally funny joke, there are a few theories to bear in mind though when telling or constructing a joke. These can also help with effective storytelling.

Incongruity theory

Oddities make people laugh. If you've ever seen videos of the London marathon, we bet you've smiled at the unusual costumes (a man dressed as a dustbin springs to mind). Similarly, often the photos and videos in our social media feeds that make us laugh are strange, unexpected, or 'incongruous' in comparison to the norm – hence the name incongruity theory (Forabosco, 1992).

Marketers know this too. So many adverts involve something unusual happening. The Cadbury Gorilla is a famous example that many people laughed at, but then also remembered many years later. Perception of nonsense humour is affected by prior emotion: those feeling positive are more likely to appreciate humour (Soh et al., 2024).

Superiority theory

Many jokes involve a so-called fall guy. Whether people are laughing at the slapstick visual comedy of Laurel and Hardy, Homer Simpson's obsession with beer and doughnuts, or funny online calamitous videos, feeling superior to the person we're observing often makes people laugh and demonstrate superiority theory (Duncan, 1985) in action. Brands can even tease their customers to build connection, as long as the tone is friendly or 'prosocial' (Oba et al., 2024).

Benign violation theory

McGraw and Warren (2010) suggest that humour occurs when the normal order is 'violated', but that this is funny only in situations that are benign or non-threatening. More recent research shows that such 'benign' humour benefits underdog brands in particular, with prominent brands benefiting more from more aggressive 'malign' humour (Béal et al., 2024).

Relief theory

Another theory, researched by Arthur Shurcliff in 1968, is that people laugh through a sense of relief after a moment of high emotional arousal. For example, if you feel anxious about a sinister silhouette at nighttime, you might laugh when you discover the real cause.

APPLYING THE THEORY: KEY QUESTIONS

Is your brand suited to a humorous marketing campaign? Funny, short videos are incredibly popular online.

5.9 MEMORY AIDES

Very often, words can deliberately trigger memories. We refer to these as memory aides.

a) Timing messages to appeal to your customers' memory
The timing of any messaging can affect the way the information is received.

Priming
Priming is when prior information affects a subsequent behaviour (Bargh and Chartrand, 2000). Even if not processed consciously, the memory of the information seems to have an effect. This theory has been disputed in some academic circles as part of psychology's 'replicability crisis' (the problem that some findings are not replicated when experiments are repeated). Our view is that, unless the data was actually fraudulent, it's accurate to report that these previous studies do seem to show the effect of priming. For example, priming people to think about

the future increases pro-environmental behaviour (Essl et al., 2024). However, asking people about past experiences increases pessimism for the future (Novella and Ramirez, 2024).

Precommitment

People tend to have some idea of their own values and beliefs, i.e., their 'selves'. They also try to keep a consistent sense of self. Explicitly asking customers to state and commit to a deadline, therefore encourages them to stick to that decision and avoid straying from the self that a commitment represents (Ariely and Wertenbroch, 2002). If someone signs up online for a sports event, they will probably take the training more seriously. In fact, people even try to find additional reasons to support a previously made choice (Zemborain et al., 2024). Similarly, working 'in tandem' to complete a challenge with a friend can increase the likelihood of success (Gershon et al., 2024). This is something we've experienced firsthand while co-authoring this book – collaborating has ensured our commitment, made the process more enjoyable, and helped us create something much stronger than we could have on our own (we hope you agree!).

Peak-end rule

You can probably remember the bit in *Toy Story* where Buzz 'flies' for the first time and wins over the other toys. You probably remember too that the movie ends with Woody and Buzz becoming friends, then chasing the removals van and flying into Andy's car. So, you recall the 'peak', most intense point, and you recall the end, but perhaps not many of the details in between. This is the essence of the peak-end rule (Kahneman et al., 1993). As described in Chapter 3 for example, DCUK use this theory to leave customers on a positive final impression. More recent research also shows that negative incidents at the end of an experience particularly affect customers (Blecic and Kuester, 2024).

b) Referring to old memories

You can also ask people to think back into the past.

Nostalgia

Very often we view the past with so-called rose-tinted glasses; we often recall positive times and long for them to return. Many of you will recall your favourite toy (Transformers for Tom, Spirograph for Luan), the car your parents owned, and the brands of food that no longer exist.

Your customers' childhood experiences generate emotional attachments to brands that persist into adulthood (Shields and Johnson, 2016). People even feel a sense of 'communal nostalgia', identifying with products that others recall (Han and Newman, 2022).

This is why heritage brands often deliberately refer to their historic roots – demonstrating their link to your past. Nostalgia can be persuasive (Cheng and Yan, 2022). Inevitably, many of the events you recall will also have involved other people. Therefore, remembering events together also helps people to feel additional positivity through a sense of social connectedness (Sedikides and Wildschut, 2019).

Repetition

Unsurprisingly, the more a customer hears something, the higher the likelihood of it being remembered, especially when the format of the information (an advert) varies slightly (Unnava and Burnkrant, 1991).

If you've purchased a Costa Coffee from a machine recently, it's likely that a repeated message has again influenced you. On display at prominent locations where Costa machines serve Barista-style hot drinks, you may have seen posters reminding you that the coffee provided is very much 'real'. The message? "Real beans, Real milk, Real quick".

Repetition by different voices is also particularly effective in attracting attention and then message processing (Chang et al., 2023). For example, using multiple influencers in a campaign can amplify the message, as each influencer brings their unique voice and audience, reinforcing the core message from various perspectives.

c) Deliberate forgetting

Research shows that people can be encouraged to forget certain information.

Directed forgetting

It appears that some people can intentionally forget information. A study first published by Bjork et al. (1968) showed that when people are asked to memorise a list, telling them to forget the first item before then giving them a second item to remember resulted in the second item becoming easier to recall. This study therefore demonstrated the ability of an instructor to modify short-term memory – known as 'directed forgetting'.

APPLYING THE THEORY: KEY QUESTIONS

Can you time your message to prepare a customer, or end on a high?

Can you tap into nostalgia by referencing shared experiences or cultural touchpoints that evoke warmth and connection?

5.10 VISUAL SENSES

Many marketers focus on visuals when communicating a brand. Although customers clearly also receive information via other senses, we focus first on visual information. Be careful though: Complex visual aesthetics are associated with higher assumed production costs (Min et al., 2024).

Most people know what kind of artwork they like. Maybe they also have specific dislikes. What they might not know though is what governs their tastes. Whether pleasurable or not, aesthetics is a combination of an emotional reaction, the application of meaning to the experience, plus the initial information communicated to the brain via a sensory reaction (Chatterjee and Vartanian, 2014), known as the aesthetic triad.

In this section we focus on the reaction of the senses, starting firstly with visual information. This is likely to consist of either images or text – or both.

a) Images that appeal

Picture superiority effect

There is much evidence to show that customers' brains particularly process imagery. Pictures are also easier to recall compared to written information (Childers and Houston, 1984). This is a theory known as the 'picture superiority effect'. Consider for example if we showed you some old photos of people you went to school with. You could probably pick out your classmates' faces, but there is also a strong possibility that you won't remember everyone's name. A similar effect would probably occur if you had to spot content you engaged with yesterday on social media. Pictures are powerful. In fact, pictures are so powerful that they can even affect other senses such as evoking smells (Sharma and Estes, 2024)!

Colour

Research has shown that more than half of an initial visual assessment is based on the colour of whatever a person is viewing (Singh, 2006). Most people have a favourite colour. For many people that colour is blue (Eysenck, 1941). In fact, there is a collection of bright colours, including many primary colours, that research shows are among the top favourite colours (for example, brown isn't one of them). There is also separate research demonstrating that brighter colours are more arousing, i.e., affect the autonomic system in the brain (Valdez and Mehrabian, 1994) and bright lighting increases adoption of new products (Zhang *et al.*, 2024). Yet, darker logos make a brand appear older (Zeng *et al.*, 2025) and darker packaging makes products seem more effective (Zheng *et al.*, 2024).

The use of colour also affects perceptions of a brand's personality, with red being perceived as 'exciting' and blue as 'competent' for example (Labrecque and Milne, 2012). Plus, there is specific research (Kwon *et al.*, 2022) showing that social media posts featuring 'cooler' colours (such as blue) generate more positive 'word of mouth' for a business brand, whilst 'warmer' colours (such as red) work best for consumer brands. AI influencers also get better responses when they use warmer colours (Chan *et al.*, 2023).

The background colour (black or white) also affects perceptions of a brand logo (Celhay and Luffarelli, 2024), and use of intense (highly saturated) colours is effective for encouraging a sentimental purchase in particular (Huang, Xu and Jiang, 2023).

Figure-ground

When viewing an image, customers' minds seek to establish the focal point within the image (Wagemans et al., 2012). Often this is obvious, such as a person standing in front of a beautiful backdrop. There are many examples of the mind seeking resolution when the object (or 'figure') and scene (or 'background') are not obvious. You may have seen examples where the mind is deliberately confused, such as the so-called Rubin's Vase (shown in figure 5.4). The lesson for marketers is to keep it simple – make the focal point obvious.

There is also evidence that 3D product images are perceived as larger than 2D images (Kwon et al., 2024), blurry backgrounds make products appear bigger (Meng et al., 2022), and curved shapes get more clicks on websites (Biswas et al., 2024).

Figure 5.4 Rubin's Vase

Sex

You've probably heard the familiar saying that in advertising "sex sells". Well, that may well be the case for certain products and services – or perhaps certain product and service categories.

To support this, there is also evidence that customers are more likely to process and recall sexual imagery (King et al., 2015) and erotic adverts grab attention (Kilijanek and Ozga, 2022) although perhaps distract from other elements of the brand. Yet, people from individualistic cultures in particular are more likely to like or share sexual brand content (Choi et al., 2022).

However, it's not a universal rule, as the effectiveness of such tactics can depend heavily on the brand, its target audience, and the context in which the ad is presented.

Video speed

Slow-motion videos make the viewing experience more 'hedonic' (Stuppy et al., 2024) and also make products appear more luxurious (Jung and Dubois, 2022).

White space

Recent research suggests that customers appreciate white spaces. Websites that space out the information displayed are aesthetically pleasing, as are brand logos that allow plenty of space (Sharma and Varki, 2018). Yet, reducing white space between products (and increasing 'circumspace' around the products) increases online clicks and purchase intention (Yu et al., 2024).

b) Gestalt

Isn't it odd that some people can look at an apparently random scattering of stars in the night sky and spot shapes. Why draw lines between those

Figure 5.5 The Law of Closure

specific stars and not others? This is gestalt theory (Köhler, 1967), or in other words the tendency of the mind to perceive meaning by grouping individual visual elements. There are many principles (or 'laws') within this theory, but here are a couple.

Law of closure

If we were to place four 'Pacmans' (Pacmen?) together, each with their mouths wide open, we could position them in such a way that you would see a square shape between the smaller Pacman shapes (as shown in figure 5.5). Is it really there? No. People like to see a 'complete' picture, even when viewing an incomplete collection of elements (Graham, 2008). You are assuming that this design was an intentional attempt to create a square.

This is the same principle behind the famous hidden arrow in the FedEx logo – created by the negative space between the 'E' and the 'x'. It's not drawn explicitly, but once seen, it's hard to unsee. The Guild of Food Writers logo features a spoon cleverly hidden within a fountain pen nib – blending the ideas of writing and food. These designs don't shout their message – they whisper it, trusting your brain to fill in the blanks.

Proximity

People assume that shapes placed next to each other are related (Brunswik and Kamiya, 1953). Eleven people standing next to each other wearing yellow sports kit? Probably part of the same team.

This is similar to the 'law of similarity' whereby similar visual elements are perceived to be part of the same group (Graham, 2008).

c) Using text effectively

Getting the words right is obviously top priority. However, you should also consider how the text appears.

Text superiority effect

This might sound like a contradiction, given that we previously told you about the picture superiority effect. The text-superiority effect is really about people's tendency to notice changes in text (such as within a paragraph of a book) compared to changes to pictures – specifically changes related to the size of the text (Pieters and Wedel, 2004). Like this! Larger font size also seems to make numbers in adverts more persuasive (Huang, 2025).

Font

If you are considering a font to adopt within your brand guidelines, perhaps think about adopting a style that your competitors don't use. Many brands even create their own. Why do you think Times New Roman has the word 'Times' in its name? Because it was created for *The Times* newspaper in the UK. The psychological evidence in this area also suggests that unusual fonts make a brand appear unique (Doyle and Bottomley, 2004), although perhaps less attractive. A typeface is then a collection of fonts. Again, the research suggests that certain typefaces have a psychological effect, perhaps even conveying the power of the brand (Kim et al., 2021).

Numbers

When it comes to presenting written numbers to a customer, they tend to prefer numerical digits rather than written numbers (Romero et al., 2024). In a review format, using stars leads to a perceived higher rating than numbers (Abell et al., 2024) for average scores ending between .5 and .9.

APPLYING THE THEORY: KEY QUESTIONS

Do your chosen brand colours evoke the right emotional response and reflect your brand's personality?

Have you selected an imagery style – for example photography or illustrations – that you can use consistently?

Consider how your font choices convey tone and professionalism – will you avoid the much-hated font Comic Sans for example, or would it support a humorous approach?

5.11 AURAL SENSES

In an age where smartphones and headphones are ubiquitous, sonic branding is now recognised as an area of study in its own right. ASMR sounds (very popular on social media) can also increase brand recall (Sands et al., 2022), brand perception (Gotsch and Gasser, 2024) and purchase intention (De Kerpel et al., 2021). Think of the sounds associated with well-known brands such as the introduction music on a Netflix series or the famous 'Intel inside' jingle.

a) Which sounds will customers associate with your brand?

There are some specific studies associated with the way people use language as well as reactions to music.

Rhyming

Messages that rhyme appear to be more likeable, more memorable, and ultimately more persuasive (Filkuková and Klempe, 2013). This is known as the 'rhyme is reason' effect (or the 'Keats heuristic') because the rhyme appears to affect how a customer cognitively absorbs the information. In English, for example, people use phrases such as "a stitch in time saves nine" (demonstrating the benefit of solving an issue early). This is perfectly sensible, sounds nice, and is easy to memorise, and therefore considered more than a non-rhyming equivalent. Whether red skies the previous night really signal good weather is irrelevant – people believe that it does (McGlone and Tofighbakhsh, 2000).

Saying is believing

Putting an idea into words affects perception. The original 'saying is believing' research (Higgins and Rholes, 1978) showed that the person giving a message is more likely to absorb the message themselves and repeat the version of the message that they had given (rather than alternative perspectives).

Music

According to Les Binet's research with the IPA, music can increase the effectiveness of an advert by 20–30% (McCrostie, 2015).

Melody

Songs with simple melodies might feel a bit annoying, but they are catchy. Sometimes people call these 'earworms'. If you consider some of the hit songs within your lifetime, the chances are that the melody was simple. Take for instance 'Baby Shark', which is YouTube's most watched video of all time.

Jakubowski et al. (2017) found that songs with generic melodies (described as 'common global melodic contours'), as well as being generally upbeat, are likely to be easier to remember.

Tempo

The speed and 'beat' of the music is referred to as the tempo. There is research showing that people react physically to music with a clear 'groove' (such as tapping their foot), through a process called 'sensorimotor coupling' (Janata et al., 2012). Faster tempos also increase arousal (Husain, Thompson, and Schellenberg, 2002).

Volume

Unsurprisingly, the volume of the music being played has an effect on the listener. Loud music, for example, makes it difficult to concentrate on reading words. This is also affected by tempo (Thompson et al., 2012).

Mode

In musical terms, mode is often used to explain whether the music is in a major or minor key. In turn, the mode of the music has been shown to affect the mood of the listener (Husain et al., 2002).

Audio logo

Some brands use a piece of music as part of their brand identity. The evidence shows that this is effective in driving brand recognition (Das et al., 2023) and music affects perceptions of innovativeness when using 'irregular contours' or 'unstable tonality' (Zoghaib et al., 2023). Musical cues can then lead people to buy brands associated with the cue (Anglada-Tort et al., 2022).

Does hearing McDonald's 'I'm Lovin' It' jingle make you desire some fast food?

APPLYING THE THEORY: KEY QUESTIONS

Can you create a distinctive sonic logo or jingle that immediately signals your brand whenever it plays?

Can you use rhyming or simple lyrical hooks in scripts to boost memorability and shareability?

For social media content, can you select music tracks that align with your audience's tastes and the emotions you want to evoke?

Chapter Summary

In this first chapter about brand, we've focused on how to shape brand perception by tapping into the way people process information and form emotional connections. You've learned how to capture attention, make content relevant, and engage both cognitive and emotional responses. We've explored how brand messaging – through storytelling, language, and even humour – can influence customer attitudes and encourage new behaviours. The use of memory aids and consistency in branding also play a vital role in how your brand is remembered and recalled.

As you develop your marketing content, ask yourself: Are you making it easy for your audience to notice, understand, feel connected, and remember your brand? Apply the questions from this chapter to build stronger, more resonant brand experiences.

What's Next?

In the next chapter we explore some of the external influences on brand perception, including individuals conveying a message.

CHAPTER 5 REFERENCES

Aaker, J. L. (1997). Dimensions of brand personality. *Journal of Marketing Research, 34*(3), 347–356.

Abell, A., Morgan, C., & Romero, M. (2024). The Power of a Star Rating: Differential Effects of Customer Rating Formats on Magnitude Perceptions and Consumer Reactions. *Journal of Marketing Research.*

Ajzen, I. (1991). The Theory of planned behaviour. *Organizational Behaviour and Human Decision Processes.*

Anglada-Tort, M., Schofield, K., Trahan, T., & Müllensiefen, D. (2022). I've heard that brand before: The role of music recognition on consumer choice. *International Journal of Advertising, 41*(8), 1567–1587.

Ariely, D., & Wertenbroch, K. (2002). Procrastination, deadlines, and performance: Self-control by precommitment. *Psychological Science, 13*(3), 219–224.

Arndt, J., Lieberman, J. D., Cook, A., & Solomon, S. (2005). Terror management in the courtroom: Exploring the effects of mortality salience on legal decision making. *Psychology, Public Policy, and Law, 11*(3), 407.

Avni-Babad, D., & Ritov, I. (2003). Routine and the perception of time. *Journal of Experimental Psychology: General, 132*(4), 543.

Bargh, J. A., & Chartrand, T. L. (2000). The mind in the middle. *Handbook of research methods in social and personality psychology, 2,* 253–285.

Barrett, L. F. (2017). *How emotions are made: The secret life of the brain.* Pan Macmillan.

Béal, M., Lécuyer, C., & Guitart, I. (2024). Humour in Online Brand-to-brand Dialogues: Unveiling the Difference between Top Dog and Underdog Brands. *Journal of Interactive Marketing.*

Beard, E., Henninger, N. M., & Venkatraman, V. (2024). Making ads stick: Role of metaphors in improving advertising memory. *Journal of Advertising, 53*(1), 86–103.

Begg, I. (1972). Recall of meaningful phrases. *Journal of verbal learning and verbal behavior, 11*(4), 431–439.

Berendt, J., Uhrich, S., Borah, A., & Kilduff, G. J. (2024).: The Rivalry Reference Effect: Referencing Rival (vs. Non-Rival) Competitors in Public Brand Messages Increases Consumer Engagement. *Journal of Marketing Research.*

Berns, G. S., Cohen, J. D., & Mintun, M. A. (1997). Brain regions responsive to novelty in the absence of awareness. *Science, 276*(5316), 1272–1275.

Binet, L., & Field, P. (2013). *The long and the short of it: Balancing short and long-term marketing strategies.* Institute of Practitioners in Advertising.

Biswas, D., Abell, A., & Chacko, R. (2024). Curvy digital marketing designs: virtual elements with rounded shapes enhance online click-through rates. *Journal of Consumer Research, 51*(3), 552–570.

Bjork, R. A., LaBerge, D., & Legrand, R. (1968). The modification of short-term memory through instructions to forget. *Psychonomic Science, 10*(2), 55–56.

Blečić, A., & Kuester, S. (2024). Which moments matter most? Investigating boundary conditions of the effect of specific moments on overall evaluations of customer experiences. *Journal of Consumer Behaviour.*

Booker, C., *The Seven Basic Plots,* Continuum 2006

Boster, F.J. Mongeau. P. (1984) Fear-arousing persuasive messages. *Annals of the International Communication Association, 8*(1), 330–375,

Broadbent, D. E. (1954). The role of auditory localization in attention and memory span. *Journal of Experimental Psychology, 47*(3), 191.

Brunswik, E., & Kamiya, J. (1953). Ecological cue-validity of 'proximity' and of other Gestalt factors. *The American journal of psychology, 66*(1), 20–32.

Cascio Rizzo, G. L., Berger, J., De Angelis, M., & Pozharliev, R. (2023). How sensory language shapes influencer's impact. *Journal of Consumer Research, 50*(4), 810–825

Celhay, F., & Luffarelli, J. (2024). Competent or Sad Blue? Lively or Aggressive Red? Why, How, and When Background Color Shapes the Meanings of Logo Hues. *Journal of Consumer Research,* Article ucae019.

Chan, K. W., Septianto, F., Kwon, J., & Kamal, R. S. (2023). Color effects on AI influencers' product recommendations. *European Journal of Marketing, 57*(9), 2290–2315.

Chang, H. H., Mukherjee, A., & Chattopadhyay, A. (2023). More voices persuade: The attentional benefits of voice numerosity. *Journal of Marketing Research, 60*(4), 687–706.

Chatterjee, A., & Vartanian, O. (2014). Neuroaesthetics. *Trends in cognitive sciences, 18*(7), 370–375.

Cheng, Y., & Yan, X. (2023). Effects of nostalgic messages on ad persuasiveness: a meta-analysis. *International Journal of Advertising, 42*(2), 263–287.

Cherif, E., & Baccino, T. (2022). How Consumers Process Unexpected Online Advertisements: the effects of motion and abrupt onset on consumers' attention and attitude. *Journal of Advertising Research, 62*(3), 219–240.

Chernev, A. (2001). The impact of common features on consumer preferences: A case of confirmatory reasoning. *Journal of Consumer Research, 27*(4), 475–488.

Childers, T. L., & Houston, M. J. (1984). Conditions for a picture-superiority effect on consumer memory. *Journal of Consumer Research, 11*(2), 643–654.

Choi, H., Yoo, K., Reichert, T., & Northup, T. (2022). Sexual ad appeals in social media: Effects and influences of cultural difference and sexual self-schema. *International Journal of Advertising, 41*(5), 910–929.

Cialdini, R. B., Cacioppo, J. T., Bassett, R., & Miller, J. A. (1978). Low-ball procedure for producing compliance: commitment then cost. *Journal of Personality and Social Psychology, 36*(5), 463.

Cimbalo, R. S., Beck, K. L., & Sendziak, D. S. (1978). Emotionly toned pictures and color selection for children and college students. *The Journal of Genetic Psychology, 133*(2), 303–304.

Clear, J. (2020). How to build new habits by taking advantage of old ones. *Atomic Habits*.

Compton, J. (2024). Inoculation theory. *Review of Communication*, 1–13.

Cruz, R. E., Leonhardt, J. M., & Pezzuti, T. (2017). Second person pronouns enhance consumer involvement and brand attitude. *Journal of Interactive Marketing, 39*(1), 104–116.

Dai, H., Milkman, K. L., & Riis, J. (2014). The fresh start effect: Temporal landmarks motivate aspirational behaviour. *Management Science, 60*(10), 2563–2582.

Daryanto, A., Alexander, N., & Kartika, G. (2022). The anthropomorphic brand logo and its effect on perceived functional performance. *Journal of Brand Management, 29*(3), 287–300.

Das, M., Balaji, M. S., Paul, S., & Saha, V. (2023). Being unconventional: The impact of unconventional packaging messages on impulsive purchases. *Psychology & Marketing, 40*(10), 1913–1932.

Das, S., Sandhu, K., & Mondal, S. R. (2023). Music logos drive digital brands: An empirical analysis of consumers' perspective. *Journal of Strategic Marketing, 31*(8), 1397–1412.

Davis, B. P., & Knowles, E. S. (1999). A disrupt-then-reframe technique of social influence. *Journal of Personality and Social Psychology, 76*(2), 192.

De Kerpel, L., Van Kerckhove, A., & Tessitore, T. (2024). Can you feel the advertisement tonight? The effect of ASMR cues in video advertising on purchase intention. *International Journal of Advertising, 43*(4), 716–745.

Defau, L., & Zauner, A. (2023). Personalized subject lines in email marketing. *Marketing Letters, 34*(4), 727–733.

De Saussure, F. (1989). *Cours de linguistique générale* (vol. 1). Otto Harrassowitz Verlag.

Desolneux, A., Moisan, L., & More, J. M. (2003). A grouping principle and four applications. *IEEE Transactions on Pattern Analysis and Machine Intelligence, 25*(4), 508–513.

Dickert, S., Västfjäll, D., Kleber, J., & Slovic, P. (2015). Scope insensitivity: The limits of intuitive valuation of human lives in public policy. *Journal of Applied Research in Memory and Cognition, 4*(3), 248–255.

Diener, E., Lucas, R. E., & Scollon, C. N. (2006). Beyond the hedonic treadmill: revising the adaptation theory of well-being. *American psychologist, 61*(4), 305.

Doyle, J. R., & Bottomley, P.A. (2004). Font appropriateness and brand choice. *Journal of business research, 57*(8), 873–880.

Duncan, W. J. (1985). The superiority theory of humour at work: Joking relationships as indicators of formal and informal status patterns in small, task-oriented groups. *Small Group Behaviour, 16*(4), 556–564.

Dunn, L., White, K., & Dahl, D. W. (2020). A little piece of me: When mortality reminders lead to giving to others. *Journal of Consumer Research, 47*(3), 431–453.

Eisend, M. (2009). A meta-analysis of humor in advertising. *Journal of the Academy of Marketing Science, 37*, 191–203.

Ekman, P. (2004). Emotions revealed. *Bmj, 328*(Suppl S5).

Essl, A., Hauser, D., & von Bieberstein, F. (2024). Let's think about the future: The effect of positive and negative future primes on pro-environmental behaviour. *Journal of Behavioural and Experimental Economics, 109*, Article 102166.

Eyni, A., Thongpapanl, N., Ashraf, A. R., & Wang, K. Y. (2023). The logo 'visual thickness effect': When and why it boosts brand personality. *Journal of Consumer Behaviour, 22*(2), 343–364.

Eysenck, H. J. (1941). A critical and experimental study of colour preferences. *The American Journal of Psychology, 54*(3), 385–394.

Farrington, D. P., Osborn, S. G., & West, D. J. (1978). The persistence of labelling effects. *Brit. J. Criminology, 18*, 277.

Fielding, D. (2022). *The Brand Book: An insider's guide to brand building for businesses and organizations.* Laurence King Publishing.

Filkuková, P., & Klempe, S. H. (2013). Rhyme as reason in commercial and social advertising. *Scandinavian Journal of Psychology, 54*(5), 423–431.

Forabosco, G. (1992). Cognitive aspects of the humour process: The concept of incongruity.

Formanowicz, M., Beneda, M., Witkowska, M., Nikadon, J., & Suitner, C. (2023). Mobilize is a Verb: The Use of Verbs and Concrete Language is Associated with Authors' and Readers' Perceptions of a Text's Action Orientation and Persuasiveness. *Personality and Social Psychology Bulletin*, 01461672241238418.

Fritze, M. P., Völckner, F., & Melnyk, V. (2024). Behavioural Labeling: Prompting Consumer Behaviour Through Activity Tags. *Journal of Marketing, 88*(4), 22–39.

Galai, D., & Sade, O. (2006). The "ostrich effect" and the relationship between the liquidity and the yields of financial assets. *The Journal of Business, 79*(5), 2741–2759.

Ganassali, S., & Matysiewicz, J. (2021). Echoing the golden legends: Storytelling archetypes and their impact on brand perceived value. *Journal of Marketing Management, 37*(5–6), 437–463.

Gerrig, R. (2018). *Experiencing narrative worlds*. Routledge.

Gershon, R., Cryder, C., & Milkman, K. L. (2024). Friends with Health Benefits: A Field Experiment. *Management Science.*

Gobrecht, F., & Marchand, A. (2023). The finitude of life – How mortality salience affects consumer behavior: A review. *Journal of Consumer Behaviour, 22*(1), 199–216.

Gotsch, M. L., & Gasser, F. (2024). The effect of autonomous sensory meridian response (ASMR) messages on consumer brand perceptions and intentions. *Journal of Consumer Behaviour.*

Graham, L. (2008). Gestalt theory in interactive media design. *Journal of Humanities & Social Sciences, 2*(1).

Grigsby, J. L., Jewell, R. D., & Zamudio, C. (2023). A picture's worth a thousand words: Using depicted movement in picture-based ads to increase narrative transportation. *Journal of Advertising, 52*(4), 594–612.

Gupta, T., Chen, S., & Mohanty, S. (2024). More the merrier: Effects of plural brand names on perceived entitativity and brand attitude. *Journal of Consumer Psychology.*

Han, M., & Newman, G. E. (2022). Seeking stability: Consumer motivations for communal nostalgia. *Journal of Consumer Psychology, 32*(1), 77–86.

Hastings, G., Stead, M., & Webb, J. (2004). Fear appeals in social marketing: Strategic and ethical reasons for concern. *Psychology & Marketing, 21*(11), 961–986.

Healy Jr, J. M. (1989). Emotional adaptation to life transitions: Early impact on integrative cognitive processes. In *Personality psychology: Recent trends and emerging directions* (pp. 115–127). New York, NY: Springer US.

Hernandez, J. M. D. C., da Costa Filho, M. C. M., & Strano, M. P. V. (2023). When transparency pays off: Enticing sceptical consumers with two-sided advertising. *International Journal of Consumer Studies, 47*(1), 317–333.

Higgins, E. T. (1997). Beyond pleasure and pain. *American psychologist, 52*(12), 1280.

Higgins, E. T., & Rholes, W. S. (1978). "Saying is believing": Effects of message modification on memory and liking for the person described. *Journal of Experimental Social Psychology, 14*(4), 363–378.

Hoang, C., Knöferle, K., & Warlop, L. (2023). Using different advertising humour appeals to generate firm-level warmth and competence impressions. *International Journal of Research in Marketing, 40*(4), 741–759.

Howe, H. S., Zhou, L., Dias, R. S., & Fitzsimons, G. J. (2023). Aha over Haha: Brands benefit more from being clever than from being funny. *Journal of Consumer Psychology, 33*(1), 107–114.

Huang, J., Xu, F., & Jiang, Y. (2023). I want to remember: Preference for visual intensity in sentimental purchases. *Psychology & Marketing, 40*(7), 1361–1371.

Huang, Y. (2025). Numbers Speak Louder When They Are Larger: The Impact of Font Size on the Persuasiveness of Numerical Stimuli in Advertising. *Journal of Consumer Behaviour.*

Husain, G., Thompson, W. F., & Schellenberg, E. G. (2002). Effects of musical tempo and mode on arousal, mood, and spatial abilities. *Music Perception, 20*(2), 151–171.

Hüttl-Maack, V., Sedghi, T. M., & Daume, J. M. (2024). Through rose-tinted glasses: How inducing and resolving curiosity makes consumers less skeptical and improves their product evaluations. *Journal of Consumer Psychology, 34*(1), 92–100.

Jakubowski, K., Finkel, S., Stewart, L., & Müllensiefen, D. (2017). Dissecting an earworm: Melodic features and song popularity predict involuntary musical imagery. *Psychology of Aesthetics, Creativity, and the Arts, 11*(2), 122.

Janata, P., Tomic, S. T., & Haberman, J. M. (2012). Sensorimotor coupling in music and the psychology of the groove. *Journal of Experimental Psychology: General, 141*(1), 54.

Jarvis, M., & Okami, P. (2019). *Principles of psychology: contemporary perspectives.* Oxford University Press.

Jenni, K., & Loewenstein, G. (1997). Explaining the identifiable victim effect. *Journal of Risk and Uncertainty, 14*, 235–257.

Jonauskaite, D., Epicoco, D., Al-rasheed, A. S., Aruta, J. J. B. R., Bogushevskaya, V., Brederoo, S. G., … & Mohr, C. (2024). A comparative analysis of colour–emotion associations in 16–88-year-old adults from 31 countries. *British Journal of Psychology, 115*(2), 275–305.

Jones, N., & Hamby, A. (2024). It's Written on Your Face: How Emotional Variation in Super Bowl Advertisements Influences Ad Liking. *Journal of Advertising, 53*(3), 463–472.

Jung, S., & Dubois, D. (2023). When and how slow motion makes products more luxurious. *Journal of Marketing Research, 60*(6), 1177–1196.

Kahneman, D., Fredrickson, B. L., Schreiber, C. A., & Redelmeier, D. A. (1993). When more pain is preferred to less: Adding a better end. *Psychological science, 4*(6), 401–405.

Kapferer, J. N. (2008). *The new strategic brand management: Creating and sustaining brand equity long term.* Kogan.

Keller, K. L., Heckler, S. E., & Houston, M. J. (1998). The effects of brand name suggestiveness on advertising recall. *Journal of Marketing, 62*(1), 48–57.

Khan, U., & Dhar, R. (2006). Licensing effect in consumer choice. *Journal of Marketing Research, 43*(2), 259–266.

Kilijanek, A., & Ozga, W. K. (2022). Impact of various types of provocative advertisements on brand recall and attention engagement: Pilot study report. *Applied Cognitive Psychology, 36*(4), 946–953.

Kim, S., Jung, A. R., & Kim, Y. (2021). The effects of typefaces on ad effectiveness considering psychological perception and perceived communicator's power. *Journal of Marketing Communications, 27*(7), 716–741.

Kim, K., Ryoo, Y., Manika, D., Yoon, N., & Yoon, S. (2024). From ugly to attractive: Leveraging anthropomorphism to increase demand for irregular-appearing produce. *Psychology & Marketing.*

King, J., McClelland, A., & Furnham, A. (2015). Sex really does sell: The recall of sexual and non-sexual television advertisements in sexual and non-sexual programmes. *Applied Cognitive Psychology, 29*(2), 210–216.

Koerner, E. K. (1992). The Sapir-Whorf hypothesis: A preliminary history and a bibliographical essay. *Journal of Linguistic Anthropology, 2*(2), 173–198.

Kohout, S., Kruikemeier, S., & Bakker, B. N. (2023). May I have your Attention, please? An eye tracking study on emotional social media comments. *Computers in Human Behaviour, 139*, Article 107495.

Köhler, W. (1967). Gestalt psychology. *Psychologische forschung, 31*(1), XVIII–XXX.

König, L. M. (2023). Debunking nutrition myths: An experimental test of the 'truth sandwich' text format. *British Journal of Health Psychology, 28*(4), 1000–1010.

Koukova, N. T. (2025). The Effect of Messages Emphasizing Fantasies and Expectations on Brand Evaluations and Behavioral Intentions. *Psychology & Marketing.*

Kuai, L., & Wei, H. (2025). The Role of Serendipity in Narratives: How Serendipitous Story Promotes Product Interest. *Psychology & Marketing.*

Kwon, J., Chan, K. W., Gu, W., & Septianto, F. (2022). The role of cool versus warm colors in B2B versus B2C firm-generated content for boosting positive eWOM. *Industrial Marketing Management, 104*, 212–225.

Kwon, S., Suda, T., & Nomura, T. (2024). 3D versus 2D: Effects of the number of dimensions of product images on perceptions of product size. *Journal of Consumer Behaviour.*

Labrecque, L. I., & Milne, G. R. (2012). Exciting red and competent blue: the importance of color in marketing. *Journal of the Academy of Marketing Science, 40*(5), 711–727.

Langer, E., Blank, A., & Chanowitz, B. (1978). The mindlessness of Ostensibly Thoughtful Action: The Role of "Placebic" Information in Interpersonal Interaction. *Journal of Personality and Social Psychology, 36*(6), 635–642.

Lembke, A. (2021). *Dopamine nation: Finding balance in the age of indulgence.* Penguin.

Lerner, J. S., & Keltner, D. (2000). Beyond valence: Toward a model of emotion-specific influences on judgement and choice. *Cognition & emotion, 14*(4), 473–493.

Li, X., & Shah, A. (2020). The Last Hurrah Effect: End-of-Period Temporal Landmarks Increase Optimism and Financial Risk-Taking. *Nanyang Business School Research Paper*, (20–24).

Light, N., & Fernbach, P. M. (2024). Keep It simple? Consumer perceptions of brand simplicity and risk. *Journal of Marketing Research, 61*(6), 1152–1170.

Lim, S., van Osselaer, S. M., Goodman, J. K., Fuchs, C., & Schreier, M. (2024). The Starbucks effect: When name-based order identification increases customers' store preference and service satisfaction. *Journal of Retailing, 100*(2), 316–329.

Liu, J., Hong, X., Zheng, Z., & Zhong, J. (2024). When consumers have difficulty understanding ads: How technical language lowers purchase intention. *Journal of Consumer Behaviour, 23*(2), 796–807.

Loewenstein, G. (2005). Hot-cold empathy gaps and medical decision making. *Health psychology, 24*(4S), S49.

Loewenstein, G. F., Weber, E. U., Hsee, C. K., & Welch, N. (2001). Risk as feelings. *Psychological Bulletin, 127*(2), 267.

Loomes, G., & Sugden, R. (1982). Regret theory: An alternative theory of rational choice under uncertainty. *The Economic Journal, 92*(368), 805–824.

Lowrey, T. M., Shrum, L. J., & Dubitsky, T. M. (2003). The relation between brand-name linguistic characteristics and brand-name memory. *Journal of Advertising, 32*(3), 7–17.

Macintosh, G., & Gentry, J. W. (1999). Decision making in personal selling: Testing the "KISS Principle". *Psychology & Marketing, 16*(5), 393–408.

Maschmann, I. T., Körner, A., & Topolinski, S. (2024). Consonant beginnings and vowel endings lead to higher liking judgments. *Journal of Experimental Psychology: Learning, Memory, and Cognition, 50*(11), 1862–1873.

Mathy, F., & Feldman, J. (2012). What's magic about magic numbers? Chunking and data compression in short-term memory. *Cognition, 122*(3), 346–362.

Mayer, J. D., Gaschke, Y. N., Braverman, D. L., & Evans, T. W. (1992). Mood-congruent judgment is a general effect. *Journal of personality and social psychology, 63*(1), 119.

McCann, C. D., Higgins, E. T., & Fondacaro, R. A. (1991). Primacy and recency in communication and self-persuasion: How successive audiences and multiple encodings influence subsequent evaluative judgments. *Social Cognition, 9*(1), 47–66.

McCrostie, J. (2015). You can't turn your ears off, so listen up. Campaign https://www.campaignlive.co.uk/article/cant-turn-ears-off-so-listen/1330821#05g6qw1OKo4DqdvH.99

McGlone, M. S., & Tofighbakhsh, J. (2000). Birds of a feather flock conjointly (?): Rhyme as reason in aphorisms. *Psychological science, 11*(5), 424–428.

McGraw, A. P., & Warren, C. (2010). Benign violations: Making immoral behavior funny. *Psychological science, 21*(8), 1141–1149.

Melumad, S., & Meyer, R. (2024). EXPRESS: How Listening versus Reading Alters Consumers' Interpretations of News. *Journal of Marketing Research*.

Melzner, J., & Raghubir, P. (2023). The sound of music: The effect of timbral sound quality in audio logos on brand personality perception. *Journal of Marketing Research, 60*(5), 932–949.

Meng, L., Kou, S., Duan, S., Jiang, Y., & Lü, K. (2022). How a blurry background in product presentation influences product size perception. *Psychology & Marketing, 39*(8), 1633–1645.

Meyer, W. U., Niepel, M., Rudolph, U., & Schützwohl, A. (1991). An experimental analysis of surprise. *Cognition & Emotion, 5*(4), 295–311.

Min, L., Liu, P. J., & Anderson, C. L. (2024). The Visual Complexity= Higher Production Cost Lay Belief. *Journal of Consumer Research*, Article ucae044.

Mylius, B. (2018). Three types of anthropocentrism. *Environmental Philosophy, 15*(2), 159–194.

Novella, R., & Ramirez, E. G. R. (2024). Question-order effects on judgements under uncertainty. *Journal of Behavioural and Experimental Economics, 109*, Article 102159.

Oba, D., Howe, H. S., & Fitzsimons, G. J. (2024). Brand Teasing: How Brands Build Strong Relationships by Making Fun of Their Consumers. *Journal of Consumer Research, 52*(1), 70–92.

Oppenheimer, D. M. (2006). Consequences of erudite vernacular utilized irrespective of necessity: Problems with using long words needlessly. *Applied Cognitive Psychology: The Official Journal of the Society for Applied Research in Memory and Cognition, 20*(2), 139–156.

Packard, G., & Berger, J. (2021). How concrete language shapes customer satisfaction. *Journal of Consumer Research, 47*(5), 787–806.

Packard, G., Berger, J., & Boghrati, R. (2023). How verb tense shapes persuasion. *Journal of Consumer Research, 50*(3), 645–660.

Palla, P. J., Kyriacou, E., & Zarkada, A. K. (2022, April). The Product Involvement Effect on Thought Elicitation and Attitude Strength in The Online Environment. In *Corporate and Marketing Communications Conference*.

Petty, R. E., & Cacioppo, J. T. (1986). The elaboration likelihood model of persuasion. In *Advances in experimental social psychology* (Vol. 19, pp. 123–205). Academic Press.

Pezzuti, T. (2023). Highlighting Discrepancies in Brand Messaging Increases Social Media Engagement. *Journal of the Academy of Marketing Science*, 1–22.

Piaget, J. (1952). The origins of intelligence in children. *International University*.

Pieters, R., & Wedel, M. (2004). Attention capture and transfer in advertising: Brand, pictorial, and text-size effects. *Journal of marketing, 68*(2), 36–50.

Pool, E., Brosch, T., Delplanque, S., & Sander, D. (2016). Attentional bias for positive emotional stimuli: A meta-analytic investigation. *Psychological Bulletin, 142*(1), 79.

Provine, R. R. (1992). Contagious laughter: Laughter is a sufficient stimulus for laughs and smiles. *Bulletin of the Psychonomic Society, 30*(1), 1–4.

Rathee, S., Yu-Buck, G. F., & Gupta, A. (2023). It is not just a name: Effects of proper name for high-quality versus low-quality brands. *Psychology & Marketing, 40*(7), 1388–1404.

Rizzolatti, G., & Sinigaglia, C. (2016). The mirror mechanism: a basic principle of brain function. *Nature Reviews Neuroscience, 17*(12), 757–765.

Rogers, R. W. (1983). Cognitive and physiological processes in fear appeals and attitude change: A revised theory of protection motivation. In J. Cacioppo & R. Petty (Eds.), *Social psychophysiology.* Guilford Press

Romero, M., Craig, A. W., Mormann, M., & Kumar, A. (2024). Are '10-Grams of Protein" Better than' Ten Grams of Protein"? How Digits versus Number Words Influence Consumer Judgments. *Journal of Consumer Research,* Article ucae030.

Sahni, N. S., Wheeler, S. C., & Chintagunta, P. (2018). Personalization in email marketing: The role of noninformative advertising content. *Marketing Science, 37*(2), 236–258.

Sands, S., Campbell, C., Mavrommatis, A., & Kadomskaia, V. (2022). Can a whisper boost recall of video advertisements?: Exploring the effects of autonomous sensory meridian response (ASMR) in advertising. *Journal of Advertising Research, 62*(3), 287–296.

Scacco, J. M., & Muddiman, A. (2020). The curiosity effect: Information seeking in the contemporary news environment. *New Media & Society, 22*(3), 429–448.

Schank, Roger C. & Abelson, Robert P. (1995) Knowledge and Memory: The Real Story. In: Robert S. Wyer, Jr (ed) *Knowledge and Memory: The Real Story.* Lawrence Erlbaum Associates. 1–85.

Schumacher, A., Goukens, C., Geyskens, K., & Nielsen, J. H. (2024). Revisiting surprise appeals: How surprise labeling curtails consumption. *Journal of Consumer Psychology.*

Sedikides, C., & Wildschut, T. (2019). The sociality of personal and collective nostalgia. *European Review of Social Psychology, 30*(1), 123–173.

Septianto, F., Paramita, W., & Ye, S. (2023). What's in a (first) name? Personized advertising messages enhance consumer perceived ethicality. *Journal of Advertising, 52*(2), 179–192.

Sharma, N., & Varki, S. (2018). Active white space (AWS) in logo designs: effects on logo evaluations and brand communication. *Journal of Advertising, 47*(3), 270–281.

Sharma, V., & Estes, Z. (2024). Seeing is smelling: Pictures improve product evaluations by evoking olfactory imagery. *International Journal of Research in Marketing, 41*(2), 282–307.

Shields, A. B., & Johnson, J. W. (2016). Childhood brand nostalgia: A new conceptualization and scale development. *Journal of Consumer Behaviour, 15*(4), 359–369.

Shin, H., Bunosso, I., & Levine, L. R. (2023). The influence of chatbot humour on consumer evaluations of services. *International Journal of Consumer Studies, 47*(2), 545–562.

Shu, S. B., & Carlson, K. A. (2014). When three charms but four alarms: Identifying the optimal number of claims in persuasion settings. *Journal of Marketing, 78*(1), 127–139.

Shulman, H. C., Markowitz, D. M., & Rogers, T. (2024). Reading dies in complexity: Online news consumers prefer simple writing. *Science Advances, 10*(23), Article eadn2555.

Shurcliff, A. (1968). Judged humor, arousal, and the relief theory. *Journal of Personality and Social Psychology*, *8*(4, Pt.1), 360–363

Simons, D. J., & Chabris, C. F. (1999). Gorillas in our midst: Sustained inattentional blindness for dynamic events. *Perception*, *28*(9), 1059–1074.

Singh, S. (2006). Impact of color on marketing. *Management Decision*, *44*(6), 783–789.

Sivanathan, N., & Kakkar, H. (2017). The unintended consequences of argument dilution in direct-to-consumer drug advertisements. *Nature Human Behaviour*, *1*(11), 797–802.

Slovic, P., Finucane, M. L., Peters, E., & MacGregor, D. G. (2007). The affect heuristic. *European Journal of Operational Research*, *177*(3), 1333–1352.

Smith, S. L., Ward, R. T., Allen, L. K., Wormwood, J. B., & Mills, C. (2022). Mind your words: Affective experience during reading mediates the effect of textual valence on comprehension. *Applied Cognitive Psychology*, *36*(5), 1131–1141.

Soh, R., Wu, C. L., Tsai, P. H., & Chen, H. C. (2024). Influence of emotional states on incongruity-resolution and nonsense humour processing. *International Journal of Psychology*, *59*(6), 1091–1100.

Speer, N. K., Reynolds, J. R., Swallow, K. M., & Zacks, J. M. (2009). Reading stories activates neural representations of visual and motor experiences. *Psychological Science*, *20*(8), 989–999.

Strongman, L. (2007). The anthropomorphic bias: How human thinking is prone to be self-referential.

Stuppy, A., Landwehr, J. R., & McGraw, A. P. (2024). The art of slowness: slow motion enhances consumer evaluations by increasing processing fluency. *Journal of Marketing Research*, *61*(2), 185–203.

Talebi, A., Mukherjee, S., & Das, G. (2024). Unmasking the pivotal role of ad–target ethnic congruence in driving consumers' response to fear appeals. *Psychology & Marketing*, *41*(6), 1346–1362.

Tang, F., & Hou, J. (2024). Show me the outputs! The influence of charitable outputs and charitable cause phrasing on charitable giving. *Psychology & Marketing*, *41*(10), 2368–2380.

Thompson, W. F., Schellenberg, E. G., & Letnic, A. K. (2012). Fast and loud background music disrupts reading comprehension. *Psychology of Music*, *40*(6), 700–708.

Tok, D., Chen, X., Chang, C. T., & Chu, X. Y. (2024). "Ascorbic Acid" or "Vitamin C?" When and how scientifically or commonly named ingredients enhance product evaluations. *Psychology & Marketing*, *41*(10), 2537–2550.

Tse, C. S., & Altarriba, J. (2022). Independent effects of word concreteness and word valence on immediate serial recall. *British Journal of Psychology*, *113*(3), 820–834.

Unnava, H. R., & Burnkrant, R. E. (1991). Effects of repeating varied ad executions on brand name memory. *Journal of Marketing Research*, *28*(4), 406–416.

Valdez, P., & Mehrabian, A. (1994). Effects of color on emotions. *Journal of experimental psychology: General*, *123*(4), 394.

Von Restorff, H. (1933). On the effect of area formation in the trace field. *Psychological Research*, *18*, 299–342.

Wagemans, J., Elder, J.H., Kubovy, M., Palmer, S. E., Peterson, M.A., Singh, M., & Von der Heydt, R. (2012). A century of Gestalt psychology in visual perception: I. Perceptual grouping and figure–ground organization. *Psychological Bulletin*, *138*(6), 1172.

Wansink B. *Mindless Eating – Why We Eat More Than We Think*. Bantam Dell: New York, 2006.

Warren, Caleb; McGraw, A. Peter (2 February 2015). *"Benign Violation Theory"*. Rochester, NY.

Weber, E. H. (1948). The sense of touch and common feeling, 1846. In W. Dennis (Ed.), *Readings in the History of Psychology* (pp. 194–196). Appleton-Century-Crofts.

Wen, T. J., Choi, C. W., Wu, L., & Morris, J. D. (2021). Empowering emotion: The driving force of share and purchase intentions in viral advertising. *Journal of Current Issues & Research in Advertising*, *43*(1), 47–67.

Wijland, R., Hansen, P., & Gardezi, F. (2016). Mobile nudging: Youth engagement with banking apps. *Journal of Financial Services Marketing*, *21*, 51–63.

Wiseman, R. (2008). *Quirkology: the curious science of everyday lives*. Pan Macmillan.

Witte, K. (1992). Putting the fear back into fear appeals: The extended parallel process model. *Communications Monographs*, *59*(4), 329–349.

Wood, O. (2019) *Identifying and measuring the Fluent Device*. WARC. https://www-warc-com.uwe.idm.oclc.org/content/article/identifying-and-measuring-the-fluent-device/130035

You, Y., Wang, L., Yang, X., & Wen, N. (2024). Alleviating hedonic adaptation in repeat consumption with creative thinking. *Journal of Consumer Psychology*.

Yu, Z., Ponomarenko, V., & Liska, L.I. (2024). How to allocate white space in ad design? The impact of product layouts on perceived entitativity and advertising performance. *Journal of Advertising*, *53*(2), 215–229.

Zaltman, G. (2003). *How customers think: Essential insights into the mind of the market*. Harvard Business Press.

Zane, D. M., Reczek, R.W., & Haws, K.L. (2022). Promoting pi day: Consumer response to special day-themed sales promotions. *Journal of Consumer Psychology*, *32*(4), 652–663.

Zemborain, M. R., Johar, G. V., Roggeveen, A.L., & Ansari, A. (2024). Choice bolstering changes attribute importance and affects future choices. *Journal of Behavioural Decision Making*, *37*(4), Article e2401.

Zeng, S., Wu, S., Yuan, Y., & Xu, X. (2025). Designing age: the impact of logo color lightness on brand age perception and brand attitude. *Psychology & Marketing*, *42*(4), 1188–1200.

Zhang, Y., Fishbach, A., & Kruglanski, A.W. (2007). The dilution model: how additional goals undermine the perceived instrumentality of a shared path. *Journal of Personality and Social Psychology*, *92*(3), 389.

Zhang, Y., Xia, L., Du, J., & Zhao, M. (2024). Curiosity under bright light: The influence of bright lighting on new product adoption. *International Journal of Research in Marketing*.

Zheng, X., Liu, C. and Zheng, L. (2024), Is darker more effective? The effect of package color lightness on consumer judgment of product efficacy. *Psychology & Marketing, 42*(4), 1018–1034.

Zhu, Y., Wang, Y., Wei, J., & Hao, A. (2023). Effects of vividness, information and aesthetic design on the appeal of pay-per-click ads. *Journal of Research in Interactive Marketing, 17*(6), 848–864.

Zillmann, D. (1996). Sequential dependencies in emotional experience and behaviour. *Emotion: Interdisciplinary Perspectives,* 243–272.

Zoghaib, A., Luffarelli, J., & Feiereisen, S. (2023). Branding with music: How can music contour and tonality enhance perceived brand innovativeness and brand evaluations?. *Psychology & Marketing, 40*(10), 1965–1985.

Zwicky, A. (2006). *Why are we so illuded.* Stanford University. https://web.stanford.edu/~zwicky/LSA07illude.abst.pdf

6 Brand: Finding the Right Voices

In this chapter we explore how a customer's perception of a brand is guided by the people representing the brand. Very often messages are conveyed by a person, so what difference does this make? Here we present evidence that people make quick judgements about others, including assessing whether we like them, believe them, or respect them. This knowledge will help you select appropriate people to communicate your brand messages.

Jonathon Ford is the Vice President of Digital at global sports marketing agency IMG. His role involves working with a range of world-famous sports stars who represent both sports teams and global brands. Although these talented individuals are stars in their own right, whilst wearing their club kit they help to shape perceptions of the team brand. Often these stars are also asked to work with brands outside of their natural field of expertise i.e. outside of sport. In our conversation, Jon shared why this is such a valuable asset to harness ...

THE HUMAN ELEMENT: USING PEOPLE AS BRAND REPRESENTATIVES IN SPORTS MARKETING

Sports teams have increasingly established themselves as major global enterprises, with valuations reaching unprecedented heights. Manchester United, for example, is valued at approximately $6.5 billion, making it one of the most valuable football clubs in the world. This remarkable growth began decades ago but surged in the 2000s with the rise of global media deals, online engagement, and the expansion of fanbases beyond local markets. Today, value is driven by a combination of factors including

DOI: 10.4324/9781003541226-7

lucrative media rights, expansive global fanbases, and diversified revenue streams such as sponsorships and merchandise sales.

What once was primarily about what happened on the pitch now extends far beyond that, with athletes becoming key brand assets both on and off the field. Star players – through their personal brands – are pivotal in driving engagement, especially online. Their ability to connect with fans through social media platforms has redefined how teams and athletes engage with their audience, creating deeper relationships that significantly boost brand value.

THE HALO EFFECT IN ACTION

The halo effect – where positive impressions in one area extend to other contexts – is heavily used in sports marketing. This psychological theory allows famous individuals to effectively promote brands across various domains.

Sports brands increasingly pursue collaborations with influential figures to reach new audiences, effectively borrowing their 'halos' (their fame and respect) to enhance brand perception. These partnerships enable brands to access entirely new demographic segments through trusted figures who already command attention and respect in those communities. For instance, Serena Williams's partnership with Gatorade connects the brand with both female athletes and a global audience interested in empowerment and fitness, while also leveraging her credibility as a trailblazer in tennis.

Athletes represent some of the most valuable human assets for sports brands. As seen with the NBA's strategic use of players like LeBron James, who is not only a basketball legend but also a prominent figure in entertainment and activism, sports organisations maximise their use of players in a variety of campaigns – extending their influence far beyond the game itself. Sports organisations strategically navigate the constraints of rights agreements and player contracts to ensure they are capitalising on these personal brands for maximum impact.

ATHLETES BUILDING PERSONAL BRANDS

The growing ability of athletes to build their own following presents both opportunities and challenges for sports organisations looking to leverage human representatives. Social media enables athletes to own their story and build personal audiences independent of team affiliations, creating new dynamics in the relationship between players and organisations, and impacting sports marketing activities.

When players switch teams, they often bring a loyal following with them. For example, Son Heung-min, one of South Korea's most popular football players, has a large global fanbase, particularly in South Korea. When he moved to Tottenham Hotspur, the UK club saw a significant influx of followers from his home country. Following his transfer to Los Angeles FC, they will be expecting a similar effect.

CONCLUSION

IMG, advisors to the global sports industry, partner with organisations, rights holders, and owned properties to leverage the intrinsic value of their assets, brands, and fandoms. They focus on driving long-term value through strategic marketing and content creation.

One of the keys to success in this industry is identifying how to use popular athletes effectively, while also creating systems that allow organisations to keep producing content on a regular basis. This means organisations need to engage both their loyal fans and attract new ones, without leaving anyone behind.

The foundation will always be what happens 'on the pitch', but as athlete personal branding grows, it's important to find ways to align individual and organisational interests to maximise the impact of human representatives on brand perception and audience engagement.

6.1 JUDGEMENT OF PEOPLE

Many brands use spokespeople to represent their brands. Sometimes these are employees from the organisation itself, such as the company founder. For example, if we say Meta, or Facebook, you probably picture Mark Zuckerberg.

Some brands turn to celebrities to endorse their products, relying on their fame and the public's familiarity with them. Celebrities can lend status, trust, or aspirational value to a brand. Increasingly, however, brands are also working with influencers – people who may not be widely famous but have built loyal, engaged communities online.

There is evidence that celebrity attributes can be transferred to otherwise little-known brands via 'meaning transfer' (Tian et al., 2021). Richard Perloff (1993), author of *The Dynamics of Persuasion*, summarises some of the key aspects that customers use to assess a communicator, and we review topics such as credibility below. But first, it's worth understanding some common cognitive biases that shape how people perceive a brand communicator. Biases act as mental shortcuts – not always harmful, but they can lead to distorted or inequitable judgments.

a) *First impressions count*

First, what governs initial impressions of a person? When you see some-one's LinkedIn profile for example, what guides your perception? Often, it's a combination of visual cues, perceived credibility, and how closely their presentation aligns with your expectations or social norms.

Psychology tells us that we form impressions rapidly – sometimes within seconds – using heuristics or mental shortcuts, which can be influenced by everything from profile photos to job titles and mutual connections.

This is why personal branding is so important: The way individuals choose to present themselves online, shapes how they are perceived, trusted, and remembered.

Matching principle of communication

Effective communicators understand the type of conversation taking place and try to 'match' their comments to the other person's. According to Duhigg (2024), there are three fundamental considerations: the emotion being conveyed, the decision under discussion, and the social implications.

Costly signalling

We all know that some people like to show off. The class prankster at school, the daredevil at the circus, and the parkour YouTubers. In nature too, some animals have impressive plumage or other displays of courtship. What makes such displays particularly persuasive is the risk attached. When showing off is in some way costly to the show-off, people are more likely to be impressed (Fessler *et al.*, 2014). Red Bull perform-ing the highest ever freefall for example, was particularly impressive. Similarly, spending money on advertising can signal quality in a product (Kihlstrom and Riordan, 1984).

Warmth and competence

We have discussed personality traits as being fundamental axes against which we assess the personality of other people. An even more basic way of assessing a person is whether they are warm (or cold), and whether they are competent at a specific skill against which they are being assessed (Fiske et al., 2007). We bet you had teachers at school who were kind and friendly (warm), whilst others shared their expertise in a given subject but were perhaps a littler colder? Some perhaps had both warmth and competence, others had neither.

Humourbragging (conveying self-confidence in a humorous way) can increase perceptions of warmth and competence (Pai et al., 2023), and dressing consistently can increase perceptions of competence (Kim and Lee, 2024). Brands too can be assessed according to warmth and competence, with formal language more appropriate for competent brands and informal for warm brands (Leung et al., 2022).

Nonverbal communication

There are supposed scientific studies suggesting specific percentages of meaning that are derived from verbal vs non-verbal information. Whilst there may not be consensus on such statistics, there are five principal ways in which nonverbal communication affects customers (Carney, 2024). First, eye contact is important. Second, consider gestures such as hand signals. Third, appropriately touching the person you are conversing with makes a difference, e.g., a hand on the shoulder. Fourth, consider artifacts in the vicinity – perhaps even those that relate to the conversation such as the product being sold. Lastly, the general ambience or environment makes a difference.

The way each of these five is perceived, however, might vary between cultures. For example, while direct eye contact might signal confidence and trustworthiness in many Western cultures, it can be considered disrespectful or confrontational in parts of Asia.

If you haven't already checked out the Culture Factor website (www.theculturefactor.com mentioned in chapter 2), now might be a good time to take a look.

b) Filling in the gaps about others

Sometimes people make assumptions about others when details are lacking.

Monet effect

Monet is famous for impressionist paintings. You can work out what the image is intended to be, but his paintings are certainly not photographic. A bit like the gestalt theory, viewers fill in the gaps. People imagine how Monet's mind must have interpreted the surroundings to create a scene such as waterlilies in a lake. Similarly, people fill in the gaps when knowledge of another person is incomplete (Ury, 2022). In your mind you may envisage what a given celebrity eats for breakfast for example, despite not knowing anything about the facts.

Homogeneity bias

You may have noticed that in many old war films (perhaps some newer ones too), the central characters are presented in significant detail. In contrast, little is known about the faceless enemy. This plays to a bias whereby people assume that those in a so-called in-group are diverse, compared to homogeneity (similarity) among those in the out-group (Chance and Goldstein, 2014).

APPLYING THE THEORY: KEY QUESTIONS

Have you reviewed the first impressions your spokespeople make – online and in person? Do they effectively convey the personal brand and values you want to project?

Can you proactively fill information gaps – through clear bios, credentials, and social proof – so people don't leap to wrong assumptions about your representatives?

6.2 LIKEABILITY AND AUTHENTICITY

Most people want to be liked, but there are some important theories that guide assessment of whether someone is likeable. Why does it matter to be liked? Well, this may seem unfair, but whether someone is liked affects perception of their ideas. This is called reactive devaluation.

Exam scripts are usually submitted anonymously to ensure (as far as possible) that judgement is based on the merits or otherwise of the exam paper, rather than potential pre-existing views of the student. Psychological research supports this, showing that people 'reactively devalue' suggestions from those they don't like (Ross and Stillinger, 1991).

Figure 6.1 Emotional Contagion

a) *Smiling can be contagious*

Unsurprisingly, often people favour others who make them feel good.

Emotional contagion

Showing that you are happy, can make others feel happy too (see figure 6.1): Smiles convey positive emotion to customers subconsciously (Hofman et al., 2024) and happy people are generally perceived more positively, especially when their happiness is known to be changeable (Hong et al., 2023). A smiling face can positively affect attitudes towards adverts too, for men in particular (Zhang et al., 2023), and smiling in a profile photo on Airbnb is one of the aspects that increases ratings (Jang, 2022).

b) *Birds of a feather*

One important way in which people judge others is just whether they are similar in some way or at least understand their views.

Similarity

Intuitively, many customers have a pretty good idea of who they are and how others perceive them. This is referred to as 'self-schema' (Markus, 1977). In turn, customers also recognise others who are similar to them – and react well to those people. People are nicer to those they perceive to be 'similar' (Schutt, 2023). Brand engagement also increases where an influencer has both credibility and similarity to the customer (Gupta et al., 2023).

Unity

In 2021, Robert Cialdini published an updated version of his best-selling 1984 book *Influence* adding a seventh principle by which people can influence an audience. He referred to this as 'unity': The degree to which a communicator and recipient of a message share an identity.

There are many ways to show someone that they share an identity. Some obvious ones include various demographics such as age, gender, or nationality. If you have an online group, there is probably some way in which the communicator could develop unity between just about every person there, including shared hobbies, music taste, and even similar holiday destinations. For example, people feel social connection with those who make the same 'experiential' purchase (Kumar et al., 2024). They also prefer selling to others who have a 'shared past' (Christensen and Shu, 2023) and selling to those with a similar name – even just beginning with the same letter (Sherman and Barokas, 2023). People even prefer brands from their hometown (Zhang et al., 2023).

Ingratiation

Many people share the view that the best communicators are also good at relating to others. In academic terms we might describe relating to others as 'ingratiation'. This can be 'complimentary' where the listener flatters the person, 'conformity' where the listener accepts the view of the other person, or 'self-presentation' where the listener promotes themselves to increase their attractiveness (Jones, 1964). Truthful people are also perceived as more attractive (Ten Brinke et al., 2023), and influencers who appear genuine boost followers' self-esteem and purchase intention (Claeys et al., 2024).

Mimicry

Most of us have people we look up to: Role models. Whether consciously, or often non-consciously, people mimic the behaviour of role models (Chartrand and Van Baaren, 2009). This might include teenagers adopting a dance they've seen in Fortnite or on TikTok, or politicians standing behind a lectern as their peers did before them; behaviours can be contagious.

Mirroring

Unlike mimicry, mirroring behaviour occurs when two people in conversation begin to copy each other's actions, but as if a mirror was between them. You might brush your right hand through your hair, leading your partner to brush their left hand through their hair etc. This is sometimes known as the Chameleon Effect (Chartrand and Bargh, 1999) as, in effect, conversation partners try to immerse themselves into the conversation 'environment'. Some salespeople deliberately adopt mirroring behaviour to help their customers feel more comfortable – and in turn they buy the product or service being presented.

c) Everybody is human

It's also important just to be human!

Pratfall effect

Sometimes celebrities and influencers can seem a little bit too polished. Do they really wake up with perfect make-up? Do they never drop food on their outfits? Do they never trip over their shoelaces? The pratfall effect suggests that people who make small mistakes are perceived as being more attractive (Helmreich et al., 1970). Small imperfections can actually make people seem more human.

For example, perhaps 'behind the scenes' style social media content is beneficial to show the human side of your brand. Even admitting corporate vulnerability can increase customer support (Barros et al., 2023) and admitting being wrong on social media improves how people are viewed (Fetterman et al., 2022).

d) Looking good can help

Lastly, looking like a nice person also appears to guide judgement.

Physical attractiveness

As much as many people might not like to admit it, the way a person looks does affect how they are perceived (Eagly et al., 1991), although this varies across contexts. Beauty is in the eye of the beholder, but there are still general attributes that many people agree are attractive, such as symmetrical faces (Rhodes, 2006)

APPLYING THE THEORY: KEY QUESTIONS

Are you harnessing emotional contagion by sharing genuine enthusiasm or passion that your audience can catch and mirror?

Consider showcasing similarities – like shared values or past challenges – to foster unity (for example, highlighting a customer's story that mirrors your own brand journey).

Can you create moments of connection by showcasing community achievements – such as user-generated success stories or group milestones – to strengthen bonds?

Consider embracing small, human mistakes or imperfections (for instance, a behind-the-scenes blooper) to make your brand feel more approachable.

6.3 CREDIBILITY

a) A knowledgeable spokesperson often adds credibility

Credibility is an important aspect of persuasiveness. Who would you ask for advice about which new car to buy? Probably somebody who knows a lot about cars, maybe even a mechanic. According to Richard Perloff (1993) the credibility of a 'source' is dependent on not just 'expertise', but also the trustworthiness and attractiveness of the source. For example, such source credibility (expertise, trustworthiness and similarity) affects perceptions of influencers (Luarn et al., 2024). In fact, micro-influencers (i.e. fewer followers but often very specific expertise) seem to generate clicks on sponsored posts (Gross and von Wangenheim, 2022) and higher purchase intention (Van Reijmersdal et al., 2024).

Halo effect

Surprisingly, sometimes customers can be guided into thinking that a person with known expertise in a specific subject, also knows about a far greater range of topics. Consider how many sports stars appear in adverts for fashion brands, cosmetic products, or other brand ambassadorial roles that barely relate to sport for example. This is known as the halo effect (Nisbett and Wilson, 1977), given that the celebrity or influencer receives admiration from such a wide range of audiences (albeit not quite achieving the angelic status that the theory suggests). Stars increase the success of video games for example (Marchand and Weber, 2024). The same thing happens with brands, sometimes referred to as the noble edge effect: Brands that engage in socially responsible behaviour can benefit from the 'halo effect' (Chernev and Blair, 2015), or more broadly can benefit from a 'brand positivity effect' (Posavac et al., 2024).

Similarly, the halo effect suggests that when adverts appear in trusted, high-quality environments – such as LinkedIn for reaching professional audiences – customers are more likely to view the advertised brand positively.

APPLYING THE THEORY: KEY QUESTIONS

Does your organisation have credible experts who can convey a message? Perhaps you could partner with an external expertise.

Can you showcase other responsible behaviour in order to boost positive feeling towards your brand?

6.4 AUTHORITY AND STATUS

American social psychologist Stanley Milgram is famous for two particular experiments: One involving posting parcels around America to demonstrate six degrees of separation (as discussed earlier); and the other where people pretended to be electrocuted. The latter involved inviting participants to take part in an experiment where they were asked to gradually increase the voltage as they administered electric shocks to 'victims' (who were actually actors pretending to be in pain; Milgram, 1963). You may think you would never agree to this, but several people did. Why? Because a figure of authority (a scientist) told them to.

a) People trust figures of authority

There are always people who don't follow the rules but, generally speaking, people do respect authority. In a class of schoolchildren for example, most do what a teacher tells them.

Power

Power is a specific aspect of holding a position of authority. Power relates to the ability to influence others, potentially influence others, or control an outcome (Fiske and Berdahl, 2007). Authority is not necessarily a prerequisite, but authority often leads to power. Power can also affect product choice. Those who feel powerless increase their perception of threats and therefore choose products that are less likely to harm them (such as healthier food; Zhang and Chan, 2024). We also mention power in chapter 3 as one of Schwartz's ten common values.

Status

The recognition that somebody holds a position of authority (and perhaps also 'power'), means that people ascribe status to that person. Status really means that the person has influence and prominence and receives respect from their peers – often a whole population of people (Anderson et al., 2001). The leader of your country is probably the person with the highest recognised status within the nation, and that person likely has the authority to create laws and the power to impose them. Status can be connected to wealth too, but trying hard to gain wealth leads to higher status perceptions than effortless wealth (Warren and Warren, 2024).

Attention

Many people just want to go about their daily lives without any bother; they would rather avoid significant attention. However, those with status receive more attention (Foulsham et al. 2010).

Dominance

Often, the person nominated to be the captain of a sports team for example is also the person who stands out as being particularly vocal and perhaps the 'dominant' character in the group. How do they attain their influence? As discussed above, warmth and competence are fundamental aspects of judgement. There is specific research suggesting that 'dominance' is related to perceptions of competence (Anderson and Kilduff, 2009).

Extraversion

The five traits are fundamental aspects through which people assess the personality of others as referred to in chapter 2. These also relate to assessment of status, as extraverts are more likely to attain status (Anderson et al., 2001).

Red sneakers effect

Many years ago, Tom went for an interview at a famous entertainment company and was surprised at how casual the boss was. Well, many years later he discovered that there is a psychological theory to explain this, called the Red Sneakers Effect (Bellezza et al., 2014). When people see someone wearing clothes that don't conform to expectations (such as a senior person wearing red sneakers), research shows that these people are assumed to have higher competence and higher status than otherwise.

Self-control

If you've ever had to look after young children, you may have experienced times when you feel far angrier than you let on. Swearing in front of children is usually frowned upon! Research shows that being seen to have a high degree of self-control can help a person to appear more powerful (Wu et al., 2024).

Well-being

Unsurprisingly, it is generally better not to be completely subordinate in society. Relatively higher status in fact relates to higher levels of subjective well-being (Anderson et al. 2012).

> **APPLYING THE THEORY: KEY QUESTIONS**
>
> Consider how you present figures of authority – are you highlighting credentials, experience, or endorsements that build trust without feeling out of reach?
>
> Can you signal status in a way that resonates with your audience – through confident design, strong positioning, or association with respected voices?
>
> Can you find the right balance between approachability and authority, so you're seen as both credible and relatable?

Chapter Summary

In this chapter, we've explored how to find and use the right voices to represent your brand – whether through influencers, spokespeople, or your own team. You've learned how first impressions are formed quickly and how factors like likeability, authenticity, credibility, authority, and status all contribute to how your brand is perceived. We've looked at how these traits can build trust and influence decision-making. As you consider who speaks for your brand, ask yourself: do they reflect the values and tone you want to convey? Use the suggested application questions from this chapter to ensure your brand voices not only capture attention but also build lasting, meaningful connections with your audience.

What's Next?

In the brand-focused chapters, we've unpacked how perception is shaped through attention, emotion, storytelling, and the voices that represent your brand. With a stronger understanding of how to connect, influence, and build trust, we'll now move on to C, Choice.

CHAPTER 6 REFERENCES

Ackerman, J.M., Shapiro, J.R., Neuberg, S.L., Kenrick, D.T., Becker, D.V., Griskevicius, V., ... & Schaller, M. (2006). They all look the same to me (unless they're angry) from out-group homogeneity to out-group heterogeneity. *Psychological Science, 17*(10), 836–840.

Anderson, C., John, O. P., Keltner, D., & Kring, A. M. (2001). Who attains social status? Effects of personality and physical attractiveness in social groups. *Journal of Personality and Social Psychology, 81*(1), 116.

Anderson, C., & Kilduff, G. J. (2009). Why do dominant personalities attain influence in face-to-face groups? The competence-signaling effects of trait dominance. *Journal of Personality and Social Psychology, 96*(2), 491.

Anderson, C., Kraus, M. W., Galinsky, A. D., & Keltner, D. (2012). The local-ladder effect: Social status and subjective well-being. *Psychological Science, 23*(7), 764–771.

Barros, L. S. G., Braga, F. D. A., Chammas, C., & Costa Filho, M. (2023). When and why are consumers willing to help for-profit companies in distress?. *Journal of Advertising Research, 63*(3), 290–308.

Bellezza, S., Gino, F., & Keinan, A. (2014). The red sneakers effect: Inferring status and competence from signals of nonconformity. *Journal of Consumer Research, 41*(1), 35–54.

Carney, D. (2024) *When Words Aren't Enough: How to Excel at Nonverbal Communication.* https://www.gsb.stanford.edu/insights/when-words-arent-enough-how-excel-nonverbal-communication.

Chance, J. E., & Goldstein, A. G. (2014). The other-race effect and eyewitness identification. In *Psychological issues in eyewitness identification* (pp. 153–176). Psychology Press.

Chartrand, T. L., & Bargh, J. A. (1999). The chameleon effect: The perception–behaviour link and social interaction. *Journal of Personality and Social Psychology, 76*(6), 893.

Chartrand, T. L., & Van Baaren, R. (2009). Human mimicry. *Advances in Experimental Social Psychology, 41*, 219–274.

Chernev, A., & Blair, S. (2015). Doing well by doing good: The benevolent halo of corporate social responsibility. *Journal of Consumer Research, 41*(6), 1412–1425.

Christensen, K. L., & Shu, S. B. (2024). The Role of Heritage Connection in Consumer Valuation. *Journal of Marketing Research, 61*(3), 571–586.

Cialdini, R. B. (2021). *Influence: The psychology of persuasion.* Harper Business.

Claeys, P., Charry, K., & Tessitore, T. (2024). To be real or not to be real? The effect of genuine (vs. nongenuine) depictions of social media influencers on followers' well-being and brand purchase intention. *Psychology & Marketing, 41*(1), 203–222.

Duhigg, C. (2024). *Supercommunicators: how to unlock the secret language of connection.* Random House.

Eagly, A. H., Ashmore, R. D., Makhijani, M. G., & Longo, L. C. (1991). What is beautiful is good, but …: A meta-analytic review of research on the physical attractiveness stereotype. *Psychological Bulletin, 110*(1), 109.

Fessler, D. M., Tiokhin, L. B., Holbrook, C., Gervais, M. M., & Snyder, J. K. (2014). Foundations of the Crazy Bastard Hypothesis: Nonviolent physical risk-taking enhances conceptualized formidability. *Evolution and Human Behavior, 35*(1), 26–33.

Fetterman, A. K., Muscanell, N. L., Wu, D., & Sassenberg, K. (2022). When You Are Wrong on Facebook, Just Admit It. *Social Psychology, 53*, 34–45.

Flacandji, M., Cusin, J., & Lunardo, R. (2023). When and why signaling front-line employee inexperience can prove to be an asset: Effects on consumer forgiveness for service failure. *Psychology & Marketing, 40*(12), 2728–2742.

Fiske, S. T., & Berdahl, J. (2007). Social power. *Social psychology: Handbook of basic principles, 2*, 678–692.

Fiske, S. T., Cuddy, A. J., & Glick, P. (2007). Universal dimensions of social cognition: Warmth and competence. *Trends in Cognitive Sciences, 11*(2), 77–83.

Foulsham, T., Cheng, J. T., Tracy, J. L., Henrich, J., & Kingstone, A. (2010). Gaze allocation in a dynamic situation: Effects of social status and speaking. *Cognition, 117*(3), 319–331.

Gintis, H., Smith, E. A., & Bowles, S. (2001). Costly signaling and cooperation. *Journal of Theoretical Biology, 213*(1), 103–119.

Gross, J., & Von Wangenheim, F. (2022). Influencer marketing on Instagram: empirical research on social media engagement with sponsored posts. *Journal of Interactive Advertising, 22*(3), 289–310.

Gupta, S., Mahajan, R., & Dash, S. B. (2023). The impact of influencer-sourced brand endorsement on online consumer brand engagement. *Journal of Strategic Marketing*, 1–17.

Helmreich, R., Aronson, E., & LeFan, J. (1970). To err is humanizing sometimes: Effects of self-esteem, competence, and a pratfall on interpersonal attraction. *Journal of Personality and Social Psychology, 16*(2), 259.

Hofmann, V., Stokburger-Sauer, N. E., & Wetzels, M. (2024). The role of a smile in customer–employee interactions: Primitive emotional contagion and its boundary conditions. *Psychology & Marketing, 41*(10), 2181–2196.

Hong, E. K., Kim, J., & Choi, I. (2023). Implicit theories of happiness: When happiness is viewed as changeable, happy people are perceived much more positively than unhappy people. *Personality and Social Psychology Bulletin, 51*(2), 185–202.

Jang, H. (2022). Judging an Airbnb booking by its cover: How profile photos affect guest ratings. *Journal of Consumer Marketing, 39*(4), 371–382.

Jones, E. E. (1964). *Ingratiation: A social psychological analysis.* Appleton-Century-Crofts.

Kihlstrom, R. E., & Riordan, M. H. (1984). Advertising as a Signal. *Journal of Political Economy, 92*(3), 427–450.

Kim, M., & Lee, J. C. (2024). CEO fashion matters? Effect of consistent versus variable fashion style on perceived competence. *Psychology & Marketing*.

Kumar, A., Mann, T. C., & Gilovich, T. (2024). The Aptly Buried "I" in Experience: Experiential Purchases Promote More Social Connection Than Material Purchases. *Journal of Behavioural Decision Making, 37*(2), Article e2376.

Leung, E., Lenoir, A. S. I., Puntoni, S., & Van Osselaer, S. M. (2023). Consumer preference for formal address and informal address from warm brands and competent brands. *Journal of Consumer Psychology, 33*(3), 546–560.

Luarn, P., Chen, C. C., & Chiu, Y. P. (2024). Fashion influencers' credibility on Instagram: the stimulus–organism–response (SOR) perspective. *Journal of Strategic Marketing*, 1–14.

Marchand, A., & Weber, N. R. (2024). How Star Power Drives Video Game Success. *Journal of Interactive Marketing*, 60(3), 237–249.

Markus, H. (1977). Self-schemata and processing information about the self. *Journal of personality and social psychology*, 35(2), 63.

Milgram, S. (1963). Behavioural study of obedience. *The Journal of Abnormal and Social Psychology*, 67(4), 371.

Nisbett, R. E., & Wilson, T. D. (1977). The halo effect: Evidence for unconscious alteration of judgments. *Journal of Personality and Social Psychology*, 35(4), 250.

Pai, J., Chou, E. Y., & Halevy, N. (2023). The Humour Advantage: Humourous Bragging Benefits Job Candidates and Entrepreneurs. *Personality and Social Psychology Bulletin*, 51(8), 1330–1344.

Perloff, R. M. (1993). *The dynamics of persuasion: Communication and attitudes in the 21st century*. Routledge.

Posavac, S. S., Gaffney, D. R., & Kardes, F. R. (2024). On the robustness of the brand positivity effect: Is impulsivity a moderator of overly favorable judgments and choices of focal options?. *Journal of Behavioural Decision Making*, 37(2), Article e2371.

Rhodes, G. (2006). The evolutionary psychology of facial beauty. *Annu. Rev. Psychol.*, 57(1), 199–226.

Ross, L., & Stillinger, C. (1991). Barriers to conflict resolution. *Negotiation Journal*, 7(4), 389–404.

Schütt, C. A. (2023). The effect of perceived similarity and social proximity on the formation of prosocial preferences. *Journal of Economic Psychology*, 99, 102678.

Sherman, A., & Barokas, G. (2023). The effect of name letter on market prices: Field experiments on seller behaviour. *Journal of Behavioural and Experimental Economics*, 106, Article 102058.

Ten Brinke, L., Raymundo, I., Mukherjee, M., & Carney, D. R. (2023). Some evidence that truth-tellers are more attractive than liars. *Personality and Social Psychology Bulletin* 51(6), 900–909.

Tian, S., Tao, W., Hong, C., & Tsai, W. H. S. (2022). Meaning transfer in celebrity endorsement and co-branding: meaning valence, association type, and brand awareness. *International Journal of Advertising*, 41(6), 1017–1037.

Ury, L. (2022). *How to Not Die Alone: The surprising science that will help you find love*. Simon and Schuster.

Van Reijmersdal, E. A., Aguiar, T. D., & Van Noort, G. (2024). How Is Influencer Follower Size Related to Brand Responses?: Explaining Influencer Follower Size Success through Cognitive, Affective, and Behavioural Responses. *Journal of Advertising Research*, 64(4), 451–464.

Warren, N. B., & Warren, C. (2024). Trying too hard or not hard enough: How effort shapes status. *Journal of Consumer Psychology*, 34(4), 660–669.

Wu, S., Smallman, R., & Smith, P. K. (2024). Self-control signals and affords power. *Journal of Personality and Social Psychology*, 127(6), 1189–1214.

Zhang, L., & Chan, E. (2024). Why go gluten-free? How the feeling of low power increases preferences for free-from products. *Psychology & Marketing, 42*(2), 279–291.

Zhang, K., Wang, S., Yang, H., & Chen, L. (2023). Do Consumers Prefer Sad Faces On Eco-Friendly Products?: How Facial Expressions on Green Products In Advertisements Influence Purchase Intentions. *Journal of Advertising Research, 63*(3), 274–289.

Zhang, G., Wang, C. L., Liu, J., & Zhou, L. (2023). Why do consumers prefer a hometown geographical indication brand? Exploring the role of consumer identification with the brand and psychological ownership. *International Journal of Consumer Studies, 47*(1), 74–85.

7 Choice: Embedding Your Brand in Memory

We now look at how customers assess options to make a decision. What affects choices? In this chapter, we consider how memories can affect decision-making.

According to Charan Ranganath (2025), the key to making memories stick in the brain is 'attention' and 'intention': Attract attention to the information and encourage an intention to remember that information. Memories are then held within the brain as 'engrams' (Semon, 1921), electrochemical structures that capture cognitive information. However, some memories might relate to a general idea, whereas others are very precise such as facts and figures about a product.

Memories can be gained through experiences, but people vary in the degree to which they seek and retain new information. Relying on memory can also be problematic when memories are inaccurate. There is much to think about here, including the influence of existing memories and ability to make new information memorable.

We in the UK all love to talk about the weather – it's somewhat of a national obsession. But when the weather turns dangerous, clear communication becomes more than small talk; it becomes a matter of public safety. Behind the scenes at the UK's national weather and climate service (Met Office) are experts like Helen Roberts, Socio-Meteorologist and part-time PhD student, and Ross Middleham, Creative Lead overseeing both internal and external communications. We spoke to them both about storms and memory (alongside other considerations) ...

DOI: 10.4324/9781003541226-8

THE PSYCHOLOGY OF STORM NAMING: HOW NAMES HELP PEOPLE STAY SAFE

Giving an identity to severe weather events might not seem intuitive, but since 2014, the Met Office has been naming storms. The goal? To help people stay safe by making important weather updates more memorable and easier to understand.

When a storm is expected to cause disruption or damage, particularly from strong winds, it's given a name. This isn't unique to the UK; similar systems are used across the world. Each year, a list of names is created in alphabetical order, ready to be used when needed.

As soon as a storm is named, the Met Office spreads the word – through social media, traditional news outlets, and direct communication with government agencies and emergency services. But naming a storm does more than just make it memorable – it changes how we respond.

According to the Sapir-Whorf hypothesis, the language we use can shape the way we think. Giving a storm a name makes it feel more real, more tangible, and often more urgent. By giving a storm a human name, it becomes anthropomorphised – made to feel more familiar and relatable.

This efficiency benefits both the public and meteorologists. For meteorologists, being able to reference 'Storm Darragh' created a shared reference point that's more accessible than technical descriptions of weather systems. For the public, this approach simplifies communication about weather-related risks and recommended actions such as changing travel plans or staying indoors.

THE SCIENCE BEHIND STORM NAMING

The Met Office employs a structured approach to selecting storm names. Each year, they collect public suggestions, creating a list that alternates between male and female names and runs through the alphabet (excluding letters Q, U, X, Y, and Z for global consistency). This practice mirrors the long-established convention used for hurricanes.

Storm naming must strike a delicate balance: the name should be memorable and humanising, but not so light-hearted that it undermines the seriousness of the event.

THE HUMAN FACE OF WEATHER: CREATING CONNECTION AND TRUST

During severe weather events, there is an increased demand for trusted information from the Met Office, which presents both challenges due to urgency, but also opportunities for storytelling narratives.

Weather is dynamic and changeable. When multiple events (or 'systems'), such as heavy rain or high winds, occur in quick succession, they can easily lead to public confusion. On top of that, regional variations in impact make consistent messaging even more difficult. A storm might hit northern areas hard while leaving southern regions relatively untouched, leading to very different public perceptions of how severe it really was.

To navigate this, the Met Office constantly works to balance scientific accuracy with clear, accessible language. One of the biggest shifts for the organisation in recent decades has been moving from threshold-based warnings (such as when 'winds exceed 65 mph') to impact-based warnings about potential disruptions. This followed research (Potter et al. 2018) that impact-based (vs phenomena-based) messages have been linked to greater warning comprehension and intention to undertake protective behaviours (Casteel 2016, 2018; Morss et al., 2018; Weyrich et al., 2018). Since late 2023, the Met Office has also included behavioural science (psychology) informed action advice.

Tone of voice is also important, shifting from a light-hearted approach when sharing a new list of storm names, through to a more serious language when it comes to using a storm name to communicate information about a weather event.

In addition, the Met Office has embraced more human-centred communication, recognising that trust is built through emotional connections with relatable, credible presenters. By putting trained meteorologists with strong communication skills in front of a camera, the use of personality helps to create more authentic and trusted connections with the public.

CONCLUSION

The Met Office's decision to name storms demonstrates how psychology can be effectively applied to public communication. By giving identity to weather events, creating clear signals, and connecting with audiences, they've developed a powerful tool for public engagement, safety messaging and appropriate actions.

Their focus on behavioural science research and expert decision-making processes further illustrates the importance of understanding how audiences perceive and respond to information, particularly during high-risk situations.

7.1 IMPLICIT AND EXPLICIT MEMORY

Most of the time, people have no control over what they remember or recollect. Memories suddenly come to them, triggered by a specific stimulus such as a conversation with a long-time friend. These are implicit memories.

Explicit memory involves the conscious recollection of specific information. There are thought to be two types of explicit memory. The first, known as episodic, involves recalling a specific chain of events. For example, in court a witness might be asked to recall what they saw occur. The second involves recalling specific facts. Many British people will recall that the Battle of Hastings was 1066 for example. This type of memory is known as semantic memory.

a) Sometimes memories appear, without effort
Many memories are 'undirected' and are often general concepts rather than specific facts.

Fuzzy trace theory
Often, when recalling specific information, people remember the general meaning but not the details. For example, if we ask you to remember a trip you took many years ago you would probably remember the country or city you visited; few people would recall specific details of the trip such as food eaten or music listened to. This idea that people recall the 'gist' or a 'fuzzy trace', is known as 'fuzzy trace' theory (Brainerd and Kingma, 1984).

b) Recalling facts and figures might take more effort
In contrast to 'undirected' memories, there are other times when people intentionally try to recall details. This is referred to as 'directed' memory.

Generation effect

If you have ever revised for an exam, you may have made your own notes based on a textbook or your tutor's original information. There is reason behind this apparent replication. The 'generation effect' (Slamecka and Graf, 1978) shows that people find it far easier to remember information that they have 'generated' themselves in comparison to information given to them by another.

APPLYING THE THEORY: KEY QUESTIONS

Can you design content that sticks in implicit memory – like a distinctive tagline, jingle, or visual style your audience recalls without realising why?

Consider how you're helping people build explicit memory by repeating key messages clearly and consistently across all touchpoints.

Can you use storytelling to help your audience consciously remember product benefits while also embedding emotional associations they'll recall later without effort?

7.2 LONG-TERM VERSUS SHORT-TERM MEMORY

Short-term memory relates to information gained in the recent past, but long-term memories are snippets of information retained from long ago. Most people can remember a simple list of requests for five minutes, but few of us hold onto this unimportant information days or weeks into the future. This demonstrates how brains can store information differently.

a) Drawing on memories

Very often, memories play an important role in shaping future decision making. This presents marketers with valuable opportunities to create memorable brand experiences that influence future choices.

Availability heuristic

Humans use their memories to make judgements (Tversky and Kahneman, 1973). For example, when asked to judge risk, people often try to imagine a risky event happening. This is obviously not an accurate way to ascertain risk. If asked how likely it is that their next plane trip will end in disaster, many will accurately reel off statistics such as aviation being the safest mode of transport. Yet, recent high-profile plane crashes create vivid memories in the days and weeks afterwards, the 'availability' of which alters judgement of safety.

Byron Sharp and Jenni Romaniuk (2016) also discuss the effect of mental availability – that is, the likelihood of a brand being recalled in a buying situation – when customers make a brand choice, with research from the Ehrenberg-Bass Institute (Vaughan et al., 2021) showing that advertising affects this mental availability. For example, consistent exposure to a brand's distinctive assets – like the orange EasyJet logo or the shape of the Coca-Cola bottle – helps keep the brand front-of-mind when purchase decisions are made.

Observer-expectancy bias

Again, this bias is another example of selecting information to support a pre-existing viewpoint. Scientists (even social scientists) are supposed to be objective and rigorous. Yet, just as the congruence bias involved selecting information congruent with a hypothesis, the observer-expectancy bias suggests that scientific 'observers' might intend to achieve a desired finding (Cordaro and Ison, 1963) – even if subconsciously.

Recognition heuristic

If you're in need of a quick sugary boost, would you rather grab a bag of Haribo Tangfastics or try Tom and Luan's red velvet cupcakes? Most people go for the product they recognise – even if the alternative looks or sounds better. Familiarity is reassuring. When asked to estimate chance, people use memory to assess various likelihoods. What is the chance of Brazil winning the football World Cup? Quite high. What is the chance of San Marino winning the same cup? Not so high (sorry to any Sammarinese readers). Importantly, familiarity with the topic affects this assessment (Gigerenzer and Goldstein, 2011).

Mere exposure effect

It's odd that in experiments people prefer the taste of Pepsi. Yet, people actually consume much more Coca-Cola. One explanation for this is the strength of the Coke brand, in other words familiarity with the brand. The mere exposure effect (Zajonc, 1968) shows that just being 'exposed' to a brand increases preference for it. Familiarity also makes things easier to remember (Chung et al., 2024). Continuous online adverts therefore probably have this effect.

Consistency

People want to act consistently with previous selves, especially when they have made a commitment. Very often people behave or make choices that fit with a pre-existing idea of the self (Sadler and Woody, 2003). This is known as a 'consistency bias'. If a customer likes hip hop music for example, they may well choose to follow fashion brands associated with that genre because they believe their love of hip hop is continuous and consistent.

Public statements

The effect of consistency appears to be even stronger when that commitment is made publicly. It appears that even more than wanting to stay consistent with themselves, people want to stay consistent with their public selves (Schienker et al., 1994). One helpful aspect of memories is that people don't like memories that suggest an inconsistent 'self'. In other words, by making a commitment to adopt a new behaviour at a later date, the memory of that commitment is likely to be a powerful aide (Ariely and Wertenbroch, 2002). If your previous self said you would do it, you'd better remain consistent. For example, taking an oath can increase the probability that a person acts honestly (Zickfeld et al., 2025).

Confirmation bias

Although people like to think that every decision is made by carefully, rationally, and objectively assessing the options, often they use memory to make a choice. Consider the purchase of new clothing. Emotionally, a customer's memory tells them which brand they want to be seen wearing, perhaps in photos. They still assess all the information available, but really, they are seeking information that confirms their pre-existing desire. This is confirmation bias (Nickerson, 1998).

Information bias

At work, your manager might say to you something like, "OK, let's not make a quick decision. Let's take our time to gather all the facts". So far, so sensible you might think. But often information gathering is reassuring but ineffectual. The new information doesn't alter the decision that the decision-maker had already mentally made (Baron et al., 1988).

Congruence bias

This is very similar to confirmation bias, and also called also called 'expectation bias' (Jeng, 2006). Whereas confirmation bias refers to the seeking of information to confirm an existing choice, 'congruence bias' instead refers to seeking information that is congruent with an existing hypothesis. Murder mysteries are very good at playing to this bias, encouraging you to find reasons why the most obvious suspect committed the crime – finding congruent information to support your initial hunch.

Semmelweis reflex

Although information may be sensed and processed, the so-called Semmelweis Reflex suggests that new information may be rejected if it contradicts other evidence (Gupta et al., 2020). Dentists generally advise that fruit can cause tooth decay, yet for years people have eaten apples to stay healthy – e.g., 'an apple a day keeps the doctor away'!

Recommendation

Similar to the effect of commitment, making a recommendation about a product or service appears to affect future choices too. Customers pay more when a product is recommended by influencers or previous customers (Tuncer and Kartal, 2023). Social media platforms recommend accounts that your friends like for example. Yet, one specific finding is that customers are less likely to repeat a purchase recommended to a friend if the friend rejected their recommendation (Hall et al., 2023). Recommendations work both ways!

b) How customers forget

Of course, remembering information relating to a brand may be a top priority for marketers. But people also let many memories go over time.

Ebbinghaus forgetting curve

Memories fade over time, although repetition helps to prevent this. This is known as the 'forgetting curve', named after Hermann Ebbinghaus (Murre and Dros, 2015). Sometimes this is upsetting, like memories of great holidays or experiences that feel like they are fading. Organisations, on the other hand, need to keep communicating with a customer to stay 'front of mind'. The curve is fairly steep (shown in figure 7.1), showing that over just a few days around half of new

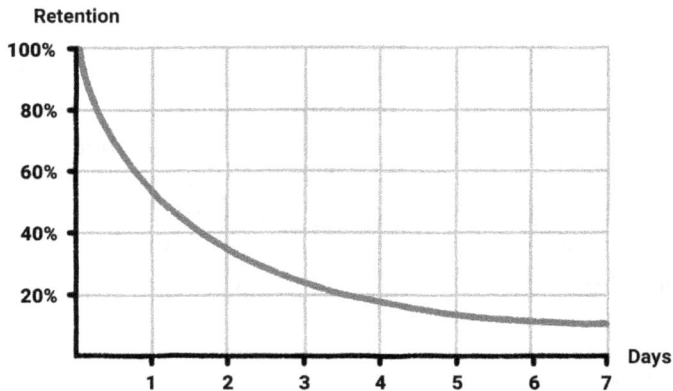

Figure 7.1 Ebbinghaus' Forgetting Curve

information learned can be forgotten. If you want people to remember more, they'll need to be prompted!

Fading effect bias
Memories fade over time according to the forgetting curve. However, memories involving positive emotions don't seem to fade as quickly (Walker et al., 2003).

Google effect
The ability to answer queries efficiently with a couple of taps (or a voice prompt) has been transformational, but some believe that it is detrimental for memory, given the assumption that information will be stored elsewhere (Sparrow et al., 2011). Why would someone try to learn information when it can be searched for online anyway?

Short-term memory
Often people hold information in their minds for a short duration, then discard that information shortly afterwards. Shopping lists are a common example. But did you know that around seven items is usually the maximum that the brain can hold in the short term (Miller, 1956)?

Transience
Transient thoughts are those that occur in a moment, but are quickly forgotten (Richards and Frankland, 2017).

Blocking

As well as remembering a remarkable variety of information, there is plenty of information that people discard. Why, for example, does a person's brain remember certain dates in history, but perhaps not their best friend's birthday? Why remember one number (a date) and not another? This theory is known as 'blocking'. When directed to focus on specific information, other similar information is blocked (Brown, 1968). To recall important information, people's brains seem to need guidance, for example with reminders and repetition.

Selective perception

Blocking occurs when certain information is retained at the expense of other 'blocked' information. Similarly, some information never goes in in the first place. This is called selective perception when people only actually acknowledge certain aspects of their environment (Massad, Hubbard and Newstson, 1979). You may remember the smell of your school classroom, but can you remember anything the headteacher said in school assemblies? More recently, research has shown a 'selective exposure bias' where people are motivated to support existing beliefs (De keersmaecker and Schmid, 2022).

Absent-mindedness

Some people appear to generally have memory-failures, as measured through the Cognitive Failures Questionnaire for example (Broadbent et al., 1982). People who know they are absent-minded might try to counter this, for example by creating rhymes for important information.

APPLYING THE THEORY: KEY QUESTIONS

Can you design messaging that creates mental availability – ensuring your brand or product is easily recalled when needed?

Consider how you're reinforcing consistency in your messaging across channels to align with your audience's preexisting beliefs, tapping into confirmation bias.

How does your content fit into the forgetting curve – are you reminding your audience of important information at key intervals to keep it top-of-mind?

Can you make your brand a mental shortcut for your audience, so they automatically think of you when they encounter a relevant need or trigger?

7.3 RUMINATION

When you wake up in the middle of the night considering whether you should have bought the green shoes instead of the blue ones, that's rumination (Luan does this a lot!) Some people might call it "mulling things over", but rumination really just means 'replaying' events in the mind.

a) People often dwell on past experiences
When considering moments in their life, people often replay and reconsider them.

Hindsight bias
Sometimes, on reflection (with hindsight), we reframe a memory (Fischhoff, 1975). What felt like a bad experience at the time, perhaps led to a longer-term positive outcome. This might lead a person to remember positive aspects of the experience. In other words, with hindsight the experience wasn't that bad.

Lag effect
The more people consider things, the more ingrained memories become. Although a dramatic event might be instantly memorable, if you want to deliberately add something new to your memory, try repeating it again and again, leaving a gap (a lag) between each repetition (Kahana and Howard, 2005).

Counterfactual thinking
Counterfactual thinking is reconsidering the past to imagine other potential courses of action that could have taken place (Roese, 1997). There are various ways of framing all the alternatives. When a customer feels like they may have taken the wrong course of action, the obvious alternative is one with a better outcome: this is 'upward' counterfactual thinking – reflecting the phrase "the grass is always greener on the other side".

Downward counterfactuals involve the same process but feeling relieved that the outcome wasn't worse. 'Omission' is when the person wishes that they had done something that they 'omitted'; 'commission' is opposite: when someone wishes they hadn't done something.

Persistence

Some memories are annoying, or even painful. Although we try to distract ourselves, the memories just won't disappear from our minds. These intrusive memories, often referred to as 'persistent' (Schachter, 2002), can impact marketing efforts. When a customer has a bad experience with a brand, despite seeing positive advertising or new products, the negative memory of the brand continues to affect their perception and buying decisions.

b) Memories change over time

Although people may not realise it, memories are not simply the accurate retrieval of stored information.

Levelling and sharpening

Raconteurs are brilliant at repeating stories. Often people pay a lot to hear from an after-dinner speaker, such as a sports star or former politician. However, the speaker's recollection of events is not a 'fly on the wall' accurate replay; more likely they have 'levelled' the memory, removing certain details – certain peaks and troughs (like levelling a piece of the landscape) – to make the story easier to tell and consistent with the chosen punchline.

Sharpening is the opposite of 'levelling' (Holzman and Klein, 1954). In other words, rather than removing details, some memories involve recalling specific details that bring the story to life.

For example, a brand might focus only on the positive aspects of a customer's experience, leaving out the challenges they faced, to make a story more digestible and impactful. On the other hand, 'sharpening' occurs when specific memorable details are emphasised to make the story more vivid, such as highlighting a particularly emotional moment or a unique feature of the product that played a pivotal role in the customer's decision-making process. Both techniques can help create more engaging and persuasive stories.

APPLYING THE THEORY: KEY QUESTIONS

Can you address rumination by using retargeting ads that gently remind your audience about your product or service?

Consider how you can use counterfactual thinking in your messaging – presenting an alternative scenario or "what could have been" to highlight the benefits your product provides.

7.4 OTHER MEMORY EFFECTS

Here are a number of further psychology theories relating to how memories are stored and recalled.

a) Filling in gaps
Sometimes people use memories to fill gaps, and sometimes people fill gaps in memories.

Context effect
If you're on holiday in a foreign country and a helpful hotel porter gives you handwritten directions to a nearby restaurant, at first you might struggle to decipher the scrawled words on the paper (Rumelhart and McClelland, 1982). However, if you know the words are French, you can use your recollection of basic French words to make sense of the instructions. Your environment or context (France) has helped you to recall relevant information (alternatively, you could find a translation app)!

Verbatim effect
The verbatim effect means the opposite of what you might expect. It's generally very difficult to recall the exact words to a speech, or every word of a song. It's much simpler to explain to someone else what the 'gist' of the message is. The meaning is more memorable than the 'verbatim' words (which also relates to 'fuzzy trace theory') – yet providing verbatim information can be a greater driver of customer behaviours associated with risk (Nolte et al., 2021).

b) Getting things wrong
Because memories often require reconstructing information in a way that makes sense, people can sometimes make errors when recalling details.

Fallibility
Rather than objective video replays, all memories are subjective mental reconstructions. Loftus and Pickrell (1995) demonstrated many years ago that sometimes people hold false memories. They might be certain

that a specific event occurred, whereas in fact the memory has been constructed.

Can you really remember childhood milestones or have photographs influenced your recollection?

Sometimes people rely on snippets of information but unknowingly fill in gaps themselves. False memories are more likely to be mistakenly held the more plausible the thought is. Loftus and Palmer (1974) conducted a study showing that the way a question is phrased can also influence how people remember an event. For example, when participants were asked about a car "smashing" into another car, their recollection of the incident was different compared to when they were asked if the car "hit" another car. The use of more intense language, like "smash" led participants to recall the event as more severe than when the word "hit" was used, demonstrating how subtle changes in wording can shape memory.

Misattribution

"A lie can travel halfway around the world while the truth is still putting its shoes on," said Mark Twain. Only he didn't. It was more likely a phrase created by Jonathan Swift. Somewhere along the line, somebody's memory played a trick on them, and plenty of others repeated the mistake. This is surprisingly common; very often people remember the information, but not the correct source (Schacter and Dodson, 2001).

Rosy retrospection

Many people say that their school days were the best of their lives. At the time though, school life can seem pretty tough. The stress of exams, anxieties about changing physical appearance through puberty, peer pressure to stay on trend etc. Yet, people tend to look back at the past through so-called rose tinted glasses, remembering events in a positive light. This is rosy retrospection (Mitchell et al., 1997).

Telescoping effect

Do you ever have the feeling that an event happened just the other week, only to be corrected – the event was last year, or perhaps even longer ago? This demonstrates the telescoping effect whereby events (rather than objects) seem nearer in time than they really were (Thompson et al., 1988).

Tip of the tongue

It's really annoying when you know what you want to say but just can't remember the word. Perhaps you can even recall the first letter, but not the rest. We sometimes refer to this feeling as the word being "just on the tip of the tongue" (Brown, 1991). This is a frequent and common occurrence, often referring to proper names in particular.

Cryptomnesia

This has nothing to do with online currency! Often Tom hums a tune to himself, believing he has written an amazing melody to a surefire number one hit. Tom isn't an international rockstar (yet). Usually, later that day it will dawn on him that the tune is actually closely related to a Depeche Mode song. This is cryptomnesia: A real memory that we mistakenly think is the work of our own imagination (Brédart et al., 2003). Being aware of this may reduce the risk of plagiarism!

c) Self-relevant memories

People remember events that involve themselves, plus they focus on themselves within the memory.

Ego-centric bias

Even if you learned this at school, it's probably much more difficult to recall the exact events leading up to World War Two than to recall how you got your first job. This is because it is easier to remember events that involve us personally (Ross and Sicoly, 1979).

Self-reference effect

We each have an idea about 'who we are'. This relates to information processing. Your customers are more likely to process information that seems to relate to how they perceive themselves (Symons and Johnson, 1997). If your information seems relevant for flapjack-loving marketing lecturers, you'll probably find it easier to grab Tom's attention, for example!

It's also easier to recall information that relates to, or includes, the person recollecting. Furthermore, when people do recall events involving themselves, they also remember details about themselves more than details relating to other people who were present (Rogers et al., 1977).

d) Helping memories to sink in

If you want to help others to remember some information, there are some ways to make recollection easier.

Elaborative interrogation

The more people 'interrogate' the information sources, such as seeking information to solve a problem, the more they recall (Jacoby, 1978). If you are trying to educate people for example, ask your audience questions. Encourage them to elaborate on the information given, perhaps identifying examples or suggesting ways the information could be used. Hagtvedt (2015) also showed that when customers are not otherwise engaged, asking a customer a question can encourage elaboration.

Modality effect

If you've ever tried remembering a 'to do' list, you may have quietly repeated the list to yourself under your breath. This is the modality effect. The mode of presentation (transforming written words to a verbal list) affects memory (Ginns, 2005).

First letter mnemonic

Making up a word to help recall otherwise complicated processes or facts is one form of so-called mnemonic device (memory aid), known as a 'first letter mnemonic' (Nelson and Archer, 1972). Such mnemonics may use the first letters of a longer name (NASA is an acronym for the North American Space Agency), or otherwise meaningless phrases. Children trying to remember the points on a compass in clockwise order for example might be given the nonsensical advice to 'Never Eat Shredded Wheat' to recall north, east, south and west. Other types of mnemonic include creating visual images or referring to keywords that are easier to recall.

Primacy effect

When explaining the modality effect, we referred to verbal lists. Further evidence of presentation modes shows that a primacy effect occurs for written lists; the first item on a written list is easier to recall (Matthews, 1927).

Recency bias

It is generally easier to recall recent information. Ask someone what they ate for lunch last week and it might take a while to remember. Ask them the same question about today's lunch and the information will probably be immediately available. Similarly, people recall the last item on a verbal list, i.e., the most recent item added. Murdock (1962) demonstrated both a primacy effect (see above) and a recency effect, together referred to as a 'serial position effect': people remember both the first few items and the most recent items on a list.

Stories

Simple this one. Stories are easier to remember than raw facts. We discussed story formats in chapter 5. Sometimes, people prefer to pay attention to easily understood anecdotes rather than complicated details; this is known as 'narrative bias' (Winterbottom et al., 2008). If you want to make information more memorable, create a story that includes this information. Story-form content online also leads to both believability and purchase intention (Cassar et al., 2021).

e) *Von Restorff effect*

Imagine a shopping list with groceries, household cleaning products, and a cuddly pink dinosaur. Which item do you think you have the least chance of forgetting? Probably the dinosaur. This demonstrates the importance of grabbing attention. The Von Restorff effect (1933) supports this, showing that distinctive items are easier to recall.

Zeigarnik effect

Strangely, events that are interrupted seem to become more ingrained in the memory (Zeigarnik, 1927). Tom was on holiday in Ireland on September 11, 2001, a date that is now recalled for tragic reasons. On that day, the plans for the evening quickly changed to incorporate watching the rolling news. That holiday is now one of the most memorable of his life. The interruption to his holiday helped to cement it in the mind more than many others.

Sensory stores

How information is received makes a difference. Information received through the eyes starts to disappear after less than a second. In comparison, sounds seem to initially stay in conscious thought for around two seconds before the information received starts to be lost (Darwin et al., 1972).

f) Truthfulness and memory

Now let's explore various theories that delve into the relationship between truth and memory. Truth is generally defined as the alignment of information with reality or facts, yet how we remember and interpret those facts can be influenced by various cognitive processes.

Belief bias

Mrs Trunchbowl in Roald Dahl's *Matilda* famously claimed that more outrageous crimes are less likely to be believed. It seems that she was on to something. Research suggests that arguments are more persuasive, even if the information is untrue, if the argument seems believable (Evans et al., 1983).

Illusory truth effect

The more often people hear a fact, the more likely they are to accept it (Hasher et al., 1977). Online conspiracy theories usually sound strange the first time you hear them, but over time they start to seep into consciousness and gradually seem less realistic. An illusion of truth is created, simply through repetition.

Subjective validation

It is far easier for someone to accept a new piece of information if it seems similar to pre-existing beliefs (Forer, 1949). This is sometimes called personal validation, the Forer Effect or the Barnum Effect (after circus leader P.T. Barnum who employed fortune tellers). If an amateur sooth sayer tells you that something bad has recently happened in your life, you'll probably search for something truthful that meets this vague statement – perhaps you stubbed your toe on the bed yesterday!

APPLYING THE THEORY: KEY QUESTIONS

Can you help make your product or service memorable, perhaps prompting them to remember positive aspects of the overall experience (rather than the details)?

Consider how misattribution might influence your audience – are there ways to shape perceptions so that positive feelings about your product are linked to the right memories or experiences?

Can you use the Von Restorff effect by highlighting a unique or unexpected feature of your product to make it stand out in your audience's memory?

7.5 INFORMATION PROCESSING

Customers sense new information around them, assess different communicators, and customers evaluate risk. We can now move on to consider ways in which people learn from these experiences.

a) Differences in information processing

People differ in the degree to which they want to know (and learn) new information, referred to as their curiosity. People also differ in the degree to which they enjoy processing information.

Need for cognition

Just as people differ in their 'openness to experience', people also differ in the degree to which they enjoy processing information. Psychologically this is referred to as a person's 'need for cognition' (Cacioppo and Petty, 1982) and there are scales and questionnaires for measuring this in each of us.

Need for cognitive closure

For some people, the unknown is simply a fact of life: we are part of something far bigger than we will ever know. For others, accepting the unknown is uncomfortable; they have a strong desire for cognitive closure and cannot live with ambiguity. This difference is known as the need for cognitive closure (Webster and Kruglanski, 1994).

b) Some customers can recognise what they don't know

Some people are better than others at recognising gaps in their own knowledge:

Intellectual humility

Nobody knows everything (except, we think, perhaps Dumbledore in *Harry Potter* and Gandalf in *Lord of the Rings*), but not everybody is prepared to admit this. Former US Defence Secretary Donald Rumsfeld famously once referred to "unknown unknowns" – in other words we need to accept that there are things that we don't know, and even things that we don't know we don't know. Accepting this requires intellectual humility (Leary et al., 2017), and this differs between people.

APPLYING THE THEORY: KEY QUESTIONS

Are your customers likely to score highly for 'need for cognition'? If they want lots of information, provide it!

Can you use the self-reference effect by framing your messaging in a way that helps your audience relate the information to their own personal experiences or needs?

Can you create a space for intellectual humility in your messaging, for example by being transparent about your product's evolution or acknowledging areas where customer feedback (rather than your own knowledge) has shaped your brand?

7.6 CONDITIONING

There are more complicated and technical words for describing this process, but conditioning really just means using feedback from previous experiences to anticipate likely future experiences.

a) *Learning through experience*

People learn from the feedback they receive, including both negative and positive feedback.

Instrumental learning

Instrumental learning is another phrase for describing 'operant conditioning' (Skinner, 1937). The theory is that behaviours can be encouraged or discouraged by providing rewards or punishment. Famously, B. F. Skinner (1938) demonstrated this with rats learning to push levers to receive food. Parents often employ this approach, using tactics such as extra pocket money for particularly dull chores or asking a child to sit on the 'naughty step' after being disobedient.

Negative reinforcers

As the name suggests, negative reinforcers are punishments for behaviours that are socially unacceptable. Once behaviour changes, the punishment is removed in order to reward compliance.

Positive reinforcers

Unsurprisingly, positive reinforcers are the opposite of negative reinforcers – rewards rather than punishments! 'Liking' social media content for example positively reinforces the behaviour of the person who posted it.

Learned associations

Sometimes people become conditioned in unexpected ways. A specific stimulus might relate to an experience that has no link to a reward or punishment. These work in a similar way, becoming learned associations or 'conditional reflexes', like a dog learning to salivate at the sound of a bell (Pavlov, 1949). For example, the smell of disinfectant reminds many people of hospital corridors – or high school in the 1990s for Tom!

b) Preferences can shift

After a while, once an association has been learned, those learned preferences can be expanded.

Peak shift

This is often a slightly complicated theory to explain, but it shouldn't be. Imagine you are told that big cars are better than small cars. You would naturally assume that a large 4x4 is better than a small city car. Now bring in a stretch limousine – even bigger than a 4x4. Remember that the supposed 'rule' is that big cars are better: suddenly, a stretch limousine seems even better than the 4x4. Your previous peak has shifted (Purtle, 1973; i.e., the car that you previously thought was the optimum [4x4] has been replaced, by the stretch limousine).

c) Customers learn socially

People also learn from others around them:

Social cognitive learning

Put simply, people often learn by observing. This is particularly important with video content in the online world. Bandura famously demonstrated this with his Bobo the clown experiment (Bandura et al., 1961) where children copied adult behaviour and attacked an inflatable clown.

Similarly, customers often learn from influencer marketing on platforms like Instagram or TikTok. When an influencer demonstrates how they use a product in a video, their followers often mimic the behaviour, leading to increased brand awareness and purchases. For example, a fitness influencer showcasing a specific workout routine using a certain brand of equipment can inspire their followers to buy the same products to undertake the routines, mirroring the influencer's actions.

APPLYING THE THEORY: KEY QUESTIONS

How could you use instrumental learning, for example by creating clear cause-and-effect relationships in your messaging – showing your audience how their actions lead to tangible rewards or benefits?

Consider how you can encourage the desired behaviours in your customers by ensuring they understand the rewards they'll receive, whether it's a discount, loyalty points, or exclusive access.

Can you take advantage of peak shift by amplifying certain attributes of your product that make it stand out?

Chapter Summary

In this chapter, we've explored how memory plays a crucial role in customer choice, and what it takes to embed your brand in both short-term and long-term memory. You've learned about implicit and explicit memory, how and why customers forget, and how factors like rumination and other memory effects can shape recall and recognition.

As you refine your marketing activities, ask yourself: are you creating memorable moments that stick with your audience over time? Use the theories from this chapter to make your brand more unforgettable and easier to choose.

What's Next?

Are you ready for our final chapter? Let's take a look at how customers determine the value of the choices they make as they complete their decision-making journey …

CHAPTER 7 REFERENCES

Ariely, D., & Wertenbroch, K. (2002). Procrastination, deadlines, and performance: Self-control by precommitment. *Psychological Science, 13*(3), 219–224.

Bandura, A., Ross, D., & Ross, S.A. (1961). Transmission of aggression through imitation of aggressive models. *The Journal of Abnormal and Social Psychology, 63*(3), 575.

Baron, J., Beattie, J., & Hershey, J.C. (1988). Heuristics and biases in diagnostic reasoning: II. Congruence, information, and certainty. *Organizational Behaviour and Human Decision Processes, 42*(1), 88–110.

Bartlett, F.C. (1932). *Remembering: A study in experimental and social psychology.* Cambridge University Press.

Bower, G.H. (1970). Analysis of a mnemonic device: Modern psychology uncovers the powerful components of an ancient system for improving memory. *American Scientist, 58*(5), 496–510.

Brainerd, C.J., & Kingma, J. (1984). Do children have to remember to reason? A fuzzy-trace theory of transitivity development. *Developmental Review, 4*(4), 311–377.

Brédart, S., Lampinen, J., & Defeldre, A. C. (2003). Phenomenal characteristics of cryptomnesia. *Memory, 11*(1), 1–11.

Broadbent, D. E., Cooper, P. F., FitzGerald, P., & Parkes, K. R. (1982). The cognitive failures questionnaire (CFQ) and its correlates. *British journal of clinical psychology, 21*(1), 1–16.

Brown, J. (1968). Reciprocal facilitation and impairment of free recall. *Psychonomic Science, 10*(2), 41–42.

Brown, A.S. (1991). A review of the tip-of-the-tongue experience. *Psychological Bulletin, 109*(2), 204.

Buehler, R., Griffin, D., & Ross, M. (1994). Exploring the "planning fallacy": Why people underestimate their task completion times. *Journal of Personality and Social Psychology, 67*(3), 366.

Cacioppo, J.T., & Petty, R.E. (1982). The need for cognition. *Journal of Personality and Social Psychology, 42*(1), 116.

Cassar, M.L., Caruana, A., & Konietzny, J. (2022). Facts or story? The impact of website content on narrative believability and purchase intention. *Journal of Marketing Communications, 28*(6), 637–656.

Chung, Y. H., Brady, T. F., & Störmer, V. S. (2024). Meaningfulness and familiarity expand visual working memory capacity. *Current Directions in Psychological Science, 33*(5), 275–282.

Cordaro, L., & Ison, J.R. (1963). Psychology of the scientist: X. Observer bias in classical conditioning of the planarian. *Psychological Reports, 13*(3), 787–789.

Darwin, C.J., Turvey, M., & Crowder, R. G. (1972). An auditory analogue of the Sperling partial report procedure: Evidence for brief auditory storage. *Cognitive Psychology, 3*(2), 255–267.

De Keersmaecker, J., & Schmid, K. (2023). Selective exposure bias predicts views on diversity over time. *Psychonomic Bulletin & Review, 30*(1), 401–406.

Evans, J.S.B., Barston, J.L., & Pollard, P. (1983). On the conflict between logic and belief in syllogistic reasoning. *Memory & Cognition, 11*(3), 295–306.

Fischhoff, B. (1975). Hindsight is not equal to foresight: The effect of outcome knowledge on judgment under uncertainty. *Journal of Experimental Psychology: Human Perception and Performance, 1*(3), 288.

Forer, B. R. (1949). The fallacy of personal validation: A classroom demonstration of gullibility. *Journal of Abnormal and Social Psychology, 44*(1), 118.

Fredrickson, B.L., & Kahneman, D. (1993). Duration neglect in retrospective evaluations of affective episodes. *Journal of Personality and Social Psychology, 65*(1), 45.

Fukuyama, F. (2015). The end of history?. In *Conflict after the Cold War* (pp. 16–27). Routledge.

Gigerenzer, G., & Goldstein, D. G. (2011). The recognition heuristic: A decade of research. *Judgment and Decision Making, 6*(1), 100–121.

Ginns, P. (2005). Meta-analysis of the modality effect. *Learning and Instruction, 15*(4), 313–331.

Gupta, V.K., Saini, C., Oberoi, M., Kalra, G., & Nasir, M. I. (2020). Semmelweis reflex: an age-old prejudice. *World Neurosurgery, 136*, e119–e125.

Hagtvedt, H. (2015). Promotional phrases as questions versus statements: An influence of phrase style on product evaluation. *Journal of Consumer Psychology, 25*(4), 635–641.

Hall, M J., Hyodo, J.D., & Kristofferson, K. (2023). How rejected recommendations shape recommenders' future product intentions. *Journal of Consumer Psychology, 35*(1), 42–60.

Hasher, L., Goldstein, D., & Toppino, T. (1977). Frequency and the conference of referential validity. *Journal of Verbal Learning and Verbal Behaviour, 16*(1), 107–112.

Holzman, P.S., & Klein, G.S. (1954). Cognitive system-principles of leveling and sharpening: Individual differences in assimilation effects in visual time-error. *The Journal of Psychology, 37*(1), 105–122.

Jacoby, L.L. (1978). On interpreting the effects of repetition: Solving a problem versus remembering a solution. *Journal of Verbal Learning and Verbal Behaviour, 17*(6), 649–667.

Jeng, M. (2006). A selected history of expectation bias in physics. *American Journal of Physics, 74*(7), 578–583.

Kahana, M.J., & Howard, M.W. (2005). Spacing and lag effects in free recall of pure lists. *Psychonomic Bulletin & Review, 12*(1), 159–164.

Leary, M.R., Diebels, K.J., Davisson, E.K., Jongman-Sereno, K.P., Isherwood, J.C., Raimi, K.T., ... & Hoyle, R.H. (2017). Cognitive and interpersonal features of intellectual humility. *Personality and Social Psychology Bulletin, 43*(6), 793–813.

Loewenstein, G., O'Donoghue, T., & Rabin, M. (2003). Projection bias in predicting future utility. *Quarterly Journal of economics*, 1209–1248.

Loftus, E.F., & Palmer, J.C. (1974). Reconstruction of automobile destruction: An example of the interaction between language and memory. *Journal of Verbal Learning and Verbal Behavior, 13*(5), 585–589.

Loftus, E.F., & Pickrell, J.E. (1995). The formation of false memories. *Psychiatric Annals, 25*(12), 720–725.

Matthews, C.O. (1927). The effect of position of printed response words upon children's answers to questions in two-response types of tests. *Journal of Educational Psychology, 18*(7), 445.

Massad, C., Hubbard, M., & Newtson, D. (1979). Selective perception of events. *Journal of Experimental Social Psychology, 15*(6), 513–532.

Miller, G.A. (1956). The magical number seven, plus or minus two: Some limits on our capacity for processing information. *Psychological Review, 63*(2), 81.

Mitchell, T.R., Thompson, L., Peterson, E., & Cronk, R. (1997). Temporal adjustments in the evaluation of events: The "rosy view". *Journal of Experimental Social Psychology, 33*(4), 421–448.

Murdock, B.B., Jr. (1962). The serial position effect of free recall. *Journal of Experimental Psychology, 64*(5), 482–488.

Murre, J.M., & Dros, J. (2015). Replication and analysis of Ebbinghaus' forgetting curve. *PloS one, 10*(7), Article e0120644.

Nelson, D. L., & Archer, C. S. (1972). The first letter mnemonic. *Journal of Educational Psychology, 63*(5), 482.

Nickerson, R. S. (1998). Confirmation bias: A ubiquitous phenomenon in many guises. *Review of General Psychology, 2*(2), 175–220.

Nolte, J., Hanoch, Y., Wood, S.A., & Reyna, V.F. (2021). Compliance with mass marketing solicitation: The role of verbatim and gist processing. *Brain and Behaviour, 11*(11), Article e2391.

O'donoghue, T., & Rabin, M. (1999). Doing it now or later. *American economic review, 89*(1), 103–124.

Pavlov, I. P. (1949). Eksperimental'naya psikhologiya i psikhopatologiya na zhivotnykh [Experimental psychology and psychopathology at animals]. *IP Pavlov, Polnoe sobranie sochineniy (2d ed., Vol. 3, Pt. 1, pp. 23–39). Moscow: Izdatel'stvo Akademii Nauk SSSR. (Original address delivered 1903).*

Peer, E. (2011). The time-saving bias, speed choices and driving behaviour. *Transportation Research Part F: Traffic Psychology and Behaviour, 14*(6), 543–554.

Purtle, R.B. (1973). Peak shift: a review. *Psychological Bulletin, 80*(5), 408.

Ranganath, C. (2025). *Why we remember: Unlocking memory's power to hold on to what matters.* Random House.

Reason, J.T., & Mycielska, K. (1982). *Absent-minded?: The psychology of mental lapses and everyday errors.* Prentice Hall.

Richards, B. A., & Frankland, P. W. (2017). The persistence and transience of memory. *Neuron, 94*(6), 1071–1084.

Roese, N.J. (1997). Counterfactual thinking. *Psychological Bulletin, 121*(1), 133.

Rogers, T.B., Kuiper, N.A., & Kirker, W.S. (1977). Self-reference and the encoding of personal information. *Journal of personality and social psychology, 35*(9), 677.

Ross, M., & Sicoly, F. (1979). Egocentric biases in availability and attribution. *Journal of Personality and Social Psychology, 37*(3), 322.

Rumelhart, D.E., & McClelland, J.L. (1982). An interactive activation model of context effects in letter perception: II. The contextual enhancement effect and some tests and extensions of the model. *Psychological Review, 89*(1), 60.

Sadler, P., & Woody, E. (2003). Is who you are who you're talking to? Interpersonal style and complementarily in mixed-sex interactions. *Journal of Personality and Social Psychology, 84*(1), 80.

Schacter, D.L. (2002). *The seven sins of memory: How the mind forgets and remembers.* HMH.

Schacter, D. L., & Dodson, C. S. (2001). Misattribution, false recognition and the sins of memory. *Philosophical Transactions of the Royal Society of London. Series B: Biological Sciences, 356*(1413), 1385–1393.

Schienker, B.R., Dlugolecki, D.W., & Doherty, K. (1994). The impact of self-presentations on self-appraisals and behaviour: The power of public commitment. *Personality and Social Psychology Bulletin, 20*(1), 20–33.

Semon, R. (1921). Chapter II. engraphic action of stimuli on the individual. *The Mneme.*

Sharp, B., & Romaniuk, J. (2016). *How brands grow.* Oxford University Press.

Skinner, B. F. (1937). Two types of conditioned reflex: A reply to Konorski and Miller. *The Journal of General Psychology, 16*(1), 272–279.

Skinner, B. F. (1938). The behavior of organisms; an experimental analysis, London, D. *Appleton-Century company, incorporated.*

Slamecka, N.J., & Graf, P. (1978). The generation effect: Delineation of a phenomenon. *Journal of Experimental Psychology: Human Learning and Memory, 4*(6), 592.

Sparrow, B., Liu, J., & Wegner, D.M. (2011). Google effects on memory: Cognitive consequences of having information at our fingertips. *Science, 333*(6043), 776–778.

Symons, C.S., & Johnson, B.T. (1997). The self-reference effect in memory: a meta-analysis. *Psychological Bulletin, 121*(3), 371.

Thompson, C.P., Skowronski, J.J., & Lee, D.J. (1988). Telescoping in dating naturally occurring events. *Memory & Cognition, 16*, 461–468.

Tuncer, İ., & Kartal, A.S. (2024). Do the importance of influencer-and customer-generated content on social media affect willingness to pay more for potential customers?. *Journal of Consumer Behaviour, 23*(2), 1002–1013.

Tversky, A., & Kahneman, D. (1973). Availability: A heuristic for judging frequency and probability. *Cognitive Psychology, 5.*

Vaughan, K., Corsi, A.M., Beal, V., & Sharp, B. (2021). Measuring advertising's effect on mental availability. *International Journal of Market Research, 63*(5), 665–681.

Von Restorff, H. (1933). Über die wirkung von bereichsbildungen im spurenfeld. *Psychologische Forschung, 18*, 299–342.

Walker, W.R., Skowronski, J.J., & Thompson, C.P. (2003). Life is pleasant – and memory helps to keep it that way!. *Review of General Psychology, 7*(2), 203–210.

Webster, D.M., & Kruglanski, A.W. (1994). Individual differences in need for cognitive closure. *Journal of Personality and Social Psychology, 67*(6), Article 1049.

Winterbottom, A., Bekker, H.L., Conner, M., & Mooney, A. (2008). Does narrative information bias individual's decision making? A systematic review. *Social Science & Medicine, 67*(12), 2079–2088.

Zajonc, R. B. (1968). Attitudinal effects of mere exposure. *Journal of personality and social psychology, 9*(2p2), 1.

Zeigarnik, B. (1927). Das Behalten erledigter und unerledigter Handlungen [The retention of completed and uncompleted actions]. *Psychologische Forschungen, 9*, 1–85.

Zickfeld, J.H., Ścigała, K. A., Elbæk, C.T., Michael, J., Tønnesen, M. H., Levy, G., … & Mitkidis, P. (2025). Effectiveness of ex ante honesty oaths in reducing dishonesty depends on content. *Nature Human Behaviour, 9*(1), 169–187.

8 Choice: Recognising Biases and Demonstrating Value

In this final chapter, we explore how customers assess the value of different choices – and how those assessments are shaped by bias.

While price is often the most visible factor, customers rarely judge a price in isolation. Instead, they compare a price to a reference point and also rely on mental shortcuts (known as 'heuristics'), such as avoiding risk and loss, valuing the efforts of themselves and others, and sometimes being influenced by emotions.

By recognising these psychological biases and understanding how customers frame value, marketers can design experiences that feel more rewarding. This can lead to small but powerful moments of positive customer behaviour, as we'll see in the next case study.

The Pennies Foundation is a charity (registered number: 1122489) which raises money for good causes when customers check out, whether online, in a store, at a kiosk, or in an app – in fact, any channel where you pay for goods and services. For example, when you buy clothing at JD Sports stores or order a pizza from Domino's via their app or online, you will be prompted to add a small donation to charity. This is the work of Pennies, led by Chief Executive Alison Hutchinson, CBE. The success of this approach is partly due to the way customers are presented with a choice to make a small donation during the checkout process. We spoke to Alison about the psychology behind this …

DOI: 10.4324/9781003541226-9

THE DIGITAL ASK: HOW TO SEAMLESSLY ENCOURAGE MICRO-DONATIONS ONLINE

Micro-donations are small, one-off charity donations. But together, they add up to a huge amount of money raised for charity.

Established in 2010, the Pennies Foundation had identified a critical challenge in charitable giving: As customers moved toward digital payments and away from cash, the traditional charity-collection box was at risk of becoming obsolete.

THE CHALLENGE

Prior to Pennies, the most popular method of small-scale charitable giving was dropping coins into a physical charity box – a simple, affordable, and emotionally satisfying way to contribute. However, two major shifts began to disrupt this long-standing practice – a serious concern for charities, as those small but frequent coin donations had long provided a reliable and meaningful source of funding.

First, the rise of digital shopping was reducing footfall in physical-retail locations, where charity boxes had traditionally encouraged impulse giving. As transactions moved online, so did the opportunity to give – offering customers a chance to enhance their purchase experience with a feel-good moment of generosity.

Second, the widespread adoption of card payments and contactless technology meant fewer people were carrying cash, reducing opportunities for spontaneous giving. At the same time, digital platforms helped overcome challenges linked to physical-donation boxes – such as theft, banking logistics, and concerns about whether funds reached the intended recipients.

Pennies needed to find a new way to present people with an option to donate.

THE SOLUTION

Pennies was founded with a clear vision: To protect the popular behaviour of small charitable donations by digitising them to reflect evolving shopping and payment methods. The concept was simple – make it easy for customers to reach a quick decision: Rounding up their purchases to the nearest pound or adding a small donation when paying by card, online or in app. When framed against the cost of the main purchase and bundled into the same checkout process, such small donations feel far more affordable to customers.

However, Pennies faced significant scepticism during its setup. Among the doubts, critics argued that the technology would not work due to fragmentation in payment systems, that retailers would resist adding friction to the checkout process, and that customers would not donate to an unfamiliar system. To overcome these challenges and generate momentum for micro-donations, Pennies adopted a comprehensive testing approach, working with merchants, fintech organisations, charities, and industry partners to implement their system across diverse retail environments – from football clubs and petrol forecourts to DIY stores and fast-food restaurants.

Pennies discovered that success was less reliant on the retail sector itself and more influenced by the clarity and efficiency of the customer journey. The most effective implementations shared several key features: Clear identification of both Pennies and the benefiting charity; a simple, one-click process to add a donation; acknowledgment of the donation on receipts; accessible feedback channels; and retailer communication that highlighted the social impact of the donations. These elements combined to create a valuable system for charities as well as a seamless and rewarding experience for customers.

IMPACT AND RESULTS

After 14-plus years in operation, Pennies has demonstrated remarkable success: Establishing micro-donations as a recognised concept in charitable giving, normalising the practice of rounding up purchases for charity and raising over £60 million from 250 million donations for more than 1,000 charities across the UK, Ireland, and beyond.

Pennies has also positioned itself particularly well for future generations who have grown up in a digital, cashless society. Research conducted by Pennies indicates that younger customers view micro-donations as a natural part of the shopping experience and expect this option to be available.

Pennies exemplifies how technological innovation can preserve valuable social behaviours even as customer habits evolve. By digitising the charity box for a cashless world, the organisation has not only protected a traditional form of giving, but enhanced it through increased transparency, scale, and impact measurement.

> The case of Pennies demonstrates that charitable giving can successfully adapt to technological change when solutions are designed with deep understanding of both customer psychology and retail environments. As digital payments continue to dominate, Pennies' model of frictionless, optional micro-donations integrated into everyday transactions represents a sustainable approach to fundraising that benefits charities and retailers alike.

8.1 UTILITY (OR USEFULNESS)

We'd like to start by explaining the word 'utility'. Whilst popular among economists, 'utility' is not a commonly used word; it might be easier to understand 'utility' as meaning 'usefulness'. There is a long-established theory of 'affordance', originally published in 1979 (Gibson, 2014) which suggests that humans judge their environment according to the benefits it offers them (i.e. its uses and benefits). Therefore, before a customer buys a product or service, they have to assess how useful it will be to them. What problem will it solve? What is the utility?

Hopefully, a marketer will have identified the problem before supporting the design team in creating the product (another of the 4 P's discussed in the introduction); and target a relevant group of potential customers for whom the problem exists.

Customers like to feel satisfied that they have made the best choice and chosen the best product or service to suit their specific requirement. In reality, they have probably made compromises along the way, perhaps when they considered practicalities and the budget. This is commonly referred to as 'satisficing': A combination of satisfying and sufficing (Simon, 1956). Let's explore some psychological theories that help to explain how customers assess utility and choose to purchase.

a) Customers use prices to judge value
First, of course, the price set by the seller sends a signal:

Money illusion
Very often customers are persuaded by price. Customers hate price rises for example. Yet, aversion to a price rise is an assessment of a product purely based on numbers (nominal value) rather than the relative value

of the product, which is far more difficult to quantify. If all prices (and perhaps wages) are rising across the country, perhaps due to economic inflation, then a small price rise should be understandable and perhaps even acceptable. This is the money illusion (Shafir et al, 1997). Sometimes the opposite occurs when people are suspicious of offers that are too generous (Vonasch et al., 2024).

b) Customers also use demand to judge value

In addition to the price, the apparent demand from other buyers increases the perceived value:

Scarcity

Aside from oxygen, what do humans need most to survive? Water. Yet how much are people in the Western world prepared to pay for a glass of tap water? Nothing, or very little. This in itself is odd, but let's also consider diamonds. How much are people prepared to pay for a tiny piece of compressed carbon that does not prolong their lives at all? Thousands! Why?

One answer to this conundrum is scarcity. Diamonds are relatively rare, yet water on earth is relatively plentiful. Natural scarcity particularly affects value (Wang et al., 2024).

There are two types of scarcity: Resource scarcity when the quantity available is limited, and time scarcity when availability is time-limited (Aggarwal et al., 2011). Anyone who has ever bought a limited-edition product, knows this very well. However, a meta-analysis showed that overall, excessive demand increases purchase likelihood more than 'urgency conditions' created by limiting time and quantity (Ladeira et al., 2023), plus offline time limits do not always seem to transfer equivalently online (Hmurovic et al., 2022).

Demand-based scarcity appeals seem most effective in Eastern cultures, yet supply-based scarcity appeals are more effective in Western cultures (Khoso et al., 2023).

Brands that don't tell the whole truth, sometimes give the impression that their products or services are scarcer than they are: "Just a few tickets left", for example, when the definition of 'a few' is actually far greater than customers would assume. This is false scarcity, but when scarcity is perceived as false the effect on consumers is reduced (Mukherjee and Lee, 2016). Brands that use these tactics can come across as duplicitous, ultimately damaging trust. It's not something we would recommend.

Winner's curse

In an online-auction situation, there is often a clamour to bid high for products that are in demand; In fact, when there are many bidders the winner competes harder, sometimes paying a price in excess of the true product value – perhaps higher even than the price they intended to pay when valuing the item in advance. This is the winners' curse (Kagel and Levin, 1986). Most of the bidders probably value the 'utility' of the item at similar levels, yet one person actually paid a lot more to win.

APPLYING THE THEORY: KEY QUESTIONS

Are you clearly communicating the problem your product solves, ensuring your audience understands its relevance to their needs or challenges?

Consider how your product's value compares to the cost – are you presenting it in a way that makes the benefit clearly outweigh the price for your audience?

Can you create a sense of scarcity by highlighting the product's popularity or exclusive offers, motivating your audience to act quickly before they miss out?

8.2 REFERENCE DEPENDENCE

It might seem obvious that a yacht is worth thousands of times more than a loaf of bread, but an alien landing on planet earth would not immediately understand why. People today have grown up in a world where certain products or services are accepted as differing in value. We even differentiate between brands offering the same product or service. When on holiday we likely compare the price of products in another country to our own currency. To understand whether the item being offered is good or bad value, customers need a point of comparison – either learned over time or provided by the marketing materials. For example, is the product cheaper than a competitor? Cheaper now than a year ago? Does spreading the cost make the product equivalent to a daily newspaper etc (this is known as 'temporal reframing'? Customers depend on these reference points in order to assess value.

One of the most successful health club marketing campaigns Luan worked on early in her career was focused on comparing the price of a health-club membership to other items – alcohol, fast food, and cigarettes. A daily price breakdown showed a health-club membership was not as expensive as potential customers expected.

a) *Budgets depend on the product*

Not only are prices reference dependent, but customers actually change their reference point depending on context. Make a cup of coffee using your coffee machine at home and you would pay very little, aside from the initial outlay on the machine and coffee beans. Yet, you'd happily pay a higher fee for pretty much the same coffee in your local coffee shop – even more in a branch of a well-known coffee-shop chain. This is partly due to the way money is allocated to certain expenditure psychologically (perhaps 'groceries' versus 'dining').

Mental accounting

Most customers probably spend a lot more each week on human food compared to pet food. In fact, they probably have a rough budget for each category of expenditure, as well as budgets for many other expenses each week, month, or year. This allocation of spending to categories is known as mental accounting (Thaler, 1985).

For example, online bank Monzo uses 'Pots' to help its customers separate money within a main account, making it easy to allocate funds for savings goals, bills, or spending budgets. Similarly, Starling Bank offers 'Spaces', which allows customers to set aside money for specific purposes, automate transfers, and even lock funds to avoid dipping into savings.

The task for marketers is to switch the allocation of the expense. For example, the usual sense of loss when spending money is reduced when customers receive money beforehand in a refund – held in a separate mental account to their usual wallet (Lee and Morewedge, 2023).

b) *The effect of free*

Of course, the ultimate way to pay less than any reference point is not to pay anything (although beware that low pricing can also signal low value as we discuss shortly).

Zero-price effect

Discounts can be interpreted differently depending on how they affect the end price. For example, you might assume that a £10 saving is appreciated by the same customer regardless of what they are buying. Yet, if that saving reduces the price to zero, the same saving is more attractive

(Shampanier et al., 2007). Getting a product for free increases the perceived benefit, even though the value saved is identical.

Foot in door

You're probably familiar with the 'freemium' concept – offering a service, such as software, for free within limits (such as within a time limit). This is an example of 'foot in door' (Freedman and Fraser, 1966), asking customers to accept a small request before asking for a larger one (like stepping into someone's doorway before being invited further into their home as the 'foot in door' name suggests).

APPLYING THE THEORY: KEY QUESTIONS

Can you present your pricing or offer in a way that taps into how people mentally account for money –like positioning it as a small, justifiable spend rather than a major purchase?

If offering a discount, consider how a discount relates to the price. Does it take the price nearer to zero?

Can you use the power of 'free' to your advantage, encouraging customers to try before they buy?

8.3 LOSS AND GAIN

When customers typically spend money, they expect to gain something in return, i.e., gain some 'utility'. But also, they are losing something: money. If the product or service doesn't provide the intended utility, then the sense of loss is even greater.

a) Customers assess gains and losses

People also judge the 'prospect' in front of them according to the chance of success or risk of loss:

Prospect Theory

Kahneman and Tversky are best-known for a principle known as 'Prospect Theory' (Kahneman and Tversky, 2013). This focuses on how customers assess the expected utility of a product or service, comparing it to a given reference point (i.e., assessing the 'prospect' of gaining value).

b) Customers amplify losses
Nobody likes to lose – especially losing money!

Loss aversion
You might be surprised at just how much people hate losing (Tversky and Kahneman, 1991). In fact, studies show that the pain of losing is twice as powerful as the pleasure of winning. In other words, the emotion of winning £10 is equivalent to losing just £5. People are therefore worried about making a wrong decision that might result in a longer-term loss.

Myopic loss aversion
This is related to plain and simple loss aversion. Myopia is otherwise known as short-sightedness. The theory here is that people tend to focus too heavily on loss in the short term, perhaps ignoring longer-term benefits (Benartzi and Thaler, 1995).

Currency
It appears that literally being reminded of the currency people are spending makes them reluctant to spend it. Yang, Kimes and Sessarego (2009) demonstrated this with an experiment comparing sales from a menu with currency symbols ($) and a menu without: Spending decreased when customers viewed the word 'dollars' or the symbol '$'. Additionally, the Rule of 100 shows that if you wish to offer your customers a discount, consider the price they will pay. If over 100, state the saving using the currency of the sale. If under 100, state the saving as a percentage (González et al., 2016).

Disposition effect
If somebody holds stocks or shares that have lost money, you might advise them to sell and instead invest the money in an industry that is on the rise. Many people don't do this (Shefrin and Statman, 1985). Instead, they are reluctant to accept a loss and instead hang on in the hope that the value will eventually rise once again. This isn't necessarily a rational decision

but occurs so often that it has its own theory, called the disposition effect. This is similar to the sunk-cost fallacy, where people feel tied and reluctant to give up a cause that they have already invested money into.

Reflection effect

The degree to which people reflect on the risk as either a gain or loss makes a difference. If a choice offers a potential gain, people tend to be cautious, preferring certainty to a high value alternative that carries risk. Perhaps a standard three-bedroom home on a housing estate is a less risky purchase than a beautiful, larger home on the banks of a river, even if both are offered at the same price. However, when faced with a decision to prevent a loss, the opposite occurs (Kahneman and Tversky, 2013). In a loss-making situation, a gamble (offering the potential of a significant solution but possibility of a loss) is preferred to a certain, but less significant, loss.

c) *Customers often hedge bets*

One way to avoid loss is to spread the risk.

1/N heuristic

If there is uncertainty about the potential for loss or gain among a variety of choices, the natural decision may be to spread the risk (Benartzi and Thaler, 2001). Invest some money in a range of different options. This is known as the '1/N heuristic' because a person is spreading one bet (1) across many options (N). The trouble with this approach is that a person's expertise may only relate to some of these options, meaning that some of these investments are sometimes referred to as being naive.

APPLYING THE THEORY: KEY QUESTIONS

Consider how your messaging might reduce risk – are you giving people a way to hedge their bets, like free trials, guarantees, or flexible terms?

Consider how your customers weigh potential gains and losses— are you framing benefits in a way that feels like avoiding a loss rather than simply gaining something new?

Can you also frame your offer in terms of what your audience stands to lose if they don't take action, rather than just what they might gain?

8.4 TIME-RELATED ASSESSMENT

As well as assessing products and services in terms of their utility and monetary value, customers also often assess time. After all, time, like money, is a risk. Who knows how our lives might be in two years' or even two months' time?

a) *Customers often focus on short-term gain*
As sensible as it may seem to plan ahead, people are often not great at doing so.

Delay (also called 'hyperbolic') discounting
It is very difficult to imagine events that might occur in the future. Who knows when our time might come to an end? In any case, something great might be just around the corner. People find it so difficult to predict the future that most prefer an immediate reward to a longer term, and even greater, reward in the future. This is also referred to as a 'present bias', 'intertemporal choice', and 'time discounting' (Doyle, 2013).

When people have the option to delay a money-saving decision, the urgency of the decision appears to decrease (Reiff et al., 2023), yet when a seller forces customers to delay a purchase, they become willing to pay even more (Desai and Jindal, 2024). People also delay tasks, but when the duration of a short task is communicated, the likelihood of postponing is reduced (Chun, Lembregts and Van den Bergh, 2023).

Duration vs dates
When setting a deadline for completing a task, should you give people a certain amount of time or give them a specific date? Should customers complete their guarantee form in five days or by the 10th of March (assuming that today is the 5th of March)? Research suggests that people feel a greater sense of urgency (an implemental mindset) when given a duration (Jeong et al., 2023).

APPLYING THE THEORY: KEY QUESTIONS

Can you make the benefits of your product feel more immediate, knowing that people tend to prefer quick rewards over long-term gains?

Consider whether you're asking your audience to wait too long for results – can you break down outcomes into shorter milestones to keep motivation high?

Can you reduce friction by highlighting how little time something takes, especially when your audience might overestimate the effort involved?

8.5 EFFORT

Let's face it, if offered the choice of a nice two-week holiday or a fortnight of exams, most of us would prefer to relax on a beach. Most of us will also choose the path of least resistance and often cut corners (sometimes literally when driving). This section explores theories relating to invested effort. For example, when reminded about the time taken to return a product, customers are less likely to do so (Lee and Yi, 2022).

a) Customers value their self effort
Firstly, people value their own effort.

IKEA effect
IKEA is a strange concept really. We choose furniture from the brochure, website, or showroom, then are presented with a box of bits. Psychologically, this is a masterstroke. By investing effort in making the product, customers feel a greater sense of attachment to the finished object (Norton et al., 2012). Lego obviously realised the same thing a few years beforehand. Despite perfect models of cars, houses, and spaceships on offer elsewhere, children feel great satisfaction in completing models themselves. This is also called 'effort justification'. Online-recipe deliveries operate on the same principle. Beware though; when a customer is asked to put lots of effort into brand interactions, their satisfaction can decrease (Ardelet and Benavent, 2022).

Incentives
One reason to invest effort is the potential of a reward at the end. In technical terms we might call this an incentive. Incentives are

particularly powerful where the task is unpleasant, or the effort required is particularly strenuous.

Escalation of commitment

"If you find yourself in a hole, stop digging" goes the popular saying. The thing is, the human tendency is to keep going, presumably in the hope that fortunes will change any moment (Staw, 1981).

Plan continuation bias

When you've spent a long time planning an event, being told to change at the last minute is difficult to accept – even when the rationale is sound. This bias to continue with a plan, such as flying a plane through bad weather (Winter et al., 2020), is simply known as plan continuation bias.

Endowed progress

At this point, you are towards the end of our book – so you may as well finish it! That's an attitude that originates from a theory known as endowed progress (Nunes and Dreze, 2006). When the end of the tunnel is in sight, the motivation to reach it increases. It can be helpful to show a customer how far they are through an online purchase or completing a survey, for example.

b) Customers value the effort of others

People also appreciate the effort put in by others.

Labour illusion

Another phrase for this theory is 'operational transparency' (Buell and Norton, 2011). Either way, the meaning is clear. Where the 'labour' or 'operations' behind the scenes can be seen, the customer's perception of the product or service changes. Many pizza restaurants, for example, allow customers to see the fresh food being prepared. Not only are the hygiene standards of the chef on display (just think about all the kitchens you never see), but we also understand the skill that goes into each step of food preparation. In turn, we value the food more highly. A good reason then to show customers 'behind the scenes' content online!

c) *Misplaced importance*

Sometimes, when deep in the details of a situation, it's difficult for people to see the wood for the trees – they become so focused on the small parts that they lose sight of the overall picture. Taking a step back can help to gain perspective, prioritise what really matters, and make more informed decisions.

Focusing illusion

Excessive focus on just one aspect of life is often misplaced (Kahneman et al., 2006). This is a focusing illusion. For instance, exam results do carry some weight, but perhaps not as much as students think at the time. For many students, exam results mean everything, and they place a huge focus on their meaning and consequence. There are many examples of people who failed their exams yet made a huge success of their lives.

APPLYING THE THEORY: KEY QUESTIONS

Consider whether involving your audience more – through customisation, choices, or contributions –might increase how much they value the final outcome.

Can you make effort feel like part of the reward, showing that the time or work involved adds meaning rather than being a barrier?

Can you spotlight the effort you've put in – behind-the-scenes work, attention to detail, or care – to build trust and appreciation?

Consider whether you're drawing too much attention to a single aspect of your offer – are you unintentionally creating a focusing illusion that might skew decisions?

8.6 OWNERSHIP

When customers pay for a product, they usually legally own it. Ownership makes a difference psychologically to the value placed on the product, as we will see in this section.

For example, customers like to think that they have chosen the best products, and perhaps even the best brands. If this is true though, why do we see a variety of car brands on the road – including many that are similarly priced? The reality is that people like to own products and brands that reflect identity rather than simply serving a purpose (Akerlof and Kranton, 2010). Utility in this sense relates to the usefulness of the brand in reflecting identity.

a) WTP and WTA differs

If customers were computers, they would automatically calculate the value of whatever product or service was on offer: In a selling situation, the price would be the same. Humans, however, are not computers. In fact, the 'willingness to pay' (WTP) price and 'willingness to accept' (WTA) price when buying or selling the same thing are often different (Hanemann, 1991).

Endowment effect

In the classroom, we often ask for a volunteer who owns a car. We ask them to write on a piece of paper how much they would sell their car for. Then, other students in the class are asked to estimate how much they would pay for the same vehicle. What do we find? The estimates are usually far lower than the volunteers' own price. This happens all the time; people over-estimate the value of their own belongings for a variety of products (Bialek et al., 2022; Colucci et al., 2024), sometimes referred to as the 'mere ownership effect' (Bialek et al., 2022). We even value information, regardless of whether it is material or immaterial (Stefanczyk et al., 2021). This is psychologically known as the endowment effect (Knetsch, 1989). Online sites, such as Gumtree and eBay, help to overcome this by letting buyers and sellers negotiate.

Sunk cost fallacy

The sunk cost fallacy is the tendency to continue investing in something – whether it's time, money, or effort – simply because you've already invested a lot, even when it's no longer the best decision. It happens when past costs, which can't be recovered, influence present choices, making it difficult to walk away even when doing so would be more rational (Thaler, 1980).

An organisation might continue pouring money into a failing advertising campaign because they've already spent thousands developing the concept and buying media space – telling themselves it would be wasteful to stop now – rather than cutting their losses and reallocating the budget to something more effective. Don't be afraid to try something different, especially now you're armed with new psychology theories to apply.

APPLYING THE THEORY: KEY QUESTIONS

Remind customers of the products they have previously purchased from you (that they now own) and the value of the products to them.

Can you shift the conversation from cost to value, helping people focus on what they'll gain by buying your product or service, rather than what they're giving up?

8.7 CHOICE

Choice architecture is a term that became famous following the publication of Thaler and Sunstein's book *Nudge* in 2008. The concept is straightforward – just as the design that architects create for a house affects how we use the building, how communicators present choice options can also affect the choices customer make.

Another important concept is 'choice satisfaction'. Many people get excited about buying something new. Perhaps they've saved for months, viewed many alternatives, and pinpointed a specific date in the diary when the purchase would finally happen. Whether that excitement remains afterwards depends on how they reflect on the decision. In academic terms, this is referred to as choice satisfaction (Wilson et al., 1993).

a) Presentation of choices to a customer

People don't always make objective decisions based on weighing up the facts. How choices are seen can direct the decision.

Decision staging

Because of choice overload, customers employ strategies such as 'chunking'. Decision staging is one such approach, dividing all options into different groups and then selecting according to specific attributes – in other words passing through specific 'stages' to reach a final choice.

Decoy effect

If people were always rational and objective, they would assess each option according to its own merits and utility. This often isn't the case. Instead, people compare one option against the alternatives (Huber et al., 1982). Therefore, sometimes customers are swayed by an option which is simply there to provide a comparison point. This is known as a

Figure 8.1 Decoy Effect

'decoy' (see figure 8.1). For example, a website may offer a product for the same price either with or without a free gift. Would anyone really turn down a free gift? Just presenting an inferior alternative can create a 'dominance effect' for the superior product (Fridman et al., 2024).

Default option

Many governments and policy makers have wisened to the fact that people don't like making choices. Whether we describe it as uncertainty or just laziness, the point is that very often people stick with the first option presented (Johnson et al., 2002). Many marketers have known this for a long time, but now public services often also operate 'opt out' policies in areas such as pension enrolment and organ donation, with 'inclusion' as the default option.

Online subscriptions often automatically renew. Defaults are also powerful when customers presume they are the most popular option (Buchanan et al., 2022). For hedonic products, the default option is also perceived as higher value (Sullivan et al., 2024).

Status quo bias

This is a similar, but subtly different theory to the default option. The default option suggests that people will often stick with the choice presented as the 'normal' or 'usual' selection. Status quo bias shows that people sometimes stick to a choice made a long time ago (Samuelson and Zeckhauser, 1988), even when new and better options emerge. For example, customers often use the same insurer for many years by simply renewing annually rather than shopping around.

No choice options

When choosing between options, one possibility is simply not to take any of them. Confusingly, this decision is actually selection of the 'no choice' option (Dhar, 1997), or 'choice deferral' when none of the available options are particularly attractive. When a country considers how to act in a wartime conflict for example, not acting at all is still a potential choice. This is sometimes referred to as 'omission' in comparison to 'commission' (taking action). People sometimes assume, perhaps wrongly, that making a bad decision (commission) is morally worse than making no decision (omission; Spranca, et al., 1991).

Temptation bundling

When people are reluctant to act, an incentive or reward can work wonders (Milkman et al., 2014) i.e. 'bundling' an indulgent pleasure with an unattractive activity.

b) Faced with too many choices

Don't assume that customers always want a wide range of options. Too many choices can actually be off-putting.

There is a famous study involving jam that you may have heard of (Iyengar and Lepper, 2000). The basic outcome is that when people are offered a wide variety of jams, they are less likely to buy anything than if they are offered a much smaller selection. The theory underpinning this is choice overload; that is, people don't like being faced with too many choices. You could use filters, for example pricing 'low to high', colour selection or sizing, on a website to avoid presenting too many choices to your potential customer.

Compromise effect

Very often there is no product or service that meets a customer's requirements exactly. If Tom wanted a fluorescent-yellow polo shirt with green polka dots but couldn't find a shop that sold one, the solution is therefore a compromise (Simonson, 1989). People buy the nearest available option offering at least some of the features they desire – a plain yellow polo shirt in Tom's case. There is sometimes a benefit in positioning a product as offering a combination of features to serve different needs, becoming a compromise option for many customers.

Procrastination

Most of us are happy to put off a difficult decision. This is procrastination and again is a known bias by those who study decision-making

(Ariely and Wertenbroch, 2002), although self-imposed deadlines can help to overcome such delay. In his 2016 TED Talk, Tim Urban shared his journey of waiting until the last minute to get things done – if you have a tendency to procrastinate, it is recommended viewing!

c) *Common ways of making decisions*

Humans try to be as logical as they can, and we all learn from people around us. If we spot for example that Nike seems to be more popular than Adidas, but that Adidas is more popular than Puma, we can also assume that Nike is more popular than Puma. We can reach conclusions by developing hierarchies and ascertaining how choices might then be made. These are known as transitive preferences.

Very often, preferences are revealed rather than stated. It's well-known in the social sciences that sometimes participants' actions and thoughts differ. The answer people might give to a 'self-report' question about their behaviour might not match their actual behaviour. Sometimes this is referred to as social desirability bias.

In the marketing world, observation of behaviour is therefore a better way to reveal their preferences. Choice selection is not objective. Humans can be guided by psychological 'nudges'. In the real world too, customers sometimes find solutions that 'satisfice', meeting perhaps a range of minimum requirements rather than being perfect.

Making quick decisions

People often rely on 'rules of thumb' – simple, general principles or guidelines that help them make quick decisions, especially when faced with complex or uncertain situations.

Fast and frugal

Fast and frugal is an easy way to think about how decisions tend to be made as quickly and painlessly as possible (Gigerenzer and Goldstein, 1996), sometimes using just one reason for the basis of a decision. Unlike computers, people can't assess many datapoints at once so rely on 'biases' to guide them. Controversially, some psychologists refer to this as irrationality. We prefer the term 'bounded rationality'. Taken in isolation, many choices appear rational and reasoned; it's just that the terms of reference are often limited because the brain can't possibility consider all the potential information.

First instinct fallacy

Humans like to make decisions efficiently, then stick to them. Sometimes, people are even encouraged to 'follow their gut instinct'. This can be a mistake though. It might actually be better to review an initial decision rather than trust the first instinct (Kruger et al., 2005).

Take-the-best heuristic

If we ask you to choose the best footballer in the world, you'll probably immediately think of a goal scorer, or at least an attacking player. It's unlikely you would consider a defender, or even a goalkeeper. The 'take the best' theory (Gigerenzer and Goldstein, 1999) is a 'fast and frugal mechanism' suggesting that people arrive upon a specific chosen attribute (e.g. goal scoring) and then select options based on this one characteristic.

Take-the-first heuristic

This sounds similar to the theory above, but this theory instead suggests that people often 'take the first' option that springs to mind (Johnson and Raab, 2003). Fancy a burger? You'll perhaps google 'McDonalds' before considering Burger King, Wimpy, or other more local brands. Sometimes there is just no need to spend time considering additional possible options.

Representativeness heuristic

In a famous Daniel Kahneman experiment, participants are asked to decide whether a quiet, 'meek and tidy soul', chosen at random, is more likely to be a farmer or librarian. Most people say librarian, although logic dictates that there are many, many more farmers than librarians. This is because people are guided by how representative (Kahneman and Tversky, 1972) the description is of 'librarian' rather than carefully considering the question, which is really about probability.

Making decisions systematically

When decisions are taken more carefully, here are some alternative ways of assessing options:

Elimination by aspects

One rule that can be used to filter out options is to develop a series of mental filters. In this way, each option can be assessed according to specific 'aspects' in turn (Tversky, 1972), leaving just a small pool of products or services that meet the criteria.

Weighted additive
The weighted additive approach to comparing options involves scoring each item for importance, then comparing the final scores (Churchman and Ackoff, 1954).

Avoiding risks
Just as people prefer to avoid losses, they also avoid even the risk of a loss.

Extremeness aversion
Would you buy the most expensive watch on a jeweller's website? Well, even if they could afford it, most people probably wouldn't spend thousands on something that just tells the time. But would you buy the cheapest option? Probably not! You never know how long it will last. Ignoring either end of the spectrum is known as extremeness aversion (Simonson and Tversky, 1992).

Diversification bias
A natural way to avoid making a wrong decision is for a person to spread the risk. As the saying goes, "don't put all your eggs in one basket". For example, when stocking up for the month in a sweet shop, people perhaps buy a variety of products. Yet, when buying smaller quantities of sweets for immediate consumption, people are less likely to diversify.

This apparently natural instinct is known as diversification bias (Read and Loewenstein, 1995). Yet, when faced with a collection of diverse consumables (such as listening to songs), repeating the consumption of similar items together (listening to the same song several times) helps to prevent 'hedonic decline' whereby enjoyment of each purchase decreases over time (Chen and Redden, 2023).

Risk aversion
People are generally risk averse. Therefore, when considering a range of choices, an important consideration is what the potential downsides are (Kahneman and Tversky, 1984). People avoid bad outcomes rather than seek good outcomes (Ryan et al., 2024). Those who work

harder seem especially risk averse (Bechler et al., 2024) and many particularly avoid risky decisions where the outcome is complex (Oberholzer et al., 2024) as well as using mental visualisations to imagine risky actions (Smieja et al., 2023).

Uncertainty aversion

Alongside risk, another key determining factor in distinguishing between multiple choices is the likelihood that one will be more reliable. You may have found the most talented developer to create your new website, but if there is any chance they might stop working halfway through, many of us would rather avoid that uncertainty regardless of their skills. This is also referred to as 'ambiguity aversion' (Ellsberg, 1961). In a retail environment, shoppers seeking to avoid uncertainty are more brand loyal (Guo and Wang, 2023).

There are two potential types of uncertainty (Jackson, 2023): Aleatory uncertainty (fear of the unknown) and epistemic uncertainty (being unsure although the possibilities are known).

Zero-risk bias

Just like with the zero-cost effect, people prefer reduction of risk when it leads to no risk at all (Raue and Schneider, 2019). Reducing the risk of a product breaking by 20% for example ought to be very attractive. However, if another product effectively eradicates all risk (even if this risk was just 10% originally), this is preferable. Money-back guarantees are a good example of this risk reduction.

d) Things people 'neglect' to consider

Because a human's ability to consider information is limited (hence the phrase 'bounded rationality'), people often exclude important information.

Domain neglect

People can learn all sorts of scientific principles at school or college, but sometimes they struggle to apply them to real life. They struggle to understand how specific situations (known as domains) might affect their application (Mike and Hazzan, 2022). Perhaps customers fail to see how different buying behaviours are required in different situations (as marketers we know all about this!).

Waiting for a sale is a good idea when buying clothing for example, but not when buying festival tickets.

Common source bias

As the name suggests, this is a bias where people or organisations continue to rely on the same source, such as academics undertaking research upon the same population continuously.

Opportunity cost neglect

Missed opportunities 'cost' people, as they potentially miss out on a variety of benefits. Sticking to a 'tried and tested' brand, means that customers 'neglect' the cost of missing better options elsewhere (Frederick et al., 2009).

Subtraction neglect

Sometimes the solution to a problem is to stop doing something, that is, to take something away (Adams et al., 2021). The solution to a poorly performing team for example, might be to remove a disruptive influence. The tendency is to think firstly of solving problems through adding something new, such as buying a new product or service. This is therefore also sometimes referred to as 'additive bias' as well as subtraction neglect.

Less is better effect

Consider receiving a dinner set as a gift – 31 dinner plates and bowls; however, in the same box are a few extra broken plates too: a bit disappointing. But compare this to a perfectly intact dinner set with just 24 pieces and suddenly the 31-piece dinner set looks pretty good! This is exactly what Christopher Hsee (1998) found. The effect was that, in isolation, the lesser set looked better. In comparison, the preference was reversed.

e) *Comparison of choices*

Is a lasagne good for you? Well, the answer is, "it depends". If you are promoting a specific product or service, customers need to know what to compare it to. Humans are reference dependent.

Anchoring

Would many people pay £10 for a banana? Most customers use experience to value many products, even if this is not consciously processed. Comparing a price to a reference point is known as anchoring because it links a current value to an established one like a chain to an anchor. There are many other ways in which people 'anchor' comparison points, beyond numerical values (Furnham and Boo, 2011).

Conservatism bias

It's very difficult to shift mindset, especially when certain beliefs have been held for a long time. Imagine a scientist discovering today that, rather than gravity pulling people down, space is pushing us towards Earth. Now imagine how difficult it would be to convince the world of this new finding! Conservatism bias affects human's reluctance to change beliefs in many, many contexts, including financial decisions (Barberis et al, 1998).

Functional fixedness

What is a Wellington boot for? Keeping your feet dry? Yes. But did you know that in parts of England, welly boots are also used for traditional 'welly wanging' competitions? This involves throwing (known as wanging) a welly as far as possible. Functional fixedness shows that people generally identify an object's use and stick to it, but with a little imagination many objects have alternative purposes (German and Barrett, 2005).

Framing

When you look through a camera lens, whatever you see has a 'frame' around it. When you spin around the frame now shows you something different, even if your geographical location hasn't changed. The resulting photograph also looks very different depending on where the camera points. This is the gist of framing – drawing attention to different aspects of a whatever is being discussed (Kahneman and Tversky, 1984).

Contrast effect

Imagine that you somehow manage to scrape together the cash to purchase a pretty nice, seaworthy boat. It seems luxurious, with a kitchen, beds, and a sundeck. Your friends on social media are

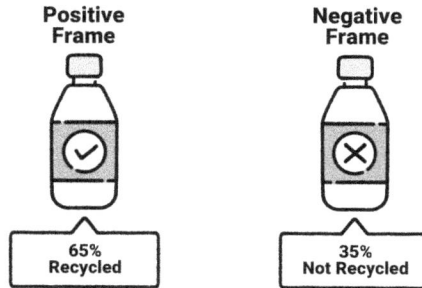

Figure 8.2 Framing Effect

impressed. But then you see pictures from the South of France of the huge yachts (by which we really mean ships) moored in Cannes, Nice, Antibes, and Monaco. The effect is that in contrast to alternatives, you might feel like a pauper. Judgement differs when something can be contrasted, as Bower (1961) demonstrated among rats.

Gain/loss framing

We discussed gains and losses earlier in this chapter. Understanding perceptions of gains and losses can also affect how the benefits of a product or service are framed. Framing can be used to focus on positivity or negativity, such as offering the customer either the potential to gain something or avoid losing something (see figure 8.2). However, framing the positive aspects of a purchase (such as ingredients being 95% natural) has less effect when a customer is emotionally driven (Poor and Isaac, 2023).

Distinction bias

Options tend to be 'framed' by whatever they are compared against (Hsee and Zhang, 2004). This means that two or more options viewed separately may actually be assessed differently (perhaps more favourably) than when they are held against one another to allow comparison.

Salience bias

Sometimes it's very easy to look for clear differences between two choices, known as salience (Bordalo, Gennaioli and Shleifer, 2013). When looking for a new home for example, people often focus on the visual 'perceived' differences between houses (often called 'kerb appeal') rather than how each house has been constructed. This is an example of cognitive ease – allowing the brain to be easily guided, rather than interrogating the information presented.

APPLYING THE THEORY: KEY QUESTIONS

Can you simplify decision-making by staging choices, guiding your audience through a clear, step-by-step process instead of overwhelming them with too many options at once?

How can the presentation of your options can nudge people towards your preferred choice – are you using a decoy option to make your main offer seem more appealing?

Can you pair your product or service with something tempting to encourage customers to choose it, using temptation bundling to make it harder to resist?

Consider whether your audience might experience choice overload – are you limiting options to a manageable number to avoid overwhelming them and causing decision fatigue?

What are you using as an anchor – does the first price or product your audience sees set the tone for how they judge everything else?

Consider whether the way you're framing options changes how people feel about them – are you encouraging action or unintentionally creating hesitation?

8.8 PRESENTATION OF PRICES

Customers generally don't enjoy parting with their money – for personal or professional purchases. In many cases seeing money disappear from a wallet (physical or digital) is seen as a loss. Even online notifications such as email or text messages can cause this feeling of discomfort (Gu and Chen, 2023).

a) How customers pay
The price of a product is important, but so is the method of payment.

Payment format
Spending money is mentally 'painful'. Where payment is especially 'painful' (such as parting with physical cash) this also seems to reduce the desire for variety as customers feel the need to justify each choice

(Huang et al., 2024). However, credit or debit cards appear to soften the effect of spending money (Prelec and Simester, 2001). Although the outcome is the same, tapping a piece of plastic is far more comfortable than literally giving away coins or notes. Online payment for physical products reduces negative emotion compared to payment on delivery (Yu et al., 2022) and paying on mobile can even lead to overspending (Ahn and Nam, 2022).

Denomination effect

In the UK, many of our traditional seaside amusement arcades have what we call 2p (two-pence) machines. Players roll in 2p coins, which gradually stack up and eventually topple over to reward a lucky winner with a small prize – probably around 20p in coins. It's a simple game, which presumably makes money for the owners over a very long run. People play for long periods of time because emptying their pockets of copper coins doesn't feel like spending money. People feel discomfort holding large quantities of coins and are therefore happy to spend them. Many would be more reluctant to spend the equivalent value in £5 banknotes (Zenkic et al., 2024). This preference for spending smaller denominations demonstrates the denomination effect (Raghubir and Srivastava, 2009).

b) Assessment of numbers

The way numbers, such as prices, are presented can affect the way people consider them.

Precise numbers

Schindler and Yalch (2006) use the term 'sharp' numbers in comparison to 'round' numbers, but the practical application of their work is that customers are less likely to think that precise numbers are an estimate. If you were quoted exactly £495 for a repair to your car, you might be suspicious. Did each part, the oil, and the labour, total exactly £495.00? £495.42 is far more convincing (Thomas et al., 2010). When a discount is rounded up (e.g. 8% rather than 7.7%), it also reduces purchase intention (Jha et al., 2024).

Left digit effect

Setting a price just below a round number can increase purchase decisions (Troll et al., 2023). You've probably seen plenty of examples of prices being deliberately set just below a whole number (e.g., £9.99 rather than £10.00). In academic terms, this is referred to as 'left-digit effect' (Thomas and Morwitz, 2005). In other words, customers focus on the number at the far left and don't take as much notice of the extra 99p.

Ratio bias

Humans are generally not brilliant at objectively assessing numbers – or to be more specific, assessing statistics. When asked to compare probabilities, people tend to focus on the number rather than the ratio (Denes-Raj, Epstein and Cole, 1995). If offering a prize draw for instance, perhaps consider a lump-sum cash prize rather than an equivalent value per week.

Even a penny

Very often, charities collecting money suggest that passersby donate whatever they can. They might say that 'even a penny' will make a difference (Cialdini and Schroeder, 1976). From one perspective, this approach works: Donations do increase when donors are asked for a low value.

c) Price and branding

The price you set, also sends a message about your overall brand.

Signalling

Many people make assumptions about products or services based on price. You might assume for example that a £20 bar of chocolate will taste better than a £2 bar of chocolate. Why should it though? Perhaps the £20 chocolate just costs more to import, or perhaps the seller is just making a huge profit! It's not unusual to expect higher quality when the price is higher (Kurz et al., 2023). This is also sometimes called the Veblen effect.

Discounting the brand

Offering a promotion (such as a free gift) can actually reduce purchase intention, unless the promotion is perceived to add significant value (Simonson et al., 1994). In addition, collaborating with another brand to offer your product as a free gift can reduce the perceived value of the product (Raghubir, 2004). Trying too hard seems to cheapen the product.

APPLYING THE THEORY: KEY QUESTIONS

Can you make it easier for people to say yes by offering flexible payment options – like Klarna or PayPal's 'Pay in 3' options that reduce the immediate cost and friction of purchase?

Consider how your use of precise numbers (rather than rounded figures) might increase trust and make your pricing feel more considered.

Can you signal premium quality or exclusivity through your pricing, knowing that higher prices can sometimes suggest greater value or status?

8.9 SELF-CONTROL AND DECISION-MAKING

Self-control or self-regulation is the ability to restrain behaviour when required.

a) A desire to be in control

Many people like to feel that they master of their own destiny.

Action bias

Many people don't like feeling out of control. When faced with a dilemma or a threat, the instinct is to react in some way (Bar-Eli et al., 2007) – even when the action taken in response doesn't improve the situation.

Control premium

Studies even suggest that customers will pay a premium if they are able to control an outcome (Owens et al., 2014). In terms of stocks and shares for example, investors will sometimes pay more when investment results in a controlling stake.

Illusory control

People like to feel a sense of control. Sometimes that leads to a mistaken belief that a person's own actions can make a difference, known as the 'illusion of control' (Langer, 1975). If a large airliner crashes into icy waters for example, the lifejackets stowed under the seat won't make a huge difference – but the important point is that passengers think they can save themselves (and feel reassured as a result). How many people really take advantage of a moneyback guarantee when an organisation offers this on an online purchase? Again, this provides reassurance.

Reactance theory

Sir Isaac Newton first posited that every action has a reaction. Well, there is some evidence that something similar happens in human psychology. People generally don't like being completely restrained and fight to retain some autonomy: They 'react' (Brehm, 1966), as can be seen through the revolutions that sometimes occur against authoritative regimes. Asking customers to behave a certain way is likely to be more acceptable than telling them to do so.

But you are free...

As described in the 'action bias', people like to feel that they are in control of their actions – even if studies of free will suggest that this is an illusion. In marketing terms, giving customers the option to walk away (Carpenter, 2013) increases the feeling that a subsequent choice to purchase is their own.

Learned helplessness

It's pretty uncomfortable to acknowledge that a situation can't be changed – or at least can't be changed by the person themselves. The first thought of many Prisoners of War may be how to escape. Over time, people learn to accept their fate; they accept a feeling of helplessness. This is learned helplessness (Maier and Seligman, 1976).

Placebo effect

Whilst other theories demonstrate a desire for self-control, the placebo effect demonstrates the effect of self-control. Of course, medicine works. Yet, there are surprising findings that people's minds are also able to overcome some medical conditions (Wampold et al., 2005). After swallowing a pill that is in fact a 'placebo' (contains no medicine), some people still notice benefits. This effect can even occur when people know the placebo is a placebo (Charlesworth et al., 2017)! Perhaps the same effect occurs when people purchase a brand that they expect to benefit them.

b) Fatigue and decision-making

Over time, the ability to consider information carefully seems to diminish.

Decision fatigue

If you've ever had to organise a big event, or place a complicated order, you might recall that after a while some decisions just seem unimportant. What colour do the napkins need to be? Who cares when you've just spent hours carefully creating a menu to cater for every possible requirement! After a while you pay less attention to the decisions you make. The theory is that over time a person's ability to make decisions worsens. As people make decisions, they get fatigued and therefore don't pay sufficient attention to subsequent information. As a result, people make mistakes, such as making less accurate forecasts (Hirshleifer et al., 2019).

Ego depletion

Ego depletion is a close cousin of decision fatigue, but it relates more to self-control than decision making. The theory is that after spending a lot of effort being disciplined, such as following a careful diet, subsequent self-constraint is more difficult (Baumeister et al., 2007). Self-control is a limited resource (Vohs et al., 2018).

c) Self-perception and decision-making

When people evaluate choices, how they think of themselves can affect their decision.

Ego-centric bias

Selfishness is generally considered an unpleasant characteristic, but the truth is that most people think about themselves at some point in their decision-making. In fact, ego-centric thinking is a known bias (Greenberg, 1983) affecting perception of fairness. Children for example often complain that they are hungry, forgetting that their siblings ate lunch at the same time.

G.I. Joe phenomenon

You might think that somebody who teaches or researches customer behaviour (or reads a book like this) ought to be immune from many of the biases we discuss. Well, we can tell you from personal experience that this is not true! In fact, belief that knowledge of psychological effects is sufficient to avoid them is referred to as the G.I. Joe phenomenon (Kristal and Santos, 2021).

Optimism bias

Thankfully, humans are optimistic creatures. Otherwise, incredible feats such as moon landings would never be considered. This becomes more of an issue though when estimating the likelihood of future events. People tend to overestimate the probability of positive outcomes (Sharot, 2011). Eskreis-Winkler et al. (2024) also refer to this tendency for optimism in relation to dealing with 'big problems', known as the 'big problem paradox'.

This is applied, for example, to household budgets. Forecasted spend on food and basic utilities may be fine, but estimates of unusual one-off goods and services will be too optimistic. "The washing machine? No, it's only ten years old so it'll probably be fine". What happens? Customers underestimate their exceptional purchases (Sussman and Alter, 2012).

Overconfidence

Although the level of self-confidence that people feel can vary, humans generally tend to apply optimism about the future to confidence in their own success. Subjective confidence in the likelihood of a positive outcome is therefore often higher than an objective assessment of statistics would warrant (Moore and Healy, 2008). People are particularly overconfident when they feel passionate (Bailey et al., 2024), but sharing a decision with others can reduce overconfidence (Piehlmaier, 2023).

d) Trying to be consistent

People like to feel a relatively stable sense of who they are.

Cognitive dissonance

The theory of cognitive dissonance (Festinger, 1962) suggests that people feel mental discomfort holding two conflicting thoughts. For example, most people know that alcohol isn't nutritious, yet alcoholic drinks are consumed across the world. People need to find some way of resolving the discomfort, such as ignoring the dissonance between competing thoughts, justifying the behaviour, adding 'consonance' to show that the behaviour is beneficial in some way, or just adopting a change to avoid the dissonance. In the case of drinking, this might mean selecting a drink with lower (or no) alcoholic content. People can even experience cognitive dissonance vicariously when observing inconsistent behaviour in others (Jaubert et al. 2024).

Habit

Habits are recurring or patterns of behaviour (Wood and Rünger, 2016). Often, they are linked to a context, such as always eating the same breakfast cereal when at home (but branching out when on holiday). As discussed in chapter 5, bundling habits together (habit stacking) can be an effective way of encouraging behaviour change.

Inertia

It's very easy, and perhaps reassuring, to repeat established patterns of behaviour. Where this prevents new (perhaps better) behaviours, this is referred to as inertia. Phoning somebody is more sociable (and maybe more efficient), but perhaps you normally just WhatsApp your friends. Some people score more highly than others for 'openness' to new experiences. In fact though, the tendency to prefer consistency to change is common (Gal, 2006). This conservative approach is also known as status quo bias.

Normalcy bias

When viewing a derelict building, some people find it very hard to visualise the building in any other state until they are shown an image. Similarly, when looking into the future, some people find it difficult to plan for an eventuality that they are unfamiliar with. This is known as 'normalcy bias' (Omer and Alon, 1994).

Dishabituation

People develop the habit of ignoring adverts and need to be 'dishabituated' and encouraged to pay attention to the screen again. Banner blindness is a term used to describe the effect when people fail to notice online 'banner' adverts. For example, highly creative adverts can dishabituate viewers and grab their attention again (Abedi and Koslow, 2022).

APPLYING THE THEORY: KEY QUESTIONS

Can you help your audience feel in control of their decisions by giving them simple, low-effort actions – or an option to withdraw within a certain timeframe (e.g., 28 days cooling off)?

Consider whether your messaging plays into your audience's perspective – are you showing them how *they* benefit, not just what your product does?

Can you keep your content feeling fresh – rotating visuals and messages to avoid banner blindness and prompt renewed attention?

Can you make using your product or service a habit by integrating it seamlessly into your audience's daily routine, so it becomes second nature?

8.10 ASSESSMENT OF CHANCE AND LOGICAL FALLACIES

Whether it's predicting the weather or the likelihood of winning a prize, life often requires people to assess potential events. For many people though, without training in mathematics or statistics, this is very difficult, often leading to errors.

a) Deriving meaning from information

People like to make sense of their surroundings, which can lead to errors when judging cause and effect.

Apophenia

Tom used to attribute any bad 'luck' (we use inverted commas here, because really there is no such thing as luck) to walking over three drain covers. This was apophenia – giving meaning to events that are actually unconnected. This is sometimes referred to as 'illusory correlation' (Chapman, 1967).

Clustering illusion

If you're looking at data online you might notice patterns. In basketball for example, high scoring by one player is known as having a 'hot hand', which is why this is sometimes also called the 'hot hand' fallacy (Gilovich, Vallone and Tversky, 1985). The truth, however, is that even random events show small patterns or clusters of results. These should be seen for what they truly are: Random rather than meaningful. Many people look for patterns that aren't there.

Pareidolia

Just like giving meaning to data, people sometimes attach meaning to inanimate objects, such as seeing shapes in clouds. This tendency to celebrate a random stimulus or stimuli (such as water droplets in a cloud) is known as pareidolia. For example, 'face pareidolia' is when people see faces in objects (Palmer and Clifford, 2020). There is evidence though that the human brain prioritises images featuring faces, such as those identified through pareidolia (Caruana and Seymour, 2022).

Extension neglect

Assessing one thing on its own is likely to lead to errors in judgement. For example, telling a young musical artist or sports player that they will be the 'next big thing' could be an example of extension neglect: Failure to consider a wider sample. Every town has good sports players and guitarists, but only some will reach a national or international level. Similarly, products and services should be assessed against a range of alternatives.

Nonproportional thinking

If inflation leads to the price of a £1 chocolate bar rising by five pence, some customers will expect other items in the store to also rise by five pence too. But, proportionately (5% inflation), a £2 loaf of bread is likely to have risen by 10 pence, and a £3 box of cereal by 15 pence. Failure to account for this is nonproportional thinking (Shue and Townsend, 2021).

Neglect of probability

Tom is scared of flying but loves driving. Fear of flying is often driven by a fear that the plane will crash and kill the passengers. This is statistically unlikely (especially compared to deaths caused by cars), but this is a typical example of humans neglecting probability. Sunstein (2003) suggests that this occurs in reaction to terrorist attacks too, for example.

Base rate neglect

If two of your friends receive the same expensive gift for Christmas, such as a watch, it's tempting to draw conclusions from this information. For example, you may assume that the value of Christmas presents is increasing. If so, you are ignoring wider data and neglecting the true 'base rate' of probability (Lyon and Slovic, 1976).

Insensitivity to sample size

Statisticians know that small samples are more likely to include variation. If you have just a very small number of people, it's unlikely that their characteristics (such as their average age) will be representative of the whole country. People do not always remember this though (Hamil et al., 1980).

Subadditivity effect

When buying insurance online, a customer might consider the general risk of a fire starting in their house and choose appropriate cover. Yet, ask them what the chance is of their washing machine, or dishwasher, or another electrical item catching fire and the perceived overall chance combined may well be higher than the overall chance of a fire in the house – which is illogical. The same may occur for the chance of theft too for example. This error in assessment is known as the subadditivity effect (Tversky and Koehler, 1994).

Misplaced faith in chance

Because humans are emotional beings, they don't make accurate assessments of probabilities.

Gambler's fallacy

Multiple occurrences that happen purely by chance, are not connected. On a roulette wheel, landing on red five times in a row might lead a gambler to assume a strong likelihood of a sixth red, but this assessment is mistaken (Tversky and Kahneman, 1974). Even statisticians have to remind themselves sometimes that correlation is not causation.

Certainty-possibility effects
Reducing risk to zero has a greater effect than a similar reduction that does not lead to zero. In reverse, a similar effect occurs: When the chance of success increases by 10% from zero for example, the positive effect is greater than when increasing simply by 10% from 20% to 30%. Similarly, an increase to 100% chance of success has a particularly positive effect (Tversky and Kahneman, 1981), and a decrease from 100% chance has a particularly negative effect (Tversky and Kahneman, 1986).

Survivorship bias
In World War II, many bomber planes were shot by enemy fire from below. If asked to consider reinforcement of planes, one approach could be to strengthen the areas where returning planes appeared to be shot. There is a logical problem with this though; those planes that returned had survived despite their bullet holes. It would probably be better to work out where the fatally damaged planes were hit and protect against recurrence (see Mangel and Samaniego, 1984).

Texas sharpshooter fallacy
Imagine an archer shooting many arrows at a stand, then adding a target afterwards. This would clearly be cheating, but it would also give a false picture of the archer's accuracy. This is the sharpshooter fallacy (Evers, 2017): A focus on clusters of data but ignoring differences between the results. This relates to the 'clustering illusion' above too.

b) A desire for logic
People like to feel that their choices are logical and therefore rationally sound. However, this is often not the case.

Other logical fallacies
Sometimes, when people think they are acting logically, this is a 'fallacy' – hence the phrase 'logical fallacy'. Perhaps 'false logic' is a clearer way of expressing the same meaning. Here are some examples:

Motivated reasoning
In an ideal world, everyone would assess information factually without bias. The truth is that different people can see the same information in completely different ways and find plenty of reasons why their view is

the correct one. This is motivated reasoning (Kunda, 1990) – providing a rationale that is motivated by preexisting values and beliefs.

Evaluability

When choosing between options, people often focus on aspects of a choice that they are able to evaluate. There are many aspects to this, such as being able to compare to a reference point (Hsee and Zhang, 2010). For example, people tend to evaluate clothing based on how the items of clothing look, rather than more difficult aspects to evaluate, such as durability.

Outcome bias

People sometimes use the phrase 'the ends justify the means' when reflecting on events. In fact, when the outcome is known, people assume prior actions caused the ending. This is the outcome bias (Baron and Hershey, 1988). Ultimately, customers judge products and services by whether they solve the problem they were intended to solve. If a customer leaves a restaurant feeling elated, they may attribute their emotion to the restaurant visit (when perhaps their companions played a role too).

Proportionality bias

To use another war analogy, a big bomb typically creates a big explosion. There is similarly a general assumption that big events in our lives or society are somehow proportionate to a big cause (Leman and Cinnirella, 2007). However, imagine a rat chewing through a wire and creating a large fire. Sometimes we fail to consider small causes. The butterfly effect should remind us of this, i.e., the flapping of tiny wings can apparently lead to huge consequences.

Straw man fallacy

Politicians are sometimes very good at creating a big argument about a topic by misrepresenting the opposition's point. The opposition might win the debate, but the effort was really a distraction from the main issue. This superficial discussion is known as a 'straw man' (Lewinski and Oswald, 2013) – easy to defeat. The victory is actually pretty shallow.

Zero-sum bias

Most people enjoy winning. Yet, many situations don't need a winner and shouldn't be treated as 'winner takes all' or a 'zero-sum' situation. Students often want to achieve a better grade than their peers for example, when in reality there is no limit (a nonzero-sum situation) on the number of top grades awarded (Meegan, 2010).

Continued influence effect

Misinformation is a big problem in the online world. Unfortunately, it can be very influential. Surprisingly, the influence of misinformation can persist even when people know the truth (Johnson and Seifert, 1994). Many people still believe that "space is filmed in a Hollywood basement" for example (© Red Hot Chilli Peppers).

Conjunction fallacy

When you picture a typical summer, you might think of bright sunshine overhead, blue skies and nice warm temperatures. Yet, the number of days per year when both warm temperatures and dry weather really occur together may be less than you think. For example, the UK has some warm sunny days, but it also has quite a few warm rainy days too! The probability of a conjunction can't be more than the probability of its constituents (Tversky and Kahneman, 1983).

Automation bias

Have you ever felt raindrops on your head, but told your friends that it can't be rain because your app says rain is not predicted? Or driven along a road expecting delays because your satnav showed a traffic jam that your eyes showed you had cleared? This misplaced reliance on technology is a modern phenomenon with its own name (automation bias) because of the reliance on 'automated' technology that has replaced otherwise manual processes (Mosier and Skitka, 1999).

APPLYING THE THEORY: KEY QUESTIONS

When presenting data, are you clear about what the numbers actually show? Explain proportional price rises and avoid customers misunderstanding patterns or risks.

Are you using statistics or percentages in a way that supports your message without triggering scepticism or confusion?

Can you help your audience avoid drawing the wrong conclusion from a coincidence – attributing causes, or even blame, unnecessarily?

8.11 TIME PERCEPTION WHEN MAKING DECISIONS

People are not consistent or accurate when judging time.

a) Customers do not treat time objectively

There are several biases that specifically affect decisions regarding time.

Present bias

Many people can't resist temptation. Although they know that savings may attract interest rates, resulting in an ultimately larger monetary outcome, 'present bias' leads to a preference for a more immediate payoff (O'Donoghue and Rabin, 1999).

Planning fallacy

A very common bias, associated with being too optimistic, is the underestimation of time required to undertake a given task. This is known as the planning fallacy (Buehler et al., 1994) and also frequently affects the cost of large building or infrastructure projects.

Time-saving bias

It's fair to say that in many countries, a lot of people drive faster than they should. In the UK, the motorway speed limit is 70 mph, but many people drive at 80 mph. 80 mph might feel a lot faster, but the reality is that driving around 14% faster than legally permitted doesn't make a huge difference to a journey time. This demonstrates the time-saving bias (Peer, 2011).

Duration neglect

When recalling experiences, we often fail to take account of how long the event lasted (Fredrickson and Kahneman, 1993). For example, perhaps when asked about their favourite holiday, people might compare a weekend break with a three-week road trip. The duration of the emotion doesn't affect judgement.

Time confetti

As tempting as it can be to look at your phone when it pings, frequently modern technology can distract people from more absorbing tasks. The effect is to divide big jobs into smaller chunks or 'confetti' (Whillans, 2019), which is stressful as people are forced to juggle between multiple jobs.

APPLYING THE THEORY: KEY QUESTIONS

Are you framing time in ways that feel manageable – like 'just five minutes a day' or 'in less than a week'?

If you are engaging a customer, maybe try and avoid stressful distractions for the customer – get their full attention.

8.12 INVOLVEMENT

"Tell me and I forget, teach me and I may remember, involve me and I learn." – Xun Kuang 818 AD.

At the start of this book, we focused on gaining the attention of your audience. As we near the end, we now consider how a customer's mental engagement affects the likelihood of purchase. This is known as 'involvement'. Understanding the meaning and role of involvement in purchasing decisions is important and will guide appropriate communication and marketing activity.

Customers often differ in the degree to which they think about a purchase. Ordering baked beans in the online groceries? Probably not much thought required. Many customers probably buy the same brand each time. In terms of the dual processes of cognition discussed at the beginning of chapter 5, baked beans are probably more likely to be 'peripheral', based on 'heuristics' and system 1. However, buying a new house probably requires a lot more thought and 'involvement'. In fact, the process is probably also a lot slower as different aspects of the purchase are considered, and different options compared.

One difference here between beans and houses is price. But even some non-expensive products require careful consideration. Few people throw on clothes without some consideration given to styling. This all demonstrates that people are more mentally 'involved' in some purchases than others.

The concept of 'involvement' was first developed by Judith Zaichkowsky in 1985, and was based on the perception of the product or service as being relevant in some way to the needs, values and interests of the person considering it. Whilst some products are inherently more or less interesting (Luan doesn't find grocery shopping interesting), there may of course be individual differences between people. Postage stamps are a low involvement purchase for many people, but not for a stamp collector for example. Product type can affect the degree of involvement experienced. When a product is low involvement, advertising campaigns based on facts are likely to be more effective in increasing quality perceptions (Nuweihed and Trendel, 2023).

a) *The effect of involvement on product choice*
The degree to which people consider a purchase carefully, can affect the choice that they make.

Identity-building products
In many cases, people choose products that in some way suit them. OK, some products are purely functional (e.g., a hammer), but marketers have even managed to promote some everyday household items as a reflection of identity in some way. When you buy washing detergent for example, perhaps you select the scent that suits your home. Many products are chosen therefore for reasons beyond function. Russell Belk (1988) described a link between possessions and identity. People's possessions become a reflection of themselves, known as an 'extended' self.

Try thinking about your best friend for example. Do they own a guitar? Or an air fryer? If a stranger met them, these possessions would probably give the stranger some clues about your best friend's interests. Perhaps their possessions would reveal their values too. These products weren't necessarily chosen to reflect a particular identity, but nevertheless they do affect the identity of the person. A guitar owner for example develops an identity as a guitarist, or even a musician.

Self-expression products
Self-expression is a little different to identity-building. Products chosen deliberately for self-expression are intended to send a message to others in a given social group. Think about your best friend again. Do they wear boots or trainers? Being more specific, would they wear Dr Martens boots or Nike Air Jordans? Govers and Schoormans (2005) describe this as 'symbolic meaning'. Products hold a personality (similar in concept

structure (ABC) for applying these within your marketing strategy and plans. We hope that you now begin your own deeper exploration.

If you want to stay up to date with the latest research and discussion, you should find our website helpful: www.marketingandpsychology.com.

To summarise, here's a quick reminder of all that you have learned.

We began in the first section with a discussion of the ways you can understand your audience before even attempting to communicate with potential customers.

In chapter 2 we guided you through various ways in which people differ psychologically. This included personality traits and different perspectives on intelligence. In chapter 3 we looked at how to understand your customer's disposition according to their attitude, values and beliefs, as well as what motivates their behaviour. Finally, within the 'audience' section, we explained how a customer's social situation affects their decision making, including aspects such as relationships, comparison with others, and self-evaluation.

From chapter 5 onwards we moved to looking at how a brand is perceived. We considered what people pay attention to, then looked at how to craft messages, appeal to the senses, and create memorable information. Chapter 6 then discussed psychological theories relating to the specific people who deliver a message. Are they likeable? Perhaps they have credible expertise on a specific topic or are just figures of authority.

Our final section was an exploration of theories that explain how people make choices. In chapter 7 we discussed ways in which memory affects decision-making, including both long-term and short-term memories and how customers learn. Chapter 8 then looked at how biases affect decision making and how customers assess value, covering aspects such as reference points, pricing, and self-control.

We don't expect anyone to memorise all these theories or even remember the headings within each chapter. Just keep the book to hand and dip in and out of it to remind yourself of relevant topics as and when you need to. If you identify any particularly useful theories, try reading the original research (or at least the abstract) and then searching for any papers that have since cited that paper. Just like customers, academics tend to form networks, connected through citations.

Above all, if you remember nothing else about this book, remember that there broadly three areas of your marketing plan to consider when evaluating how psychology can help you.

It's as simple as ABC!

- Audience
- Brand perception
- Choice

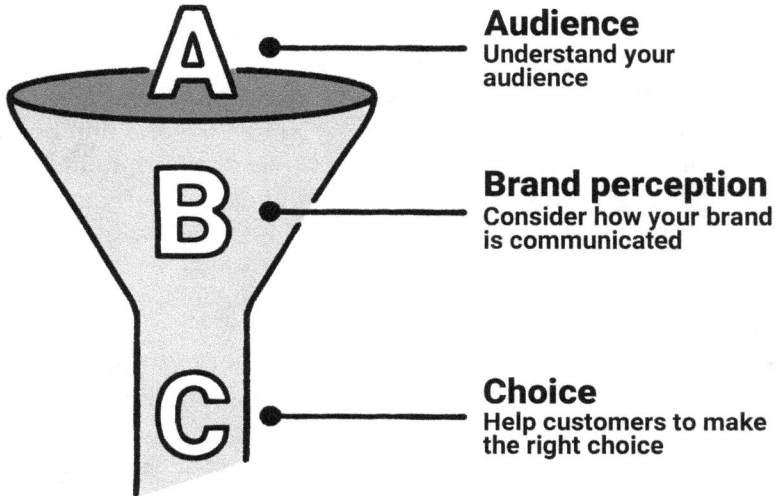

Audience
Understand your audience

Brand perception
Consider how your brand is communicated

Choice
Help customers to make the right choice

CHAPTER 8 REFERENCES

Abedi, F., & Koslow, S. (2022). Can Personalization or Creativity Reduce Banner Blindness? An Executive Functions Approach to Media an Creative Strategies. *Journal of Advertising Research, 62*(3), 201–218.

Adams, G.S., Converse, B.A., Hales, A.H., & Klotz, L.E. (2021). People systematically overlook subtractive changes. *Nature, 592*(7853), 258–261.

Aggarwal, P., Jun, S.Y., & Huh, J.H. (2011). Scarcity messages. *Journal of Advertising, 40*(3), 19–30.

Ahn, S. Y., & Nam, Y. (2022). Does mobile payment use lead to overspending? The moderating role of financial knowledge. *Computers in Human Behavior, 134*, Article 107319.

Akerlof, G.A., & Kranton, R.E. (2010). *Identity economics: How our identities shape our work, wages, and well-being.* Princeton University Press.

Alberhasky, M., & Raghunathan, R. (2023). Skills make you happy: Why high (vs. low) skill activities make consumers happier, yet they don't choose them. *Psychology & Marketing, 40*(10), 2088–2102.

Ardelet, C., & Benavent, C. (2023). Does making less effort entail satisfaction? A large empirical study on client relationship services. *International Journal of Market Research, 65*(1), 83–99.

Ariely, D., & Wertenbroch, K. (2002). Procrastination, deadlines, and performance: Self-control by precommitment. *Psychological Science, 13*(3), 219–224.

Bailey, E. R., Krautter, K., Wu, W., Galinsky, A. D., & Jachimowicz, J. M. (2024). A potential pitfall of passion: Passion is associated with performance over-confidence. *Social Psychological and Personality Science, 15*(7), 769–779.

Banerjee, P., & Minchael, S. (2024). Of happy larks and unhappy owls: Why morning versus evening types feel different levels of happiness from experiential versus material purchases. *Psychology & Marketing, 41*(10), 2493–2505.

Bar-Eli, M., Azar, O. H., Ritov, I., Keidar-Levin, Y., & Schein, G. (2007). Action bias among elite soccer goalkeepers: The case of penalty kicks. *Journal of economic psychology, 28*(5), 606–621.

Barberis, N., Shleifer, A., & Vishny, R. (1998). A model of investor sentiment. *Journal of financial economics,* 49(3), 307–343.

Baron, J., & Hershey, J.C. (1988). Outcome bias in decision evaluation. *Journal of Personality and Social Psychology, 54*(4), 569.

Baumeister, R.F., Vohs, K.D., & Tice, D.M. (2007). The strength model of self-control. *Current Directions in Psychological Science, 16*(6), 351–355.

Bechler, C.J., Lutfeali, S., Huang, S. C., & Morris, J. I. (2024). Working hard for money decreases risk tolerance. *Journal of Consumer Psychology, 34*(1), 110–118.

Belk, R.W. (1988). Possessions and the extended self. *Journal of Consumer Research, 15*(2), 139–168.

Benartzi, S., & Thaler, R. H. (1995). Myopic loss aversion and the equity premium puzzle. *Quarterly Journal of Economics, 110*(1), 73–92.

Benartzi S, Thaler RH. 2001. Naïve diversification strategies in defined contribution saving plans. *American Economic Review,* 91, 79–98

Białek, M., Gao, Y., Yao, D., & Feldman, G. (2023). Owning leads to valuing: Meta-analysis of the mere ownership effect. *European Journal of Social Psychology, 53*(1), 90–107.

Bordalo, P., Gennaioli, N., & Shleifer, A. (2013). Salience and consumer choice. *Journal of Political Economy, 121*(5), 803–843.

Bower, G.H. (1961). A contrast effect in differential conditioning. *Journal of Experimental Psychology, 62*(2), 196.

Brehm, J. W. (1966). *A theory of psychological reactance.* Academic Press.

Buchanan, T.M., Buchanan, J., Diedericks, D., & Davis, L. (2023). I'll have what she's having: (Social) perceptions of default options and implications for marketing and decision making. *International Journal of Consumer Studies, 47*(2), 509–522.

Buehler, R., Griffin, D., & Ross, M. (1994). Exploring the" planning fallacy": Why people underestimate their task completion times. *Journal of Personality and Social Psychology, 67*(3), 366.

Buell, R.W., & Norton, M.I. (2011). The labor illusion: How operational transparency increases perceived value. *Management Science, 57*(9), 1564–1579.

Carpenter, C. J. (2013). A meta-analysis of the effectiveness of the "but you are free" compliance-gaining technique. *Communication Studies, 64*(1), 6–17.

Caruana, N., & Seymour, K. (2022). Objects that induce face pareidolia are prioritized by the visual system. *British Journal of Psychology, 113*(2), 496–507.

Chapman, L.J. (1967). Illusory correlation in observational report. *Journal of Verbal Learning and Verbal Behaviour, 6*(1), 151–155.

Charlesworth, J. E. G., Petkovic, G., Kelley, J. M., Hunter, M., Onakpoya, I., Roberts, N., Miller, F. G., & Howick, J. (2017). Effects of placebos without deception compared with no treatment: A systematic review and meta-analysis. *Journal of evidence-based medicine*, *10*(2), 97–107.

Chen, J., & Redden, J.P. (2024). Better together: How clustering can attenuate hedonic decline. *Journal of Consumer Research*, *51*(2), 408–427.

Chun, L., Lembregts, C., & Van den Bergh, B. (2024). Mind over minutes: The effect of task duration consideration on task delay. *Journal of Consumer Psychology*, *34*(3), 502–509.

Churchman, C.W., & Ackoff, R.L. (1954). An approximate measure of value. *Journal of the Operations Research Society of America*, *2*(2), 172–187.

Colucci, D., Franco, C., & Valori, V. (2024). The endowment effect with different possession times and types of items. *Journal of Behavioural and Experimental Economics*, *110*, Article 102216.

Das, M., Balaji, M.S., Paul, S., & Saha, V. (2023). Being unconventional: The impact of unconventional packaging messages on impulsive purchases. *Psychology & Marketing*, *40*(10), 1913–1932.

Denes-Raj, V., Epstein, S., & Cole, J. (1995). The generality of the ratio-bias phenomenon. *Personality and Social Psychology Bulletin*, *21*(10), 1083–1092.

Desai, P., & Jindal, P. (2024). Getting a Break in Bargaining: An Upside of Time Delays. *Marketing Science*, *43*(6), 1260–1278.

Dhar, R. (1997). Consumer preference for a no-choice option. *Journal of Consumer Research*, *24*(2), 215–231.

Dominko, M., & Verbič, M. (2022). The effect of subjective well-being on consumption behaviour. *Journal of Consumer Affairs*, *56*(2), 876–898.

Doyle, J.R. (2013). Survey of time preference, delay discounting models. *Judgment and Decision making*, *8*(2), 116–135.

Duhigg, C. (2013). *The Power of Habit: Why we do what we do and how to change*. Random House.

Ellsberg, D. (1961). Risk, ambiguity, and the Savage axioms. *Quarterly Journal of Economics*, *75*(4), 643–669.

Eskreis-Winkler, L., Troncoso Peres, L. T., & Fishbach, A. (2024). The bigger the problem the littler: When the scope of a problem makes it seem less dangerous. *Journal of Personality and Social Psychology*.

Evers, J.L.H. (2017). The Texas sharpshooter fallacy. *Human Reproduction*, *32*(7), 1363–1363.

Fennis, B.M., & Stroebe, W. (2021). *The psychology of advertising*. Routledge.

Festinger, L. (1962). Cognitive dissonance. *Scientific American*, *207*(4), 93–106.

Frederick, S., Novemsky, N., Wang, J., Dhar, R., & Nowlis, S. (2009). Opportunity cost neglect. *Journal of Consumer Research*, *36*(4), 553–561.

Fredrickson, B.L., & Kahneman, D. (1993). Duration neglect in retrospective evaluations of affective episodes. *Journal of personality and social psychology*, *65*(1), 45.

Freedman, J.L., & Fraser, S.C. (1966). Compliance without pressure: the foot-in-the-door technique. *Journal of Personality and Social Psychology*, *4*(2), 195.

Fridman, A., Amir, O., & Hansen, K. T. (2024). Dominance Effects in the Wild. *Journal of Consumer Research, 50*(6), 1117–1135.

Fulmer, A.G., & Reich, T. Promoting a product without increasing the promotion budget: How chance in promotions can heighten consumer demand. *Journal of Consumer Psychology.*

Furnham, A., & Boo, H.C. (2011). A literature review of the anchoring effect. *The Journal of Socio-Economics, 40*(1), 35–42.

Gal, D. (2006). A psychological law of inertia and the illusion of lossaversion. *Judgment and Decision making, 1*(1), 23–32.

German, T.P., & Barrett, H.C. (2005). Functional fixedness in a technologically sparse culture. *Psychological Science, 16*(1), 1–5.

Gibson, J.J. (2014). The theory of affordances (1979). In *The people, place, and space reader* (pp. 56–60). Routledge.

Gigerenzer, G., & Goldstein, D.G. (1996). Reasoning the fast and frugal way: models of bounded rationality. *Psychological Review, 103*(4), 650.

Gigerenzer, G., & Goldstein, D.G. (1999). Betting on one good reason: The take the best heuristic. In *Simple heuristics that make us smart* (pp. 75–95). Oxford University Press.

Gilovich, T., & Gallo, I. (2020). Consumers' pursuit of material and experiential purchases: A review. *Consumer Psychology Review, 3*(1), 20–33.

Gilovich, T., Vallone, R., & Tversky, A. (1985). The hot hand in basketball: On the misperception of random sequences. *Cognitive Psychology,* 17(3), 295–314.

Givi, J., Grossman, D.M., & Kardes, F.R. (2024). Erroneous consumer evaluations in the marketplace: How consumer evaluations are biased by raw performance scores. *Psychology & Marketing, 41*(3), 665–676.

González, E.M., Esteva, E., Roggeveen, A.L., & Grewal, D. (2016). Amount off versus percentage off – when does it matter?. *Journal of Business Research, 69*(3), 1022–1027.

Govers, P.C., & Schoormans, J.P. (2005). Product personality and its influence on consumer preference. *Journal of Consumer Marketing, 22*(4), 189–197.

Gray, K., & Wegner, D.M. (2010). Blaming God for our pain: Human suffering and the divine mind. *Personality and Social Psychology Review, 14*(1), 7–16.

Greenberg, J. (1983). Overcoming egocentric bias in perceived fairness through self-awareness. *Social Psychology Quarterly,* 152–156.

Gu, Y., & Chen, R. (2023). Effects of payment notifications on consumer purchase decisions: The role of pain of payment. *Journal of Consumer Behaviour, 22*(4), 818–832.

Guo, B., & Wang, D. (2024). Will online shopping lead to more brand loyalty than offline shopping? The role of uncertainty avoidance. *Journal of Marketing Research, 61*(1), 92–109.

Hamill, R., Wilson, T.D., & Nisbett, R.E. (1980). Insensitivity to sample bias: Generalizing from atypical cases. *Journal of Personality and Social Psychology, 39*(4), 578.

Hanemann, W.M. (1991). Willingness to pay and willingness to accept: how much can they differ?. *The American Economic Review, 81*(3), 635–647.

Hick, W.E. (1952). On the rate of gain of information. *Quarterly Journal of Experimental Psychology*, 4(1), 11–26

Hirshleifer, D., Levi, Y., Lourie, B., & Teoh, S. H. (2019). Decision fatigue and heuristic analyst forecasts. *Journal of Financial Economics, 133*(1), 83–98.

Hmurovic, J., Lamberton, C., & Goldsmith, K. (2023). Examining the efficacy of time scarcity marketing promotions in online retail. *Journal of Marketing Research, 60*(2), 299–328.

Hsee, C.K. (1998). Less is better: When low-value options are valued more highly than high-value options. *Journal of Behavioural Decision Making, 11*(2), 107–121.

Hsee, C.K., & Zhang, J. (2004). Distinction bias: misprediction and mischoice due to joint evaluation. *Journal of Personality and Social Psychology, 86*(5), 680.

Hsee, C.K., & Zhang, J. (2010). General evaluability theory. *Perspectives on Psychological Science, 5*(4), 343–355.

Huang, M., Zhan, M., Huang, R., & Wu, J. (2023). How commuting time influences hedonic consumption: The role of perceived stress. *Journal of Consumer Behaviour, 22*(2), 439–454.

Huang, L., Siddiqui, R.A., & Ghosh, A. P. (2024). More of the same: Painful payment methods decrease variety seeking. *Marketing Letters, 35*(4), 533–545.

Huber, J., Payne, J.W., & Puto, C. (1982). Adding asymmetrically dominated alternatives: Violations of regularity and the similarity hypothesis. *Journal of Consumer Research, 9*(1), 90–98.

Iyengar, S.S., & Lepper, M.R. (2000). When choice is demotivating: Can one desire too much of a good thing?. *Journal of Personality and Social Psychology*, 79(6), 995.

Jackson, M. (2023). *Uncertain: the wisdom and wonder of being unsure*. Rowman & Littlefield.

Jaubert, S., Fillon, A. A., Souchet, L., & Girandola, F. (2024). Vicarious Dissonance: Pre-Registered Meta-Analysis. *Personality and Social Psychology Bulletin.*

Jeong, Y., Hwang, S., & Suk, K. (2023). Ten days (vs. May 10) make you rush: The effect of time descriptions on task scheduling. *Journal of Applied Social Psychology, 53*(2), 121–133.

Jha, S., Biswas, A., Guha, A., & Gauri, D. (2024). Can rounding up price discounts reduce sales?. *Journal of Consumer Psychology, 34*(2), 343–350.

Johnson, E.J., Bellman, S., & Lohse, G.L. (2002). Defaults, framing and privacy: Why opting in-opting out. *Marketing Letters, 13*, 5–15.

Johnson, J.G., & Raab, M. (2003). Take the first: Option-generation and resulting choices. *Organizational Behaviour and Human Decision Processes, 91*(2), 215–229.

Johnson, H.M., & Seifert, C.M. (1994). Sources of the continued influence effect: When misinformation in memory affects later inferences. *Journal of Experimental Psychology: Learning, Memory, and Cognition, 20*(6), 1420.

Kagel, J.H., & Levin, D. (1986). The winner's curse and public information in common value auctions. *American Economic Review, 76*(5), 894–920.

Kahneman, D., Krueger, A. B., Schkade, D., Schwarz, N., & Stone, A. A. (2006). Would you be happier if you were richer? A focusing illusion. *science*, *312*(5782), 1908–1910.

Kahneman, D., & Tversky, A. (1972). Subjective probability: A judgment of representativeness. *Cognitive Psychology*, *3*(3), 430–454.

Kahneman, D., & Tversky, A. (1984). Choices, values, and frames. *American Psychologist*, *39*(4), 341.

Kahneman, D., & Tversky, A. (1986). Rational choice and the framing of decisions. *Journal of Business*, *59*(4), 251–278.

Kahneman, D., & Tversky, A. (2013). Prospect theory: An analysis of decision under risk. In *Handbook of the fundamentals of financial decision making: Part I* (pp. 99–127).

Khoso, U., Tafani, E., & Qazi, A. (2023). Scarcity Appeals in Cross-Cultural Settings: A Comprehensive Framework. *Journal of International Marketing*, *31*(4), 53–75.

Kivetz, R., & Zheng, Y. (2017). The effects of promotions on hedonic versus utilitarian purchases. *Journal of Consumer Psychology*, *27*(1), 59–68.

Knetsch, J.L. (1989). The endowment effect and evidence of nonreversible indifference curves. *The American Economic Review*, *79*(5), 1277–1284.

Kristal, A. S., & Santos, L. R. (2021). *GI Joe phenomena: Understanding the limits of metacognitive awareness on debiasing* (No. 21-084). Harvard Business School Working Paper.

Kruger, J., Wirtz, D., & Miller, D.T. (2005). Counterfactual thinking and the first instinct fallacy. *Journal of Personality and Social Psychology*, *88*(5), 725.

Kunda, Z. (1990). The case for motivated reasoning. *Psychological Bulletin*, *108*(3), 480.

Kurz, J., Efendić, E., & Goukens, C. (2023). Pricey therefore good? Price affects expectations, but not quality perceptions and liking. *Psychology & Marketing*, *40*(6), 1115–1129.

Ladeira, W. J., Lim, W. M., de Oliveira Santini, F., Rasul, T., Perin, M. G., & Altinay, L. (2023). A meta-analysis on the effects of product scarcity. *Psychology & Marketing*, *40*(7), 1267–1279.

Lalot, F., Ahvenharju, S., & Uusitalo, O. (2024). Green dreams are made of this: Futures consciousness and proenvironmental engagement. *British Journal of Social Psychology*, *64*(1), e12799.

Langer, E. J. (1975). The illusion of control. *Journal of personality and social psychology*, *32*(2), 311.

Lee, C.Y., & Morewedge, C. K. (2023). Mental accounting of product returns. *Journal of Consumer Psychology*, *33*(3), 583–590.

Lee, S., & Yi, Y. (2022). Is returning a product worth my time? The impact of time cues on consumer product returns. *Psychology & Marketing*, *39*(7), 1413–1427.

Leman, P. J., & Cinnirella, M. (2007). A major event has a major cause: Evidence for the role of heuristics in reasoning about conspiracy theories. *Social Psychological Review*, *9*(2), 18–28.

Lewiński, M., & Oswald, S. (2013). When and how do we deal with straw men? A normative and cognitive pragmatic account. *Journal of Pragmatics, 59*, 164–177.

Lyon, D., & Slovic, P. (1976). Dominance of accuracy information and neglect of base rates in probability estimation. *Acta Psychologica, 40*(4), 287–298.

Maier, S. F., & Seligman, M. E. (1976). Learned helplessness: theory and evidence. *Journal of Experimental Psychology, 105*(1), 3.

Mangel, M., & Samaniego, F. J. (1984). Abraham Wald's work on aircraft survivability. *Journal of the American Statistical Association, 79*(386), 259–267.

Meegan, D.V. (2010). Zero-sum bias: Perceived competition despite unlimited resources. *Frontiers in Psychology, 1*, 191.

Meunier, L., Bashirzadeh, Y., & Ohadi, S. (2024). Framing the Default Option Right. *Journal of Behavioural Decision Making, 37*(3), Article e2395.

Mike, K., & Hazzan, O. (2022). What is common to transportation and health in machine learning education? The domain neglect bias. *IEEE Transactions on Education, 66*(3), 226–233.

Milkman, K.L., Minson, J.A., & Volpp, K. G. (2014). Holding the hunger games hostage at the gym: An evaluation of temptation bundling. *Management Science, 60*(2), 283–299.

Moore, D. A., & Healy, P. J. (2008). The trouble with overconfidence. *Psychological review, 115*(2), 502.

Mosier, K.L., & Skitka, L.J. (1999, September). Automation use and automation bias. In *Proceedings of the human factors and ergonomics society annual meeting* (Vol. 43, No. 3, pp. 344–348). SAGE Publications.

Mukherjee, A., & Lee, S. Y. (2016). Scarcity appeals in advertising: the moderating role of expectation of scarcity. *Journal of Advertising, 45*(2), 256–268.

Norton, M. I., Mochon, D., & Ariely, D. (2012). The IKEA effect: When labor leads to love. *Journal of Consumer Psychology, 22*(3), 453–460.

Nunes, J.C., & Dreze, X. (2006). The endowed progress effect: How artificial advancement increases effort. *Journal of Consumer Research, 32*(4), 504–512.

Nuweihed, W., & Trendel, O. (2024). The role of informational versus transformational ad appeals in building consumer-based brand equity for low involvement products. *Journal of Marketing Theory and Practice, 32*(4), 579–598.

Palmer, C.J., & Clifford, C.W. (2020). Face pareidolia recruits mechanisms for detecting human social attention. *Psychological Science, 31*(8), 1001–1012

Peer, E. (2011). The time-saving bias, speed choices and driving behavior. *Transportation Research Part F: Traffic Psychology and Behaviour, 14*(6), 543–554.

Piehlmaier, D. M. (2023). The one-man show: the effect of joint decision-making on investor overconfidence. *Journal of Consumer Research, 50*(2), 426–446.

O'donoghue, T., & Rabin, M. (1999). Doing it now or later. *American economic review, 89*(1), 103–124.

Oberholzer, Y., Olschewski, S., & Scheibehenne, B. (2024). Complexity aversion in risky choices and valuations: Moderators and possible causes. *Journal of Economic Psychology, 100*, Article 102681.

Omer, H., & Alon, N. (1994). The continuity principle: A unified approach to disaster and trauma. *American Journal of Community Psychology*, *22*, 273–287.

Owens, D., Grossman, Z., & Fackler, R. (2014). The control premium: A preference for payoff autonomy. *American Economic Journal: Microeconomics*, *6*(4), 138–161.

Palmer, C. J., & Clifford, C. W. (2020). Face pareidolia recruits mechanisms for detecting human social attention. Psychological Science, 31(8), 1001–1012.

Poor, M., & Isaac, M.S. (2023). Affective debiasing: Focusing on emotion during consumption attenuates attribute framing effects. *Journal of Behavioural Decision Making, 36*(5), Article e2347.

Pozharliev, R., De Angelis, M., & Cascio Rizzo, G. L. (2025). How Argument Numerosity Shapes Firm-Generated Content Effectiveness. *Psychology & Marketing*.

Prelec, D., & Simester, D. (2001). Always leave home without it: A further investigation of the credit-card effect on willingness to pay. *Marketing letters*, 12, 5–12.

Raghubir, P. (2004). Free gift with purchase: promoting or discounting the brand?. *Journal of Consumer Psychology, 14*(1-2), 181–186.

Raghubir, P., & Srivastava, J. (2009). The denomination effect. *Journal of Consumer Research, 36*(4), 701–713.

Raue, M., & Schneider, E. (2019). Psychological perspectives on perceived safety: Zero-risk bias, feelings and learned carelessness. *Perceived safety: A multidisciplinary perspective*, 61–81.

Read, D., & Loewenstein, G. (1995). Diversification bias: Explaining the discrepancy in variety seeking between combined and separated choices. *Journal of Experimental Psychology: Applied, 1*(1), 34.

Reiff, J., Dai, H., Beshears, J., Milkman, K.L., & Benartzi, S. (2023). Save more today or tomorrow: the role of urgency in precommitment design. *Journal of Marketing Research, 60*(6), 1095–1113.

Rifkin, J.R., Du, K.M., & Cutright, K.M. (2023). The preference for spontaneity in entertainment. *Journal of Consumer Research, 50*(3), 597–616.

Ryan, W.H., Baum, S.M., & Evers, E.R. (2024). Biases in improvement decisions: people focus on the relative reduction in bad outcomes. *Psychological Science, 35*(5), 558–574.

Samuelson, W., & Zeckhauser, R. (1988). Status quo bias in decision making. *Journal of Risk and Uncertainty, 1*, 7–59.

Schindler, R. M., & Yalch, R. F. (2006). It Seems Factual, But Is It? Effects of Using Sharp versus Round Numbers in Advertising Claims. *Advances in Consumer Research, 33*(1).

Schwartz, B. (2004). The tyranny of choice. *Scientific American, 290*(4), 70–75.

Schwartz, B., Ward, A., Monterosso, J., Lyubomirsky, S., White, K., & Lehman, D. R. (2002). Maximizing versus satisficing: happiness is a matter of choice. *Journal of Personality and Social Psychology, 83*(5), 1178.

Shafir, E., Diamond, P., & Tversky, A. (1997). Money illusion. *The Quarterly Journal of Economics, 112*(2), 341–374.

Shampanier, K., Mazar, N., & Ariely, D. (2007). Zero as a special price: The true value of free products. *Marketing Science, 26*(6), 742–757.

Sharot, T. (2011). The optimism bias. *Current biology, 21*(23), R941–R945.

Shefrin, H.M., Statman, M., 1985. The disposition to sell winners too early and ride losers too long. *Journal of Finance* 40, 777–790.

Shue, K., & Townsend, R.R. (2021). Can the market multiply and divide? Non-proportional thinking in financial markets. *The Journal of Finance, 76*(5), 2307–2357.

Simon, H. A. (1956). Rational choice and the structure of the environment. *Psychological Review, 63*(2), 129.

Simonson, I. (1989). Choice based on reasons: The case of attraction and compromise effects. *Journal of Consumer Research, 16*(2), 158–174.

Simonson, I., & Tversky, A. (1992). Choice in context: Tradeoff contrast and extremeness aversion. *Journal of Marketing Research, 29*(3), 281–295.

Simonson, I., Carmon, Z., & O'curry, S. (1994). Experimental evidence on the negative effect of product features and sales promotions on brand choice. *Marketing Science, 13*(1), 23–40.

Smieja, J., Zaleskiewicz, T., Sobkow, A., & Traczyk, J. (2023). Imagining risk taking: The valence of mental imagery is related to the declared willingness to take risky actions. *Journal of Behavioural Decision Making, 36*(4), Article e2340.

Spranca, M., Minsk, E., & Baron, J. (1991). Omission and commission in judgment and choice. *Journal of Experimental Social Psychology, 27*(1), 76–105.

Staw, B. M. (1981). The escalation of commitment to a course of action. *Academy of management Review, 6*(4), 577–587.

Stefanczyk, M.M., Rokosz, M., & Białek, M. (2022). Mere ownership effect is equally pronounced in material and immaterial objects. *Social Psychology*.

Sullivan, N.J., Breslav, A., Doré, S. S., Bachman, M. D., & Huettel, S. A. (2024). EXPRESS: The Golden Halo of Defaults in Simple Choices. *Journal of Marketing Research, 62*(2), 386–404.

Sunstein, C.R. (2003). Terrorism and probability neglect. *Journal of Risk and Uncertainty, 26,* 121–136.

Sussman, A. B., & Alter, A. L. (2012). The exception is the rule: Underestimating and overspending on exceptional expenses. *Journal of Consumer Research, 39*(4), 800–814.

Thaler, R. (1980). Toward a positive theory of consumer choice. *Journal of Economic Behaviour & Organization, 1*(1), 39–60.

Thaler, R. (1985). Mental accounting and consumer choice. *Marketing science, 4*(3), 199–214.

Thomas, M., & Morwitz, V. (2005). Penny wise and pound foolish: the left-digit effect in price cognition. *Journal of Consumer Research, 32*(1), 54–64.

Thomas, M., Simon, D. H., & Kadiyali, V. (2010). The price precision effect: Evidence from laboratory and market data. *Marketing Science, 29*(1), 175–190.

Taylor, S.E., Crocker, J., Fiske, S.T., Sprinzen, M., & Winkler, J.D. (1979). The generalizability of salience effects. *Journal of Personality and Social Psychology, 37*(3), 357–368

Thaler, R.H., & Sunstein, C.R. (2009). *Nudge: improving decisions about health, wealth, and happiness. 2008.* Yale.

Troll, E. S., Frankenbach, J., Friese, M., & Loschelder, D. D. (2024). A meta-analysis on the effects of just-below versus round prices. *Journal of Consumer Psychology, 34*(2), 299–325.

Tversky, A. (1972). Elimination by aspects: A theory of choice. *Psychological Review, 79*(4), 281.

Tversky, A., & Kahneman, D. (1974). Judgment under Uncertainty: Heuristics and Biases: Biases in judgments reveal some heuristics of thinking under uncertainty. *Science, 185*(4157), 1124–1131.

Tversky, A., & Kahneman, D. (1981). The framing of decisions and the psychology of choice. *Science, 211*(4481), 453–458.

Tversky, A., & Kahneman, D. (1983). Extensional versus intuitive reasoning: The conjunction fallacy in probability judgment. *Psychological Review, 90*(4), 293.

Tversky, A., & Kahneman, D. (1986). Rational Choice and the Framing of Decisions. *The Journal of Business, 59*(4), S251–S278.

Tversky, A., & Kahneman, D. (1989). Rational choice and the framing of decisions. In *Multiple criteria decision making and risk analysis using microcomputers* (pp. 81–126). Springer Berlin Heidelberg.

Tversky, A., & Kahneman, D. (1991). Loss aversion in riskless choice: A reference-dependent model. *The Quarterly Journal of Economics, 106*(4), 1039–1061.

Tversky, A., & Koehler, D. J. (1994). Support theory: A nonextensional representation of subjective probability. *Psychological Review, 101*(4), 547.

Urban, T. (2016, February). *Inside the mind of a master procrastinator* [Video]. TED2016. https://www.ted.com/talks/tim_urban_inside_the_mind_of_a_master_procrastinator?language+en

Vohs, K. D., Baumeister, R. F., Schmeichel, B. J., Twenge, J. M., Nelson, N. M., & Tice, D. M. (2018). Making choices impairs subsequent self-control: A limited-resource account of decision making, self-regulation, and active initiative. In *Self-regulation and self-control* (pp. 45–77). Routledge.

Vonasch, A.J., Mofradidoost, R., & Gray, K. (2024). People reject free money and cheap deals because they infer phantom costs. *Personality and Social Psychology Bulletin, 51*(10), 2050–2067.

Wampold, B. E., Minami, T., Tierney, S. C., Baskin, T. W., & Bhati, K. S. (2005). The placebo is powerful: estimating placebo effects in medicine and psychotherapy from randomized clinical trials. *Journal of Clinical Psychology, 61*(7), 835–854.

Wang, T., Liang, S., & Sun, Y. (2023). So curious that I want to buy it: The positive effect of queue wait on consumers' purchase intentions. *Journal of Consumer Behaviour, 22*(4), 848–866.

Wang, X., Sung, B., & Phau, I. (2024). How rarity and exclusivity influence types of perceived value for luxury. *Journal of Brand Management,* 1–17.

Whillans, A. (2019). Time poor and unhappy. *Harvard Business Review.*

Wilson, T.D., Lisle, D.J., Schooler, J.W., Hodges, S.D., Klaaren, K.J., & LaFleur, S.J. (1993). Introspecting about reasons can reduce post-choice satisfaction. *Personality and Social Psychology Bulletin, 19*(3), 331–339.

Winter, S. R., Rice, S., Capps, J., Trombley, J., Milner, M. N., Anania, E. C., ... & Baugh, B. S. (2020). An analysis of a pilot's adherence to their personal weather minimums. *Safety Science, 123*, Article 104576.

Wood, W., & Rünger, D. (2016). Psychology of habit. *Annual Review of Psychology, 67*(1), 289–314.

Xiang, L., (818AD). *Ruxiao: The Teachings of the Ru.* Xunzi

Yang, H., & Chakravarti, D. (2024). The discount consolidation effect: How brands can present quantity discounts more effectively. *Journal of Consumer Psychology, 34*(4), 620–631.

Yang, S.S., Kimes, S.E., & Sessarego, M.M. (2009). $ or dollars: Effects of menu-price formats on restaurant checks. *International Journal of Hospitality Management, 28*(1), 157–160.

Yu, Y., Peng, X., & Wang, L. (2023). The impact of mobile payment on hedonic preference. *Journal of Interactive Marketing, 58*(2-3), 151–166.

Zaichkowsky, J.L. (1985). Measuring the involvement construct. *Journal of Consumer Research, 12*(3), 341–352.

Zenkić, J., Mead, N. L., & Millet, K. (2024). When cash costs you: The pain of holding coins over banknotes. *Journal of Consumer Psychology, 34*(4), 641–649.

Zhu, Y., Wang, Y., Wei, J., & Hao, A. (2023). Effects of vividness, information and aesthetic design on the appeal of pay-per-click ads. *Journal of Research in Interactive Marketing, 17*(6), 848–864.

Index

For Product Safety Concerns and Information please contact our EU
representative GPSR@taylorandfrancis.com
Taylor & Francis Verlag GmbH, Kaufingerstraße 24, 80331 München, Germany